HISTORY OF LINCOLNSHIRE

Edited by

JOAN THIRSK

VOLUME VI

TUDOR LINCOLNSHIRE

by

GERALD A. J. HODGETT

PREFACE

THIS is the third book to appear in a proposed twelve-volumed series on the history of the historic county of Lincolnshire.

Lincolnshire is not one of the favoured regions of England. Unlike many other counties it has never had its own history produced by an industrious eighteenth or nineteenth century antiquary. It is not that there have been few students of history within the county. Rather the size of the county, among other factors, has presented problems in bringing together all this material into a comprehensive historical and topographical account of Lincolnshire, a basis for all future work; and the Victoria County History proceeded no further than one volume.

Conscious of this lack, the Lincolnshire Local History Society (now the Society for Lincolnshire History and Archaeology) took the first steps in 1965 towards a new county history, and in the following year the History of Lincolnshire Committee was born. The aim was to publish a series of volumes which would be at the same time both scholarly and of general interest, written by specialists already engaged in work on particular periods and subjects, and yet in their summaries of recent work aimed at the general reader as well as at the scholar.

The Committee has thus planned a series of twelve volumes to provide a more or less comprehensive account of the region from prehistoric times until the middle of the twentieth century. The series is under the general editorship of Dr. Joan Thirsk of St. Hilda's College, Oxford.

An initial financial basis for the Committee's work was provided by the Pilgrim Trust, the Seven Pillars of Wisdom Trust, the Marc Fitch Fund, the Lincolnshire Association and the Willoughby Memorial Trust. Help in other ways has been given to the project by the Lincolnshire Association, the Lincoln City and County Library and Museum Services, the Society for Lincolnshire History and Archaeology, the Lincolnshire Rural Community Council and the Department of Adult Education of the University of Nottingham. Grants received in connection with specific volumes will be acknowledged as each book appears. To all these bodies, and to many others who have assisted in so many ways, we are very grateful; it is with their help that the Committee presents the sixth volume in

THE HISTORY OF LINCOLNSHIRE
in twelve volumes

ALAN ROGERS (*Chairman, History of*
Lincolnshire Committee)

Portrait by Holbein of Katherine baroness Willoughby de Eresby, wife of Charles Brandon, duke of Suffolk, and later of the protestant, Richard Bertie.

HISTORY OF LINCOLNSHIRE

VI

TUDOR LINCOLNSHIRE

by

GERALD A. J. HODGETT, M.A., F.S.A.

*Reader in History in the University of London,
King's College*

LINCOLN

HISTORY OF LINCOLNSHIRE COMMITTEE

1975

PUBLISHED BY

THE HISTORY OF LINCOLNSHIRE COMMITTEE

86 NEWLAND, LINCOLN

© THE HISTORY OF LINCOLNSHIRE COMMITTEE

ISBN 0 902668 05 6

PRINTED IN GREAT BRITAIN

BY COX & WYMAN LTD

LONDON, FAKENHAM AND READING

In piam memoriam M.L.H.
quae hunc comitatum
et optime norat
et amabat.

CONTENTS

Figures

PLATES

ACKNOWLEDGEMENTS

This book has been published with the help of a grant from the late Miss Isobel Thornley's Bequest to the University of London.

The History of Lincolnshire Committee and the author also wish to acknowledge help as follows: the History of Parliament Trust for permission to consult its files of work in progress; Mr. Ian Beckwith for material on schools and education; Mr. E. Gillett for material on Grimsby. Donations towards the cost of illustrations have been received from Mr. P. Dover (in memory of his wife), from Mr. F. R. Wagstaffe and Mr. P. K. Dennis. Mr. K. Bowler of the Department of Geography in the University of Nottingham drew the maps, and Mr. R. A. Elliott suplied the brass rubbing for Figure 2.

We acknowledge plates as follows: Cover, L.A.O. and Hull University; Frontispiece, the Right Honourable the Earl of Ancaster; I and II, National Portrait Gallery; III, Va and VII, Lincoln City Libraries; IV, *Country Life*; VI, IX, X, XIb, XIIb, XIII, Alan Rogers; V, Sir Simon Benton Jones and University of Nottingham Photographic Department; VIII, L.A.O. and G. Tokarski, Lincoln; XIa, P. J. Wilson; XIV and XVI, David Dunn, Louth; and XV, the incumbents and churchwardens of Roxby and Frodingham, and Gerrard Studios, Scunthorpe.

BIBLIOGRAPHY AND LIST OF ABBREVIATIONS

Abbreviation or author	*Full Title*
AASRP	Associated Architectural and Archaeological Societies' Reports and Papers.
Allen, T.	The History of the County of Lincoln, 1834.
AHR	Agricultural History Review
APC n.s.	Acts of the Privy Council of England, new series, edited J. R. Dasent, Volumes 7–31, (London), 1893–1906.
BM Add. MS.	British Museum Additional Manuscript.
BM Harl. MS.	British Museum Harleian Manuscript.
BM Lansdowne MS.	British Museum Lansdowne Manuscript.
BM Sloane MS.	British Museum Sloane Manuscript.
Bodl. Lib.	Bodleian Library Oxford.
Bowker, M.	The Secular Clergy in the Diocese of Lincoln 1495–1520, Cambridge, 1968.
Bull. IHR	Bulletin of the Institute of Historical Research.
Cal. Pat. Rolls	Calendar of Patent Rolls.
Camden Soc.	Camden Society Publications, Royal Historical Society.
CSPD	Calendar of State Papers Domestic Series, 1527–1601, edited R. Lemon and M. A. E. Green, 6 volumes, London, 1856–71.
Darby, H. C.	The Draining of the Fens, London, 2nd edn. 1956.
Dodds, M. H. and R.	The Pilgrimage of Grace and the Exeter Conspiracy, Cambridge, 1915.
EHR	English Historical Review.
EcHR	Economic History Review.
Foxe, J.	The Acts and Monuments of John Foxe, 4th edn. 1867.

Abbreviation or author	*Full Title*
G.E.C. Complete Peerage	*The Complete Peerage etc., by G.E.C.*, edited by Vicary Gibbs *et al* 12 volumes (13 parts), London, 1910–59.
Gillett, E.	*A History of Grimsby*, 1970.
Hill, J.W. F.	*Tudor and Stuart Lincoln*, Cambridge, 1956.
HMC	*Reports of the Historical Manuscripts Commission.*
HMSO	His (Her) Majesty's Stationery Office.
Jnl Eccles. Hist.	*Journal of Ecclesiastical History.*
LAAS	*Lincolnshire Architectural and Archaeological Society's Reports and Papers.*
LAO (C)	Lincolnshire Archives Office (Committee).
Leland, J.	*The Itinerary of John Leland*, Centaur Press edition, 1964.
LP	*Letters and Papers, Foreign and Domestic, of the reign of Henry VIII*, edited J. S. Brewer, J. Gairdner and R. H. Brodie, London, 1862–1910.
Lincs Pedigrees	Harleian Society Publications, volumes 50, 51, 52 and 55, *Lincolnshire Pedigrees*, edited A. R. Maddison, volumes I–IV, London, 1902, 1903, 1904, 1906.
Lincs NQ	*Lincolnshire Notes and Queries.*
Lincs Wills	*Lincolnshire Wills 1500–1600*, edited A. R. Maddison, Lincoln, 1888.
LRS	Lincoln Record Society Publications.

The following volumes of the Lincoln Record Society's Publications are referred to frequently in the notes.

2. C. W. Foster, *Lincoln Episcopal Records* temp. *Thomas Cooper, 1571–84*, 1912.

5, 10, 24. C. W. Foster, *Lincoln Wills, 1271–1526*, 1914–30.

12, 13, 15. R. E. G. Cole, *The Chapter Acts of the Cathedral Church of Lincoln*, 1915–20.

23. C. W. Foster, *The State of the Church in the reigns of Elizabeth and James I*, 1926.

33, 35, 37. A. Hamilton Thompson, *Visitations in the diocese of Lincoln, 1517–31*, 1940–47.

50. R. W. K. Hinton, *The Port Books of Boston, 1601–40*, 1956.

53. G. A. J. Hodgett, *The State of the Ex-religious and Former Chantry Priests in the Diocese of Lincoln*, 1959.

54, 63. A. Mary Kirkus and A. E. B. Owen, *The Records of the Commissioners of the Sewers, 1547–1603*, 1959, 1968.

Pevsner, N. and Harris, J.	*The Buildings of England: Lincolnshire*, Penguin Books, 1964.
Pishey Thompson	*The History and Antiquities of Boston*, 1856.
PRO	Public Record Office.
PRO Exch. Aug. Off.	Exchequer, Augmentations Office.
Misc. Books	Miscellaneous Books.
Savine, A.	*English Monasteries on the Eve of the Dissolution*, Oxford Studies in Social and Legal History, I, Oxford, 1909.
SP	State Papers.
SP Dom.	State Papers Domestic.
SR	*Statutes of the Realm*, ed. A. Luders *et al.*, 1810–28.
Thirsk, J.	*English Peasant Farming*, London, 1957.
Val. Eccl.	*The Valor Ecclesiasticus*, ed. J. Caley and J. Hunter, London, 1810–34.
VCH	Victoria County History.

FOREWORD

IT gave me great pleasure to be asked by the Lincolnshire Local History Society to write the history of Lincolnshire during the Tudor period since it meant that I could return, after years of studying and teaching medieval history, to a period and to the county in which my research interests had first centred. In the course of writing this book my acquaintance with the county has deepened as my use of ordnance survey maps has increased, but I am still aware of my inadequacies in local topography. Lincolnshire is a large county with between 600 and 700 villages and, in addition, a large number of hamlets; moreover, two (or on occasion more than two) places bear the same name, and thus the pitfalls, for all but native or long-resident Lincolnshiremen, are many.

A survey of the history of a county over 118 years in a short volume must inevitably be based upon the work of other scholars, since to enter into the *minutiae* that emerge from the multifarious original sources would make the work too long and too detailed for the general reader. In three areas I have gone to these sources. When dealing with the ecclesiastical history of the early sixteenth century, and especially in my discussion of the dissolution of the monasteries, I have drawn upon original material both in Lincoln and in the Public Record Office, and also in writing about the Bertie household. Similarly, in treating of the local government of Lincoln I have used the council minutes, but, in the main, my book owes much to those scholars who, from the Tudor period onward, have written about the county. From Leland's *Itinerary*, the fruits of his travels throughout England in the late 1530s to Sir Nikolaus Pevsner's *Buildings of England*, a work which emerged from his travels throughout the country in the 1950s and 1960s of the present century, much topographical work on Lincolnshire has appeared. To such books and to the careful genealogical compilations of A. R. Maddison, as also to the list of office holders made by the late J. B. King, the writer on Tudor Lincolnshire owes an enormous debt: they provide the essential skeleton upon which the story can be hung.

An attempt has been made to study the history of Lincolnshire between 1485 and 1603 in all its facets and to avoid devoting undue attention to any one aspect. But one aspect is of paramount importance —land use. Because Lincolnshire still remains in the twentieth century an agricultural county, readers of this book resident in the county will be able to appreciate more easily than those living in large conurbations the importance of agriculture. Despite the fact that neither potatoes nor sugar beet were grown in Tudor Lincolnshire, the basics remain in many ways the same: good corn land, cattle grazing, sheep pasture and woodland were as important to the rural economy of the sixteenth century as to the twentieth. Another aspect to which special attention has been given is the way in which religious changes in the country as a whole affected the shire in particular. Whether we should completely abandon periodization in the writing of history is a matter for dispute among historians, but if there is any point to the definitions 'medieval' and 'modern', the decade between 1530 and 1540 has as good a claim to be regarded as a watershed as any other dividing partition. Not only did it see the abandonment of submission to a foreign sovereign in matters of religion, however nominal that submission might have been in practice, but it witnessed also the beginnings of greater state direction. Moreover, changes that flowed from the dissolution of the monasteries had some effect upon the social structure of the shire. Although, perhaps, the results of the acquisition of monastic property were not so important in Lincolnshire as in some other counties, yeomen and gentlemen were able to obtain new lands as a result of the Dissolution and thus to advance up the social scale. But the social structure owed more to the quality of the land and its use than to religious change or political action; nevertheless the land and religious change are the two most significant factors of the history of Lincolnshire in the Tudor period.

The reader who is looking for an account of Lincolnshire worthies in the sixteenth century will not be satisfied, since this side of the story has been played down for two reasons. First, much has been written elsewhere about prominent Lincolnshire men and women, such as Katherine Willoughby, Ann Askew, and William Cecil, and at greater length than would have been possible in this book; and, secondly, without long and detailed research little more could have been added to the biographies of lesser-known inhabitants of the shire than appears in the standard works of reference such as the *Dictionary of National Biography*. Moreover, the national careers of prominent men and women do not rightly fall within the scope of a county history.

In the aspect of fundamental importance to this survey—the land and its use—I have been guided and helped at every stage by the General Editor, Dr Joan Thirsk, whose assistance has been quite inadequately acknowledged in the footnotes. For the history of the city of Lincoln I owe a great debt, as everyone working in this area does, to Sir Francis Hill and also to Professor Kathleen Major for her general encouragement and her asking of pertinent questions. Mrs Dorothy Owen's knowledge of Church and Society in Lincolnshire has been available to me in even greater measure than appeared in volume V of this History. My thanks are also due to Mrs Margaret Bowker with whom I discussed chapters II and III and who generously placed some of her notes at my disposal. To Dr Alan Rogers who has read the manuscript and offered suggestions which have saved me from many errors, and who has put me in touch with others working on various aspects of the history of the county, particularly Mr Ian Beckwith and Mr Edward Gillett, I am most grateful. The staff of the Lincolnshire Archives Office has made my visits to Lincoln not only profitable but enjoyable and, once again, I have to thank my cousin Mrs Scott Garnet of Grantham for preparing the typescript of another book.

CHAPTER I

AGRICULTURE AND THE SOCIAL STRUCTURE UNDER THE EARLY TUDORS

LINCOLNSHIRE at the close of the Middle Ages and throughout the Tudor period was one of the most isolated of English shires: the fact that it had no royal visit between 1541 and 1617, despite the limited range of Elizabeth I's journeys, bears witness to that isolation. Henry VIII, admittedly in a mood of exasperation at events there, described its inhabitants, in a well-known phrase, as "the commons of one shire and that one of the most brute and beastly of the whole realm".[1] It was in one sense at the 'end of the line' since it was the most northerly county to be governed directly from London; in Tudor times the parts of England north of the Humber came under the control of the Council of the North centred at York. But its geographical position and inadequate transport made it a neglected county and, apart from Lincoln and Boston, both in decline, and Stamford and Grimsby, it had no large towns, although many market towns of modest size existed. Outsiders had strange views about the shire and its inhabitants, which opinions were not infrequently based upon profound ignorance. It was regarded by some as an unhealthy place, the climate of which gave rise to agues and fevers,[2] and the inhabitants of the Fens were thought by some to be scarcely human beings. Nevertheless, parts of the county contained some of the richest agricultural land in the whole country.

Lincolnshire's isolation was basically attributable to geographical factors. In the south the watery fenlands that spread from Huntingdonshire through the Isle of Ely to north-western Norfolk in one direction, and in the other to the soke of Peterborough, made the county difficult of access from those parts. Moreover, the low-lying ill-drained lands in that area joined up with the Lincolnshire fens that extended from the Norfolk boundary well to the west of Spalding and included land many miles to the north of Boston. Also three other areas of the county, beside the fenland, stood only a few feet above sea level and were

[1] *SP Hy.* VIII, I, p. 463.   [2] LP, IX, p. 380.

I

therefore liable, for various reasons, to flooding; the Marsh between the Wolds and the North Sea, the Isle of Axholme and the Ancholme valley. The marshy Isle of Axholme made access to the county difficult in the north-west, and the Humber estuary presented some hazards in approaching Lincolnshire from the East Riding. In fact, only one easy approach from the rest of the kingdom existed; this was the Great North Road which entered the county at Stamford, and after passing through Rutland, re-entered Lincolnshire east of South Witham and left it again about four miles south of Newark. Thus, only Kesteven was easily accessible to the centres of political, judicial, and governmental power and there is some evidence to show that a number of Lincolnshire families, originally settled in other parts of the county, with ambitions that might lead them to the capital, moved into this south-western part of the shire.[3]

Pre-industrial England was marked by strong regional differences and even within a county that had 'as much unity as any human division'[4] regional differences existed. The county was bounded by the great bow of the coastline, and on the west the river Trent formed a natural boundary as did the limestone ridge in the south-west, but within it many differences existed between region and region. In addition to the fenland areas and the other low-lying districts already mentioned, the upland regions of the Wolds and the claylands formed two further distinct farming regions. In fact, geographical and geological divisions did not always correspond exactly with farming regions for the marshland comprised a belt of boulder clay and a belt of silt of sea deposits.[5] Nevertheless, the marsh, sweeping round the coast from Grimsby to Wainfleet and extending to a depth of ten miles inland formed the fourth region of unified farming economy. Lincolnshire was therefore not one farming region but four.

The county was, as indeed it remains to the present day, primarily agricultural; a county where arable was, perhaps, slightly more important than animal husbandry but where both abounded.[6] In the fenlands, pasture predominated over arable which amounted in Elloe wapentake to only between 4 per cent and 25 per cent of the village land. That Holland was a place where the king's purveyors obtained supplies is known from the fact that navy victuallers in 1513–14 purchased 253 fat winter-fed oxen there and had them salted at Saltfleet.[7] Thus, although the south-eastern division of the county was noted for its excellent fish and fowl, it was meat and dairy products that formed its main contri-

[3] See J. W. F. Hill, *Tudor and Stuart Lincoln*, Cambridge, 1956, p. 8.
[4] M. W. Barley, *Linconshire and the Fens*, London, 1952, p. 10.
[5] Joan Thirsk, *English Peasant Farming*, London, 1957, pp. 49, 50.
[6] *Ibid.*, p. 22.   [7] Thirsk, *op. cit.*, p. 30.

bution to the national food supply. Probate inventories show that more farmers had livestock than in Leicestershire, and that the average herd was larger in Holland than in the inland county.[8] In the 1530s, there were horses on nine out of ten farms in Leicestershire while only three-quarters of the farms in Lincolnshire used them. Sheep were numerous since Lincolnshire remained, as it had been in the Middle Ages, a great wool-producing region. A note made in 1536 on the price of wools indicates that, although Lincolnshire wool was not the most expensive, Holland wool was fetching 4s. 8d. and that of Lindsey 5s. a tod of 28 lbs. weight.[9] Throughout the sixteenth century in Holland the herds of cattle and the flocks of sheep were increasing and the problem of finding adequate pasture and commons emerged.[10]

Today about 80 per cent of the total area of Lincolnshire is cultivated, so that the shire is one of the principal arable counties of England; in the sixteenth century, although the percentage of arable may then have been less, it was also a major grain-producing county. In Holland, barley was the principal grain crop—61 per cent of the sown land was growing it in the 1530s—and it is known that the county supplied London ale brewers with barley in 1573 and 1574.[11] Thirty per cent of the sown land in Holland was under peas and beans and only 9 per cent grew wheat. In the marshland, on the other hand, wheat was the most important crop; 32 per cent of the sown land there was devoted to wheat; a crop that was grown for markets outside the area. Barley and pulses were also important crops, but, as Leland[12] remarked, the marshland was above all noted for its good wheat. But the best region from the farming point of view was the southern end of the Wolds where the soil was a deep fertile loam.[13]

The mainstay of upland farming was, however, sheep, for John Leland's impression that the Lincoln Heath, particularly around Ancaster, was good sheep land can be amply confirmed by a study of inventories, and here wool was grown for which there was much demand among Yorkshire and East Anglian clothiers. Although the number of 200–400 sheep was a large flock for a yeoman, such flocks were not unusual.[14] Gentlemen frequently had a flock of 1,000 sheep, as did Thomas Cony of Bassingthorpe and John and Thomas Hatcham of Careby at the southern end of the Lincoln Heath. The claylands in the west of the county bordering on Leicestershire and Nottinghamshire and those in the centre between the cliff and the wolds contained some of the worst soil in the county. This was highlighted by the fact that the average fortune of a sample of clayland farmers in the 1530s

[8] Thirsk, *op. cit.*, p. 32. [9] LP VIII, X, p. 90. [10] Thirsk, *op. cit.*, pp. 35, 36.
[11] Thirsk, *op. cit.*, p. 39. [12] Leland, *Itinerary*, p. 34.
[13] Thirsk, *op. cit.*, p. 81. [14] Thirsk, *op. cit.*, p. 85.

was only about 40 per cent of that of the marsh farmers.[15] The unattractive soil conditions resulted in a sparse population in the central vale of Lindsey. The principal crops here were wheat, barley, and peas, with barley more important than on the marshland but not so important as in the fens in respect of the percentage of sown arable.[16] Rye, although only taking up 6½ per cent of the sown arable, was a more significant crop in the claylands than in the other regions of Lincolnshire. These lands were areas of mixed husbandry: in the western lowlands north and south of Lincoln the land use has been calculated as between arable and grass land at six to four.[17] At one place, Long Bennington, 67 per cent of the land was arable, 9½ per cent meadow and 19 per cent enclosed pasture. The southern claylands between the Heath and the fen, to the east of the river Witham, was the principal forest land of Lincolnshire which produced much timber as the name Timberland reminds us.

What clearly emerges from a survey of early Tudor agriculture, taking all the four farming regions of the county together, is that barley was the major crop.[18] It was sold to maltsters and brewers from outside the shire, both from London and from Yorkshire. The second largest crop was pulses and this was directly connected with livestock husbandry for they were used chiefly as winter feed for stock in a county that was an important cattle and sheep rearing district. Differences appeared from region to region and the average herds of cattle and flocks of sheep of the marshland farmer were larger than those of the clayland farmer. Lincolnshire was champion country:[19] the crops were cultivated in large open fields and in the marshland there were frequently only two fields, the East and the West field, so called because they lay on either side of the main north–south road.[20] It would appear that in some places, in particular at North Thoresby and Tetney, one field lay fallow every year and this may well have been the rule in the sixteenth century. But this keeping of half the land fallow each year provided valuable grazing especially for sheep and led to a mixed farming economy.

What was the social structure of this overwhelmingly agricultural shire? 'The want of gentlemen here to inhabit' was a fact lamented by the officials in Holland who were in charge of the muster returns in 1580, and it is true that the 'aristocracy' in the villages of that division of

[15] Thirsk, *op. cit.*, p. 56.   [16] Thirsk, *op. cit.*, p. 101.   [17] Thirsk, *op. cit.*, p. 95.
[18] Thirsk, *op. cit.*, p. 102.
[19] J. D. Gould, 'The Inquisition of Depopulation in Lincolnshire', EHR 67, 1952, pp. 393–5 and I. S. Leadam, *The Domesday of Inclosures, 1517–18*, Roy. His. Soc., 1897, pp. 243–60.
[20] Thirsk, *op. cit.*, p. 61.

the shire did not consist of a squire and his family but rather of a group of middling rich yeomen.[21] A modern map of Holland shows no gentlemen's seats in the wapentakes of Elloe and Skirbeck, and none of any size in Kirton, and there were few in those parts of Kesteven which adjoin Holland or in the Isle of Axholme. Holland for whatever reason, and Danish influence is perhaps an insufficient explanation, was a district of small but prosperous farms and remained so until the twentieth century.[22] In Lindsey and Kesteven there was a lower proportion of rich taxpayers but they might justifiably be classed as gentry. In the small Wold and Heath villages sharp differences between rich and poor are demonstrable in the Tudor period. Poor harvests had far reaching effects upon the two-thirds of the population which was below or only barely above the poverty line.[23]

The distinction between yeomen and gentry is sometimes a difficult one to determine and might frequently reflect nothing more than the way in which a man wished to style himself. Richard Taylor of Beckingham, for example, who was styled 'yeoman', left property worth £399 7s. on his death in 1590, a sum that was on the level of that left by the squirearchy. The paucity of gentlemen and esquires in the parts of Holland in a list, dated between 1550 and 1560, is remarkable, for only ten names appear on it compared with twenty-one in Kesteven and ninety-five in Lindsey.[24]

Lincolnshire was then a county with relatively few great landowners who dominated the local scene. Moreover, it was, in a sense, leaderless in the early Tudor period,[25] since no great family with clear precedence like, for example, the Percies in Northumberland emerged in the shire between the death of viscount Beaumont in 1507—and he had been insane since 1487—and the entry into Lincolnshire affairs of Charles Brandon, duke of Suffolk in the second and third decades of the sixteenth century. With viscount Beaumont's death the great Bardolf-Beaumont complex of lands within the county came into the king's hands.[26] The Welles lands came into the hands of the Crown with the death of John lord Welles in 1499, as the Cromwell estates had done on the demise of lord Cromwell in 1471. As there were extensive lands of the duchy of Lancaster in Lincolnshire,[27] notably the honour of

---

[21] Ibid., p. 47.   [22] Thirsk, op. cit., p. 44.

[23] W. G. Hoskins, 'Harvest Fluctuations and English Economic History, 1480–1619', AHR XII, 1964, p. 29.

[24] Lincs. NQ, x, 1908–9, p. 60 and B. M. Harleian MS. 2145.

[25] M. E. James, 'Obedience and Dissent in Henrician England: The Lincolnshire Rebellion 1536', Past & Present, 48, 1970, p. 40.

[26] G.E.C., Complete Peerage, sub nomine.

[27] R. Somerville, History of the Duchy of Lancaster, I, 1953, p. 134 et passim and P.R.O. Lists and Indexes, No. XXXIV, pt. II, 1910, pp. 78–81.

Bolingbroke and the manors of Sutton and Long Bennington, the result of these forfeitures was that much land in the county at the beginning of the Tudor period was under the control of the Crown. But royal authority was far away, the king himself being more and more frequently settled in or near London, and members of many local families such as the Husseys, Dymokes, Tyrwhits and Thimbelbies[28] became bailiffs of Duchy lands and of those of the late lord Cromwell. Many lands and offices in Lincolnshire were then in the hands of the Crown and no one family dominated the shire until Charles Brandon, duke of Suffolk became the guardian of Katherine, lady Willoughby in 1529 and subsequently, in 1533 or 1534, his ward's husband.[29] The Willoughby estates together with the extensive monastic property which he acquired between 1537 and 1539 made him for a time the most prominent man in the county, but his public service was so demanding that he can have spent little time in the shire. His wish to be buried at Tattershall was not fulfilled, but it may demonstrate that, up to his death in 1545, he regarded Lincolnshire as his principal home.[30]

Under the Tudor monarchs down to the 1530s Lincolnshire was a county where yeoman and gentry families, a few of which had risen to the honour of knighthood, held sway without being under the domination of one or two great territorial magnates. Many of these families remained prominent in the county in the early years of the present century and some still play their part in Lincolnshire society. There is clear evidence of yeoman families prospering and entering the ranks of the gentry in the fourteenth and fifteenth centuries; the Custs of Pinchbeck and the Skipwiths of Ormsby are two examples.[31] Two other prominent families were the Heneages and the Tyrwhits. The former had been settled at Hainton, five miles south-east of Market Rasen, in the fourteenth century, and the latter at Kettleby, three miles east of Brigg, from the same period.[32] Perhaps more prestigious, because of the part its head played as king's champion, was the Dymoke family at Scrivelsby near Horncastle.[33] The family of Thorold was already long established at Marston before the opening of the Tudor period as were

[28] James, op. cit., p. 40.

[29] G.E.C. Complete Peerage sub nomine and see SR III, 97–8 for act of Parliament confirming his title to lands.

[30] See LP XI, 569 for his acquisition of Tattershall and ibid., XII, 1103; XIII, ii, 1269; xx, ii, 189 for his monastic property and income.

[31] G. A. J. Hodgett, 'The Dissolution of the Religious Houses in Lincolnshire and the Changing Structure of Society', LAAS IV, pt. 1, n.s., 1951, p. 83.

[32] A. R. Maddison, Lincolnshire Pedigrees, Harleian Society, vols. 50, 51, 52, sub nominibus.

[33] S. Lodge, Scrivelsby, the Home of the Champions, London, 1893, p. 57.

the Cracrofts in Hogsthorpe.[32] The Copeldikes[32] of Harrington, four miles north-west of Spilsby, and the Conys[32] of Bassingthorpe near Corby in Kesteven also played a role in the history of Tudor Lincolnshire as did the Grantham[32] family of Lincoln and Goltho. The Mussenden[32] family of Healing and the Monsons[32] of Burton and South Carlton filled many offices, while the family of Ayscough (frequently spelled Askew) of Stallingborough played a role in national as well as in county history.

Social mobility was a feature of late medieval and Tudor England and many families in the county pushed their way up the social scale at this time. The Carr family of Sleaford,[34] though it may or may not be descended from an armigerous Northumberland family, is a probable example of such advancement, since George Carr who died in 1521 was undoubtedly a merchant of the Staple while his great grandsons were being knighted in the early seventeenth century.[35] The Disneys of Norton Disney were another prolific and prosperous family whose members, though never achieving knighthood, were solid gentry.

Yeoman families such as the Bellows of Great Grimsby and the Broxholmes of Owersby near Market Rasen produced two members whose purchases and sales of monastic property in the 1540s must have caused some wealth to stick to their fingers. Perhaps they should be regarded as intermediaries rather than speculators, but it is incredible to think that they did not enrich themselves as a result of their transactions.[36] It has been asserted that few great families increased their fortunes as a result of the Crown's sale of monastic lands, and that none rose entirely as a consequence of the purchase of such properties.[37] This may well be true for the alienation of monastic property did not create the land market which had been growing in extent from the later thirteenth century: the royal sales did, however, make available throughout the country millions of acres for which there was a ready demand among the yeomen and the lesser gentry. Thus, we find that, in addition to Bellow and Broxholme, many families took part in purchases of lands that had fallen to the Crown. Among the highest ranks of the gentry, Sir Robert Hussey,[38] lord Hussey's brother, acquired lands, formerly of Catley priory, not far from Sleaford. George St Paul, at one time recorder of Lincoln, his father John, and his uncle Matthew, who was married to Margery daughter of Sir Robert Tyrwhit of Kettleby, all acquired monastic property indirectly, through the duke of Suffolk's

---

[34] *The Genealogist*, III, 1879, p. 199.
[35] A. R. Maddison, *Lincs. Pedigrees, op. cit., sub nominibus.*
[36] See p. 58.
[37] Joyce Youings, *The Dissolution of the Monasteries,* London, 1971, p. 130.
[38] Hodgett, *op. cit.,* p. 92.

alienations.[39] Some of the dealers who purchased land for splitting in smaller parcels for re-sale, and who thus provided a useful service for the yeoman farmer, although described in the grants as 'of London', undoubtedly had Lincolnshire affiliations. Thomas Kydall[40] was probably a member of the Kiddall family of South Ferriby on the Humber and William Riggs 'of Clerkenwell' may have been one of the Riggs family of Stragglethorpe, a small village near Leadenham. These men co-operated with local gentry as, for example, did Riggs with Richard Disney in 1544.

At the beginning of the Tudor period then Lincolnshire was an isolated county, with an abundance of rich farm land and a much higher proportion of rich yeomen than in most other English counties. The absence of large landowners was the outstanding feature of the first forty-five years of Tudor rule and this had a profound effect upon the shire in many ways. The appearance in the county of one or two dominant landlords, and in particular of the duke of Suffolk, may have exacerbated the strife that arose in 1536 as that upheaval in turn led to, or at least was followed by, the emergence of a larger number of more powerful families in the second half of the century of Tudor rule.[41]

[39] Hodgett, *op. cit.*, p. 94.   [40] *Ibid.*, p. 89.   [41] James, *op. cit.*, p. 41.

CHAPTER II

THE CHURCH IN LINCOLNSHIRE
BEFORE THE REFORMATION

LINCOLNSHIRE men and women obtained their living, and it was a better one than in some parts of England, from the land, but man does not live by bread alone and the spiritual needs of the population were supplied by the Church. This Church down to the 1530s was the age-old institution owing allegiance to the Pope, but it was a Church which had much national and diocesan autonomy.

The shire formed part of the huge diocese of Lincoln which extended from the Humber to the Thames and within the county two archdeaconries, Lincoln and Stow, existed. The archdeaconry of Lincoln was, by far, the larger and it was divided for administrative purposes into twenty-one deaneries or rural deaneries; the archdeaconry of Stow in the north-western part of the shire comprising only four. Within the rural deaneries' boundaries were the parishes of which there were about 630[1] excluding those in the city of Lincoln and in Stamford: including these latter the total for the county was around 650. To this number should be added the chapels of ease which were designed to meet the spiritual needs of those who resided at a distance from the parish church. In addition to the parish churches served by seculars, further spiritual resources were to be found among the religious, both men and women, who lived in about 120 institutions—monasteries, friaries or hospitals.[2] Moreover, collegiate churches were established at Spilsby, Tattershall, and in Lincoln (Cantilupe College) where numbers of clerks lived and, in addition, chantries abounded whose service required the presence of more priests. In all but the smallest parishes there should have been an incumbent, resident or otherwise, a parochial chaplain who was a priest, and sometimes a deacon or sub-deacon, but, a priest and his clerk, the essential minimum, were always present.[3] The clergy in the

---

[1] A count based on H. Salter (ed.), *A Subsidy collected in the diocese of Lincoln, in 1526*, Oxford, 1909, and T. Allen, *The History of the County of Lincoln*, 1834.

[2] D. M. Owen, *Church and Society in Medieval Lincolnshire*, Lincoln, 1971, App. 3; and D. Knowles and R. N. Hadcock, *Medieval Religious Houses*, London, 2nd ed., 1972.

[3] D. M. Owen, *op. cit.*, p. 132.

parishes before the Reformation were almost certainly more numerous than after it.

Who were these parish clergy, what were their numbers, and what was the state of their life? A subsidy collected in the diocese in 1526 enables us to ascertain fairly completely the numbers of clergy in the shire in that year as well as their stipends.[4] In some larger centres of population friaries are included, in others they are not, so that we cannot be certain of the absolute accuracy of the numbers of clergy within the county, but in some 632 parishes plus some chapels at ease at least 1,312 men were theoretically available to minister to the spiritual needs of perhaps some 70,000 Lincolnshire men, women, and children. The numbers in the early Tudor period were declining for fewer ordinands seemed to be presenting themselves, and the diocese of Lincoln, it would seem, ordained relatively fewer priests than some other dioceses.[5] Yet this shortfall in numbers ordained over the number of vacancies did not result in patrons being unable to find men to serve in the parishes, for pluralism was widespread, and in fact it proved difficult for many men in orders to obtain a benefice. The result was that some had to serve as curates for many years even in some instances for life.

The social background of the clergy varied considerably:[6] a few came from noble families, many more had connections with the landed gentry, but most, probably, came from humble families since their origins, like bishop Atwater's, are often difficult to determine. As to their educational qualifications, wide variations occurred: it had been laid down that no one should be admitted to orders without an examination[7] but this was to test whether the candidate had reached the right age to be a priest, whether he was morally suitable and whether he had an adequate educational standard. Judgement on the two latter considerations lay in the hands of the bishop or, more precisely, in the hands of his examining chaplain. A similar examination was held before a priest was admitted to a benefice and, although these two examinations were not always carried out to the letter of the Canon Law, we do know that bishop Longland down to 1535 examined with great diligence both on ordination and on institution to benefices.[8] The adequacy of the ordinand's educational standards must indeed have varied and then, as now, the bishop could ordain any man he pleased, provided he was satisfied as to his qualifications. But whereas today no bishop would

---

[4] H. Salter, op. cit.

[5] M. Bowker, The Secular Clergy in the Diocese of Lincoln 1495–1520, Cambridge, 1968, pp. 38, 70–74.

[6] Bowker, op. cit., p. 41.

[7] Ibid., by the Council of Oxford, Lyndwood, Provinciale, Lib. I, tit. 5.

[8] Ex inf. Mrs Margaret Bowker.

ordain any man who had not spent some time at a theological college, in the early sixteenth century no clear definition existed as to what educational requirements were necessary. The 1526 returns do not list all the graduates, for a distinction in the form of address was made only between those who were called *magistri*, that is the Masters of Arts, and the rest who were known as *domini*, some of whom undoubtedly held a B.A. degree, some who might have come down without completing their degree course and others who had never been to a university. Out of more than 1,300 clergy in the returns of 1526, 131 were Masters of Arts and a further two, in addition to their master's degree, had doctorates.[9]

The state of the clergy is known to us principally from the visitations of parishes within the diocese which the bishop or his commissary made from time to time. Bishop Atwater's visitation[10] of the parishes in most of the rural deaneries of the two archdeaconries of Lincoln and Stow gives us a clear picture of some of the weaknesses of the local clergy. These visitations were designed to uncover faults and any account of the work of the clergy based solely on them must of necessity be biased. If the parish priest was a man of unimpeachable morals who duly celebrated mass and performed his pastoral duties nothing more than *omnia bene* was recorded and no details were given of outstandingly meritorious behaviour by the clergy.

One of the most common complaints against the clergy was non-residence[11] and the records show that both rectors and vicars did not reside. The non-residence of vicars was likely to be the more serious as alternative arrangements to have a man in the parish in priest's orders might not have been made, whereas rectors might more legitimately be non-resident. Rectories were frequently held by corporate bodies such as Oxford or Cambridge colleges or were appropriated to monastic houses: such bodies could not themselves serve the cure of souls but they were under obligation to provide a parish priest. Moreover, some rectories were tied to cathedral canonries and like offices, and arrangements similar to those made by colleges and monasteries had then to be made. Vicarages on the other hand were held to require residence[12] and, in the absence of the vicar, a parish might be left without a priest. Archdeacons in their visitations sometimes discovered non-residence,[13] but more frequently the episcopal visitation brought it to light.[14] Atwater's visitation in 1519 revealed some

[9] These figures from the edited subsidy roll of 1526 may need correction.
[10] A. Hamilton Thompson (ed.), 'Visitations in the Diocese of Lincoln 1517-31', vol. I, LRS 33, 1940.
[11] Bowker, *op. cit.*, III.   [12] Bowker, *op. cit.*, p. 85.   [13] *Ibid.*, pp. 89-90.
[14] LRS 33, pp. 55-100.

seventy-two parishes in the county where the incumbent was non-resident but nine of the rural deaneries were either unvisited or, if visited, the records have been lost; so that if the proportion of non-residents was as high there as among the visited deaneries, the true figure for the whole shire might be about 115. This would mean that in about 18 per cent of the parishes in Lincolnshire the incumbent was non-resident, but that should not be taken to imply that all those parishes were without the spiritual assistance of a priest. But some were, and it has been noted that of fifty-one cases of absenteeism recorded in 1500 in the archdeaconry of Lincoln, fourteen parishes still had a non-resident incumbent in 1519.[15] Although it may be that some of these had a resident in the intervening years, it is also highly probable that non-residence was a long term, if not a permanent, state.

Non-residence occurred especially in lucrative benefices which were in the hands of Papal or royal office-holders but absence was only possible provided dispensations allowing it had been received from the pope or the diocesan bishop.[16] The reasons for non-residence were sometimes such as might win approval, since rectories and dispensations were frequently given to young men who were students at Oxford or Cambridge or, occasionally, to those on pilgrimage. But the numbers who were pure pluralists probably exceeded the students in the ratio of three to one.[17] From episcopal records stretching over the years from 1514 to 1521 it can be seen that the rectories of Bratoft, Burton-by-Lincoln, Rand, South Collingham, and Surfleet and the vicarage of Burgh-on-Bain had, at some time or another, student incumbents;[18] but the places with no incumbent because the priest had another living mounted to fifteen at least. Moreover, probably some of a further thirty-three parishes, whose rectors or vicars did not state the reason for non-residence, were deprived because of pluralism, and another nine places had a non-resident who was absent on royal service, or because he was a chaplain, or by reason of engagement on diocesan business. Not infrequently a concomitant of non-residence was that the rector or vicar leased the rectory or vicarage to a layman with a consequent reduction in hospitality, and twenty-three such leases are recorded in bishop Atwater's visitation in 1519.[19] But on the whole we may conclude that few parishes were left without any provision having been made for them, and only Sutton in the Marsh, Clee, East Ravendale, Wilksby, and Cotes by Stow seem to have suffered in this way.[20]

Lapses other than non-residence, however, occurred. Having women

<hr>

[15] Bowker, *op. cit.*, p. 91.   [16] *Ibid.*, p. 93.
[17] Applying the diocesan figures to the shire, Bowker, *op. cit.*, p. 97.
[18] Bowker, *op. cit.*, App. IV.   [19] LRS 33, pp. 55–100.
[20] Bowker, *op. cit.*, p. 105.

in the rectory or vicarage was a perennial problem. In 1519, fifty-six allegations were made that rectors or vicars had women in the house, although in many instances it is reported either that they were not suspect or their relationship to the priest (mother, sister) was recorded. But wagging tongues were ever ready to talk in that regard, and four clerks were accused of incontinence. Some strange aberrations were noted. A priest was not supposed to take part in any other calling, and so the priest at Surfleet was noted as being a merchant and a farmer,[21] and at Saleby the vicar was accused of keeping a common tavern,[22] and of another vicar it was recorded that he worked in the fields. But the number of offences is remarkably low and of serious crime there appears to have been little apart from the foul deed of John Wymark, a former chaplain, of Sutton-on-Sea who killed his illegitimate child by drowning him in the sea.[23] Sometimes, however, priests did transgress against the common law and John Wilkinson, a priest of Grantham, was accused of attacking John Dickenson although subsequently he was acquitted.[24]

Shortcomings on the part of the clergy were duly recorded. Parishioners accused three priests of not celebrating mass as they should and many more were guilty of failure to maintain the fabric of the church. The chancel of the parish church was the responsibility of the incumbent and it is said to have been defective or 'ruined' in forty-five places. The word *ruinosus*, it has been asserted,[25] meant little more than 'in need of attention', but it is striking that a large number of rectors either could not, or would not, make the necessary repairs because of the rise in prices that occurred from the second decade of the sixteenth century. The not infrequent complaints as to the lack of fencing of the cemetery —some twenty-one are recorded—should not perhaps be regarded as a shortcoming on the part of the incumbent for, although in some instances he appears to have been responsible, the onus of maintenance probably lay with the parishioners.

How far the clergy fell short in their obligations to visit the sick and minister to the dying it is difficult to say. In the county few complaints arise on this score. Similarly, little is heard of inadequate preaching, but this is more likely to reflect the view that little was expected rather than that it was adequately performed. Outside the towns few sermons were preached[26] and, although clergy perhaps gave more sermons towards the end of the fifteenth century,[27] the parishioners of rural Lincolnshire did not expect them.

[21] Bowker, *op. cit.*, p. 106.   [22] LRS 33, p. 82.   [23] *Ibid.*, p. 83.
[24] Bowker, *op. cit.*, p. 123.   [25] *Ibid.*, p. 129.
[26] A. G. Dickens, *The English Reformation*, London, 1967, p. 29.
[27] D. M. Owen, *op. cit.*, p. 109.

The episcopal visitations which tell us so much about the Lincolnshire clergy also give much information about the lives of the laity. Much has been written about the emergence and strengthening of lay piety in the fifty years or so before the Reformation in an attempt to show that the Church was rising from its nadir and that radical reform was unnecessary. Lincolnshire men and women may perhaps not have been influenced as much as people in south-eastern England by the writings of the English mystics and by the *devotio moderna* or deepening of spiritual life that blossomed in the late Middle Ages. A quiet pietism manifested itself among some lay people and some secular clergy,[28] but it derived from the more austere and exalted mysticism that still prevailed among a small élite of the monastic order. In this, the Carthusians, the Bridgettines, and the Observant Friars led the way and these orders were not well represented in the shire. The Carthusians had a house at Epworth[29] on the isle of Axholme, founded in 1397–8, and the Observants had a friary on the edge of the county at Newark[29] which was established as late as 1507, but it is unlikely that their influence was widespread. Nevertheless, some Lincolnshire laity may have attempted to attain salvation through devout observances, laying great emphasis upon pilgrimages and saints' relics and on the means whereby the horrors of purgatory might be mitigated.

Whatever influence the *devotio moderna* may have had—and three phases of the spiritual journey,[30] the purgative, the illuminative and the unitive ways were envisaged—there can be no doubt that more weight was laid upon saints' lives, the hours of the Blessed Virgin, and the Golden Legend than upon Biblical knowledge and scholarship.[31] The purgative way pursued by means of self mortification and good works, the illuminative, the way of a progressive series of 'experiences' often interspersed with periods of 'dryness' and desolation, and the unitive way begun by advanced contemplatives in this life yet, even by them, completed only in the world to come, might be an ideal to be aimed at, but in practice most parishioners were sunk in the superstitious stories that many saints' lives contained.

A commonplace-book written by John Gysborn,[32] curate of the parish of Allington and a Premonstratensian canon, shows the important part played by saints' lives and visions, and the negligible role of scriptural teaching. His questions in the confessional, perhaps understandably, refer to the common sins of the flesh. The sins of envy,

[28] A. G. Dickens, *op. cit.*, p. 31.
[29] M. D. Knowles and R. N. Hadcock, *Medieval Religious Houses*, London, 1971, *sub nominibus*.
[30] A. G. Dickens, *op. cit.*, p. 31.   [31] *Ibid.*, pp. 18–23.
[32] BM Sloane MS. 1584.

adultery, murder were to be enquired about, along with the demand to know about any non-payment of tithes and offerings to Holy Church. He was interested to hear any confession of drunkenness on the part of men or women, and to discover from women any giving of love potions or taking of medicines to induce abortion. His different sets of questions for men, husbandmen, and man-servants illustrate clearly Mr Gysborn's consciousness of different classes in the community of his parish.

How much spiritual illumination parishioners had in the half-century before the Reformation must as yet remain an open question but undoubtedly enough enthusiasm existed among the laity to undertake work on the parish church. As against the forty-five recorded mentions of defective chancels in 1519, only one report of a defective nave and seventeen instances of broken church windows are recorded. It may well be argued that to keep the nave in good repair ministered to the parishioners' comfort, but if their attendance at church had been poor (in fact only six cases of non-attendance were recorded in 1519) or their interest in the church lukewarm, it is reasonable to suppose that more repairs would have been outstanding. At Louth, much work, including the building of the superb steeple, occurred during the period. The expenditure between 1501 and 1515 reached £305 and the *First Church-wardens' Book*[33] covering these years describes in detail the building of the steeple. The stone, quarried at Wilsford adjacent to Ancaster, was taken by water to Appletreeness on Kyme Eau, then on to Dogdyke and Coningsby and thence by cart to Louth. Not only do we know the price of the stone but also the cost of glazing and plumbing and the amount paid for writing out the music for the mass.

As might be expected among all this enthusiasm for the Church some backsliders existed. Reference has already been made to non-attenders at church and the visitation of 1519[34] revealed three instances of taverns being open during the time of divine service and two people who worked on Sundays and feast days. Church courts rather than royal courts had the responsibility for correcting moral misdemeanours and, therefore, six accusations of adultery, twenty-three of fornication, seventeen of pandering or brothel-keeping, and twenty-three alleged scolds or diffamers were made known. The returns record allegations of pregnancies outside wedlock and of illegitimate children totalling together twenty-two. But through all these episcopal records a picture emerges of a Lincolnshire laity that on the whole was satisfied with the state of the Church and that was not much affected either by new doctrines or anti-clericalism.

[33] R. C. Dudding (ed.), *First Churchwardens' Book of Louth*, 1941, p. 181.
[34] LRS 33, pp. 55–100.

Yet Lincolnshire men and women were not completely unmoved by anti-clerical or even heretical sentiment. Disputes over tithes and fees, especially mortuary and probate fees, might easily arouse anti-clerical feelings[35] but a few laymen had a burning faith which led them to question the established ways. Bishop Longland, according to Foxe the martyrologist,[36] was a notorious persecutor but none of the cases he cites comes from the archdeaconries of Lincoln and Stow. Nearly all the heretics were concentrated in Buckinghamshire and Oxfordshire, yet it is difficult to believe that no seeds of anti-clericalism and heresy were present within the county. The parishioner of Brampton who derided the ceremonial opening of the church doors with the remark: "What a sport have we towards! will our vicar run at the quintain with God Almighty?"[37] may have had some like-minded predecessor in the first three decades of the sixteenth century who spoke against the sacrament of the Lord's body or against pilgrimages and worshipping saints or the invocation of the Blessed Virgin or who possessed scriptural books in the vernacular. But if such there were, we have little or no trace of them for bishop Longland's trouble with heretics was almost entirely in the southern part of his diocese.

The state of the Church before the Reformation cannot only be assessed by a review of the secular clergy and of the laity in the parishes. Lincolnshire was a county extremely rich in monastic houses and friaries. Within the county boundaries were some fifty-one[38] monastic houses which contained some 500[39] men and women who had taken vows. All the great orders with the exception of the Cluniac had built houses within the county and the native order established by Gilbert of Sempringham, as was to be expected, flourished in Lincolnshire. There were ten Gilbertine houses, seven[40] for canons and nuns, and three[41] for canons alone. To these monasteries and nunneries (several small dependent cells have been omitted), three preceptories of Knights Hospitallers, three secular colleges and fifteen friaries divided between the towns of Grimsby, Lincoln, Boston, Grantham, and Stamford should be added

[35] Bowker, op. cit., pp. 148–9.
[36] J. Foxe, Acts and Monuments, 4th. rev. ed., 1877, vol. IV, p. 219.
[37] J. Strype, Ecclesiastical Memorials, vol. 3, pt. ii, p. 392.
[38] Knowles and Hadcock, op. cit., passim; D. M. Owen, op. cit., App. 3; VCH Lincs., II, pp. 209–37.
[39] The figure is not precise because there is no full list of the inmates of all the houses at the time of the Dissolution.
[40] Alvingham, Bullington, Catley, Haverholme, North Ormsby, Sempringham, and Sixhills.
[41] Bridgend (a cell of Semperingham after 1445), St Katherine's Lincoln and Newstead.

in order to complete the map of sites where men and women were living under some form of rule.

What was the condition of the religious living in these foundations in the half-century before the Reformation? Perpetual vows of poverty, obedience, and chastity were taken by regulars and to assess the state of their life really involves examining how far these vows were kept. The episcopal visitations of bishops Atwater (1514–21) and Longland (1521–47)[42] that tell us so much about the parishes, are also highly informative on the religious houses, at least on those that were not exempt from episcopal visitation. Some of the shortcomings undoubtedly arose from poverty. In Lincolnshire, thirty-nine houses had a clear annual income of less than £200,[43] and even this figure cloaks the grinding poverty of some houses of which the twenty-five that had an income of less than £100 *per annum* are examples. The plight of Fosse, where eight nuns were living on a net income of £7 3s. 6d.,[44] was indeed extreme, but five other houses existed with incomes of less than £20 *per annum*.[45] Numbers of inmates had been falling. Poverty led to a shortage[46] of religious in the house and, consequently, to their inability to perform the daily round of services and it should not therefore be any surprise that a feeling of apathy towards religious observance was commonly found by the visitors. Sins of omission were more frequent than sins of commission although the latter did occur.

Information given to the bishop or his deputy shows that the monks and nuns were fond of gossip and it would be well to discount some of their statements: moreover, the bishop's object was to discover faults and not to publish virtues. Nevertheless, it is obvious from frequent repetition that certain misdemeanours were common in many houses. Some Lincolnshire monks were great sportsmen, particularly fond of hunting or fowling, playing backgammon, throwing dice or shooting at the butts, and at Humberstone in June 1525 the abbot told the visitor Dr Rayne that the canons went out of the house without his licence and played tennis in the town.

Excessive drinking which had been much noted between 1420 and 1449 seems to have been less common during Longland's episcopate, but there is a reference to it at Bourne where Henry Alton and John Todd made a night of it in the local hostelry, drinking and telling yarns early and late.[47] At Newhouse,[48] in 1488 bishop Redman

---

[42] LRS 33 and 35.   [43] *Valor Eccl.* (Rec. Comm.), IV, pp. 1–144.

[44] *Ibid.*, p. 132.

[45] Gokewell, (8 nuns; £13 19s. 9d.) St. Leonard's Grimsby, (8 or 9 nuns: £9 14s. 7d.) Hyrst, Irford (7 nuns: £16 12s. 10d.) and Torksey, (4 canons: £13 1s. 4d.).

[46] VCH Lincs., II, *passim*.   [47] LRS 35, p. 83.

[48] Camden Soc., 3rd ser., XII, 1906, p. 79.

discovered four canons, John Durham, Thomas Hall, James Grimsby, and William Barlinge going out drinking after compline and there were similar incidents at Tupholme.[49] But this relative lack of evidence may not point conclusively to a decline in drinking since *omnia bene* was a frequent reply to the bishop or his representative. Complaints, usual in any community, were made that the head of the house favoured some or was unduly harsh on other members of the family. Heads of large houses were princes of the medieval Church and frequently tended to act without that co-operation with their brethren that was laid down in the monastic rule. The abbot of Bourne, John Small, gave no account of the monastery's finances according to his second in command, prior Thomas Barne.[50]

The vow of chastity taken by the religious proved for many Lincolnshire monks and nuns a vow most difficult to fulfil. Lapses are fairly frequently mentioned. At Greenfield priory in 1525, Margaret Newcome[51] was reproved by her prioress for having a child, and the prioress herself was only just cleared of being in a similar condition. At Tupholme in 1497 Thomas Pynderwelle had had a child by a woman named Philippa.[52] The presence of women, even washerwomen, in a monastery was always a cause of alarm to the visitor; at Wellow he ordered the canons to have all their dirty linen collected and taken by a servant to the washerwoman outside the enclosure,[53] and he commanded that the nuns of St Leonard's Grimsby were not to act as washerwomen for them.[54] On the other hand the prioress of Stixwold was ordered not to talk to the steward unless at least one nun was present.[55]

Apathy and neglect of religious duties are the chief faults with which the religious may be charged. Many houses, perhaps the majority, failed to maintain the complete number of services. Rising to matins at 2 a.m. was frequently not carried out; at least three houses, Bardney,[56] Bourne,[57] and Humberstone[58] did not hold services properly, and in three others it is highly doubtful whether services were fully observed. In addition to neglecting their religious duties, some houses were not fulfilling their eleemosynary functions. It has been calculated that in the country generally only about 3 per cent of monastic income was given in alms which were exempt from the 'tenth' tax.[59]

In Lincolnshire twenty-two houses gave no alms free of tenths and

[49] *Ibid.*, p. 164.   [50] LRS 35, p. 84.   [51] *Ibid.*, pp. 35, 161 *et seq.*
[52] Camden Soc., *op. cit.*, p. 164.   [53] LRS 37, p. 117.
[54] *Ibid.*, p. 119.   [55] *Ibid.*, p. 104.   [56] LRS 35, pp. 77–8.
[57] *Ibid.*, pp. 82–5.   [58] *Ibid.*, p. 167.
[59] A. Savine, *English Monasteries on the Eve of the Dissolution*, Oxf. Studies in Social and Legal Hist., I, Oxford, 1909, p. 238.

another ten with incomes of less than £50 *per annum* might be regarded as too poor to be able to offer charity.

In conclusion, the religious in the fifty years before the Reformation undoubtedly failed to reach the ideals laid down for them by the various rules they professed to follow. Their sins were, however, those of omission rather than commission and there is no evidence to show that they were unpopular with their neighbours in the countryside.

Finally, the cathedral church in Lincoln played a vital role in the spiritual life of the county. The cathedral church of the Blessed Virgin Mary at Lincoln was the most important collegiate church in the diocese and it was served by clergy whose prime duties were liturgical rather than pastoral.[60] The whole diocese had fifty-eight canons of whom twenty-eight held prebends within Lincolnshire and most of these twenty-eight prebendaries held rectories from which they were maintained either in the cathedral close or elsewhere.[61] If they were absent from their benefice they had to provide a suitable priest to attend to the spiritual needs of the parishioners. It has been pointed out[62] that by the sixteenth century most canons did not reside and that, indeed, it was rare for more than five ever to do so at the same time: prebendal stalls became the perquisite of royal or episcopal servants who thereby acquired the income that went with them. Occasionally foreigners were given prebends and Polydore Vergil, the papal collector and historian, was prebendary of Scamblesby from 1507 to 1513. But appointment to prebendal stalls was not simply a matter of finding incomes for royal or papal servants, it offered a means whereby the bishop could provide for scholars, and the overwhelming majority of cathedral canons were university men with higher degrees who were making their way to the top of the ecclesiastical ladder. To that extent cathedral canonries helped men who were going to make an above-average contribution to the life of the Church. Those who did reside had first to undertake 'major residence', which meant two thirds of a year, but could later opt for 'minor residence'—a period of one third of a year.[63]

The value of the different prebends varied greatly from St Martin's which was worth only 5s. a year to Louth at £36 3s. 4d. and so preferment from one prebendal stall to another frequently took place.[64] Resident canons after paying a sum of £40 into the common fund then

[60] Bowker, *op. cit.*, p. 155.

[61] Le Neve, *Fasti*, I, Linc. Diocese, comp. H. P. F. King, London, 1962, and *1526 Subsidy, passim.*

[62] Bowker, *op. cit.*, p. 155.   [63] Bowker, *op. cit.*, p. 161.

[64] R. E. G. Cole (ed.), 'The Chapter Acts of the Cathedral Church of Lincoln', LRS 12, 1915, p. 202 *et seq.*

shared the common income and were each assigned to a house and, on average, a resident received a little over £20 *per annum*. Below the canons were those who might be termed the 'curates of the cathedral'. A mass of clergy with lower qualifications and with far less opportunity for promotion than the canons enjoyed, filled the offices of vicars choral, poor clerks and chantry priests. The poor clerks kept the altars and assisted at mass, the vicars choral were the deputies for the non-resident canons and the chantry priests said the offices at the many chantries in the cathedral. The vicars choral although they deputized for non-resident canons were frequently not in priests' orders, and in 1514 only ten out of the thirty had been ordained priest.[65] The vicars choral usually managed in time to receive a chantry, and the income from it, together with their stipend, allowed them to live perhaps as well as most parish clergy. They must have appreciated proximity to the cathedral since most of them remained there over long periods.

The resident canons meeting in chapter conducted the business of the cathedral, taking upon themselves specific duties. The provost looked after the churches and estates belonging to the common fund. The senior canon held the office for one year before handing on to the next senior. Other canons in residence filled the offices of master of the choristers, supervisor of the fabric, and supervisor of St Hugh's shrine, while two canons audited the accounts and another was master of the Burghersh chantry.[66] Full chapter meetings were called when business demanded and the annual number held varied between nine in 1504 and fifty-six in 1508 but the most usual number was about twenty a year.[67] As the sheriff and justices of the city had no power within the close, the dean and chapter had to make arrests and keep order there and also, as they had the power of the ordinary in the exercise of ecclesiastical jurisdiction, they were obliged to grant the probate of wills. Relationships between the dean and chapter and the bishop on the one hand and with the city on the other at this period were harmonious: relationships between the canons themselves were much less cordial.

Discord arose particularly over the burdens of the treasurer who was called upon to provide goods and services which left him little from his income of about £20 *per annum*. Trouble also arose between the chapter and the lower clergy. Vicars choral were accused of neglecting the night offices—rising for matins at 2 a.m. was as irksome for them as it was in monastic houses. A fine of 1*d.* was levied for non-attendance at matins, mass, or vespers. The poor clerks were accused of being ill-educated and of attending brothels although after 1507 some improvement probably occurred. Their indiscipline may well have been partly the result of their inadequate pay (since in 1514, eleven poor clerks

[65] Bowker, *op. cit.*, p. 165.   [66] *Ibid.*, p. 166.   [67] *Ibid.*, p. 167.

received only £11 18s. 4d. between them) and their poor prospects of promotion.

But the cathedral remained a centre of pilgrimage in which were performed also a number of plays. Special sermons were preached there and attending to the needs of the laity provided *foci* of interest for the cathedral staff, although the lesser clergy may not have taken such an active part in this work as the resident canons. In conclusion, the Church in Lincolnshire in all its branches down to the 1530s seems to have satisfied the needs of the laity which it served.

CHAPTER III

THE DISSOLUTION OF THE MONASTERIES AND THE LINCOLNSHIRE REVOLT

THE old order in the Church which, as we have seen, appeared to be quite satisfactory to the majority of Lincolnshire men and women was rudely shaken in the fourth decade of the century. This is not the place to chronicle, even in the barest outline, the history of the Reformation in the country generally, but we must examine merely some of the effects of that movement upon the county. For the shire the most important consequence of the religious changes was perhaps the dissolution of the monasteries since that aspect of Henry VIII's policy principally sparked off a revolt which, although of short duration, had far-reaching effects in Lincolnshire and elsewhere. Other factors such as the examination of the clergy and a fear of increased taxation played a part, but the Dissolution was perhaps the major cause of unrest. For ten days between Monday 2 October and Thursday 12 October the king was faced with a major rebellion in the county but no analysis of the happenings of those days can be attempted before we look at the events that led up to them.

By the act of Parliament 25 Henry VIII c.25[1] the visitation of all exempt monasteries was entrusted to the king who was to appoint visitors who were to visit in the same way as the bishop or his deputy dealt with non-exempt houses in the diocese. During the year 1534 discussions took place on the dissolution of the monasteries and the forfeiture of their entire property to the Crown,[2] or so Chapuys the Imperial ambassador was informed, but when parliament met in November no act of general confiscation was introduced. The act granting first fruits and tenths to the Crown, 26 Henry VIII c.3,[3] required for its implementation a revaluation of ecclesiastical property since the last thorough one had been made in 1291. A commission collected the relevant information between January and June 1535 although the Lincolnshire returns were not ready until 3 September.[4]

[1] SR III, p. 469.   [2] LP VII, 24, 114, 871 (p. 324), 1141.
[3] SR III, pp. 493-9.   [4] J. Hunter, *Introduction to the Valor Ecclesiasticus*, IV, p. 25.

The commissioners valuing the benefices were John Longland bishop of Lincoln, the mayor of Lincoln William Palfreyman, the dean George Heneage, Robert Hussey, William Ayscough, Robert Tyrwhit, William Skipwith, William Tyrwhit, Andrew Billesby, John Copledyke, Edward Maddison, Sir Thomas Mussenden, Thomas and John Heneage, John Monson, Anthony Irby, Richard Ogle, Thomas Moigne, Vincent Grantham, and George St Paul.[5] All these were representatives of gentry families that one would expect to find being employed on such government business. But before the results of this survey were available, a decision had probably been taken, sometime before 4 June 1535,[6] to dissolve the monasteries if possible, and to this end other visitors were sent round to report on the state of the monasteries.

This second visitation which it was thought that Cromwell might undertake in July did not really get under way until the autumn, but commissioners were acting probably as early as August when Dr Layton reported to Cromwell on the state of Bath abbey.[7] Dr Richard Layton, Dr Thomas Legh, John ap Rice, Dr John London, John Tregonwell, and Thomas Bedyll acted as commissioners, and their instructions were probably those drafted earlier in the year.[8] They were similar to those that bishops had used for centuries in enquiring into the morals and the behaviour of the religious.

No extant record exists of the names of the commissioners for Lincolnshire. It is highly probable, however, that certain Lincolnshire houses, if not all, were visited by Dr Thomas Legh between the end of November and 22 December 1535 when he met Dr Richard Layton at Lichfield.[9] It is known that the two doctors started from Lichfield and purposed to visit some Trentside monasteries and to arrive in York by Twelfth Night, and it is therefore possible that they may together have visited some Lincolnshire houses during that fortnight.[10]

The reports on the state of the monasteries reached Cromwell and the king in January and February 1536. The visitors, especially Dr Legh, had been severe and it was felt by some that life was being made deliberately unpleasant for the religious so that large numbers might leave the cloister.[11] How much of the report was communicated to parliament is not certain but Henry VIII presented a bill to the house of commons on 11 March,[12] and it must have passed both houses before the last session of the 'Reformation Parliament' terminated on 14 April.

[5] *Val. Eccl.*, IV, p. 1.   [6] LP VIII, 822.   [7] LP IX, 42.
[8] LP VIII, 76.
[9] R. W. Dixon, *Hist. of the Church of England*, I, p. 335, quoting J. Strype, *Ecclesiastical Memorials*, I, p. 383, quoting B. M. Cottonian MSS. Cleop. E.IV, 5.
[10] Thomas Wright, 'Letters relating to the suppression of the monasteries', (Camden Soc. ,XXVI, 1843, p. 93.
[11] LP IX, 434.   [12] Wright, *op. cit.*, pp. 38–9.

This act, 27 Henry VIII c.28, on account of the "manifest synne, vicious, carnall and abhomynable lyving" in the smaller monasteries, dissolved all houses with a clear yearly value of less than £200.[13]

In order to make provision for the additions to the royal revenue that would result from this dissolution, a new department, the court of the Augmentations of the revenue of the king's crown, was established by 27 Henry VIII c.27.[14] The composition of the court as enacted was a chancellor, a treasurer, an attorney, and a solicitor together with ten auditors and seventeen receivers. Richard Rich was appointed as the first chancellor on 19 April and the first records of the court date from 24 April 1536.[15] A commission formed of members of the court, John Freeman and John Wiseman for Lincolnshire,[16] and of local gentry was appointed at the end of April, and it was to make another survey of the lands of the houses worth less than £200 per annum and to dissolve those houses affected by the statute.[17] The main duty of this new commission was to value the demesnes of the house, the lead, bells, jewels, plate and farm stocks and to send those who wished to remain in religion to other houses and those who were willing to serve as seculars to the archbishop of Canterbury and the lord chancellor for capacities. These commissioners valued the monastic property again and their surveys, known as the 'Suppression Accounts', usually raised the valuation figures somewhat above those of the *Valor Ecclesiasticus*. These new figures were used as a basis both for sales and leases and for the sum to be paid to the Crown by the receiver if the land remained in the king's hands.

The commissioners for the dissolution began their work in the summer of 1536, the chief representatives in the county of the court of Augmentations being John Freeman[18] and John Wiseman.[19] Freeman was at Vaudey on 7 August when he expressed his intention of pulling down roofs, battlements, and stairs as the cost of total demolition would have been excessive, amounting, in Freeman's view, to over £1,000 for Lincolnshire as a whole.[20] He proposed to sell the bells and the lead from the suppressed houses in the county which might bring in 6,000 to 7,000 marks and to leave the walls to be used for stone supplies as buyers emerged. We do not know the itinerary that was taken, though he may have begun his work as early as 1 June,[21] but there were some forty houses in Lincolnshire with an income of under £200 a year.[22]

[13] SR III, pp. 575–8; Joyce Youings, *The Dissolution of the Monasteries*, London, 1971, pp. 155–9.

[14] SR III, pp. 569–74.   [15] LP X, 721.   [16] LP XII, i, 702.

[17] Savine, *op. cit.*, p. 42 *et seq.*; LP X, 721; *ibid.*, XI, App. 15.

[18] W. C. Richardson, *History of the Court of Augmentations*, Baton Rouge, 1961, p. 49.

[19] *Ibid.*, p. 55.   [20] LP XI, 242.   [21] LP X, 1026.

[22] Savine, *op. cit.*, App. pp. 276–7.

However, by no means all of these were suppressed. If the ministers' accounts[23] for the year 1536–7 represent the full list of monastic houses that came into the Crown's possession, it would appear that only twenty houses were suppressed in the summer and autumn of 1536.[24] Stixwold was suppressed and almost immediately re-founded for the Benedictine nuns from Stainfield. But there were another fourteen houses, not counting six that were cells or dependants of other monasteries outside the county, whose income was under £200 *per annum*. Six of these belonged to the Gilbertine order which surrendered *en bloc* in the autumn of 1538, two were commandries of the Knights Hospitallers, and others, such as Fosse, may just have been too poor to bother about; the Augustinians at Kyme paid a heavy fine to continue.[25] How long it took the suppression commission to get round we do not know but it was at Legbourne on 2 October and it may well be that the task of dissolving the smaller monasteries had been completed by that date.[26]

Along with the suppression commissioners at Legbourne, at the beginning of October two other commissions were in the neighbourhood of Louth. Parliament had granted Henry a subsidy and the commissioners to assess and levy it in Lincolnshire were to meet at Caistor on Tuesday 3 October for that purpose. Thirdly Dr Richard Rayne, the bishop's commissary, had been appointed Cromwell's commissary to carry out a visitation of the clergy in the lord privy seal's capacity as the king's vicegerent in spirituals. The aim of this enquiry was to elucidate information as to the moral and political soundness of the clergy, their educational qualifications and their capacity for understanding and preaching the new doctrines.[27] Mr Frankish, the diocesan registrar, was to act as commissary in the rural deanery of Louth and Louthesk and also in that of Yarborough while Dr Rayne himself officiated in the rural deanery of Horncastle and Hill. This coincidence of the three commissions led to considerable gatherings of Lindsey men in Louth, Horncastle, and Caistor over the week-end of 30 September—2 October and among them grew the wholly understandable feeling that central government in one form or another was pressing too hardly upon them. The harvest, which had been a slightly above-average one,[28]

---

[23] PRO, *Lists & Indexes*, XXXIV, *Ministers' Accounts*, pt. II, p. 89.

[24] Bourne, Vaudey, Neubo, Swineshead, Nocton Park, Stainfield, Tupholme, Greenfield, Markby, Hagnaby, Legbourne, Louth Park, Humberstone, Wellow, Newhouse, Elsham, Newstead-next-Stamford, Thornholme, Gokewell, Torksey.

[25] Knowles and Hadcock, *op. cit.*, p. 162; LP XI, g. 519 (2).   [26] LP XII, i, 380.

[27] The injunctions given by the commissary to the clergy in N. Pocock (ed.), *Burnet's History of the Reformation*, 1865, IV, pp. 308–13.

[28] W. G. Hoskins, 'Harvest Fluctuations and English Economic History, 1480–1619', AHR XII, 1964, p. 45; T. Rogers, *Hist. of Agriculture & Prices in England*, IV, pp. 258–9.

was in, and the clergy who had gathered together for the visitation and the substantial men of the four wapentakes come to negotiate the incidence of the subsidy would have had time to talk among themselves. Rumour flew among them.

Perhaps a rebellion had been brewing if not planned for some time and some men may have come in from outside the county to take part.[29] The rebellion began on Monday 2 October after a prelude at Louth the previous evening. Several members of the subsidy commission, Sir Robert Tyrwhit, Sir William Ayscough, and others fell into the hands of the rebels.[30] Sir Robert and Sir William along with Thomas Portington, Sir Thomas Mussenden, and Thomas Moigne were detained by the rebels, as was John Heneage the brother of the dean of Lincoln.[31] The first news of the rebellion was spread by two letters, both written on Tuesday 3 October. Lord Hussey, writing to Robert Sutton, mayor of Lincoln, passed on information given him by the dean of Lincoln, George Heneage, who apparently was at Sleaford, that a company of knaves had risen in Lindsey.[32] Lord Burgh, writing to the king, informed him that the subsidy commissioners appointed to sit at Caistor that day had been forced to disperse.

On Sunday evening 1 October Dr Kendall, the vicar of Louth, preached a sermon in which he mentioned the visitation of Dr Rayne, the bishop's chancellor, and after evensong Thomas Foster, a yeoman of Louth, so stirred up the townspeople by his assertion that the crosses belonging to the parish church there would soon be taken away that they took the keys from the churchwardens and gave them for safe-keeping to one Nicholas Melton, a shoemaker. The next morning about 9 a.m. a crowd of about 100 people met outside the church and the bell was rung in order to collect men from the town and the surrounding countryside. Events moved swiftly, the bishop of Lincoln's steward, John Heneage, who was at Louth to conduct the choosing of the new town officers, tried to see Nicholas Melton, but the people carried him off and made him swear an oath.[33] It was probably the one reported a day or two later, "Ye shall swear to be true to Almighty God, to Christ's Catholic Church, to our Sovereign Lord the King, and unto the Commons of this realm; so help you God and Holydom and by this book."[34] This or similar oaths were to be tendered to many gentlemen in the following days. The next event of that eventful Monday morning was the taking of the bishop's registrar Mr Frankish by the mob and

[29] LP XI, 543.   [30] James, op. cit., p. 12, fn. 35.   [31] LP XI, 533.
[32] LP XI, 531.
[33] M. H. and R. Dodds, The Pilgrimage of Grace and the Exeter Conspiracy, Cambridge, 1915, i, p. 93; LP XI, 828.
[34] LP XI, 552.

the burning of the records and of English books. That took place despite the efforts of William Borrowby *alias* Morland, a former monk of Louth Park, who averred that he tried to stop them.[35] The third incident was the sending of some of the commons over to Legbourne priory and the capture there of John Bellow and Thomas Milisent. Bellow particularly seems to have raised the wrath of the populace as there was a shout to kill him but he ended up in the stocks. Also, Sir William Skipwith had come into Louth from Ormsby during the day and been forced to take the oath.

The following day, Tuesday 3 October, several members of the commission for levying the subsidy fell into the rebels' hands and were brought the eighteen miles or so from Caistor into Louth. These gentlemen took the oath for fear, so they said, of losing their lives and they succeeded in persuading the commons to send a letter to the king demanding a general pardon.[36] On Wednesday ugly scenes occurred twelve miles away at Horncastle where Dr Rayne and one George Wolsey were killed despite the presence of a considerable number of clergy.[37] Also on that day Alford rose and Sir Andrew Billesby was sworn. Wednesday also saw a meeting of the rebels at a cross near Louth and, doubtless, the decision to set out for Lincoln on the following day was discussed. On Thursday 5 October a large force gathered at 'Towse of the Lynge' and proceeded towards Lincoln. That night the body, strengthened by men from Market Rasen, rested, after a march of some fifteen miles, at Hamelton Hill and on Friday arrived at Grange de Lings, five miles from the county town.[38]

In the meantime, all men between sixteen and sixty from the wapentake of Wraggoe were ordered to meet at Horncastle on Thursday and these men marched to Lincoln, about 100 of them staying on the way at Barlings abbey. By Saturday 7 October, therefore, a large force of Lincolnshire men had gathered in and around the county town. What the number of the rebels actually was is indeed open to considerable doubt. The round figure of 100,000 deposed by Nicholas Melton is clearly a gross exaggeration and Christopher Ayscough's estimate of 10–12,000 spears is probably nearer the truth without his '30,000 others some harnessed and some not'.[39] The gentlemen persuaded the host to make its demands known to the king, to ask for a royal pardon and to refrain from further action until the king's pleasure was known.

Meanwhile, Henry, informed of the rising by a letter from lord Burgh who wrote after his escape from the mob at Caistor on Tuesday 3 October,[40] took prompt action to meet the rebels. The king probably

[35] LP xii, i, 380.   [36] LP xi, 553.
[37] LP xi, 828, i (2) and 975; LP xii, i, 70(ix).   [38] LP xi, 828(i).
[39] LP xi, 567, 576.   [40] LP xi, 533.

had news of the rising sometime on Wednesday morning since Sir
Robert Tyrwhit with other subsidy commissioners wrote from Louth
and dispatched Sir Edward Maddison with the letter just after midnight.[41] The earl of Shrewsbury also repeated the news in a letter to the
king in which he said 3,000 men had gathered at Horncastle.[42] On
Friday 6 October, Maddison was examined,[43] and the king gave orders
to a number of great nobles to proceed against the rebels: some of these
letters must have been dispatched shortly after midnight since the earl
of Shrewsbury received a dispatch from the Court at 11 a.m. on the
Friday. He purposed to be at Nottingham on Sunday night 8 October,
and the rebels were planning to move on Newark at the same time but
were persuaded to stay in Lincoln until they received the royal reply to
their demands. Henry's reply to the demands that no further religious
houses should be suppressed, that taxation should be reduced, and that
heretic ministers and bishops should be handed over to the Commons
was sent as a response to the subsidy commissioners' letter. In it the king
urged the gentlemen to persuade the commons to disperse and to send
one hundred of the ringleaders with halters round their necks to the
king's lieutenant. This royal reply was read to the rebels on Tuesday
10 October. By Sunday and Monday, however, authority was beginning to muster its forces. Edward Dymoke was attempting to raise a
force to meet on Ancaster heath at 2 p.m. on Sunday[44]—although its
purpose is not entirely clear—and, as we have seen, forces were gathering at Nottingham. Arrows and ordnance issued from the Tower over
the week-end and the duke of Suffolk was at Huntingdon and moving
towards Stamford on the Monday.[45] His dispatch showed how weak
the position of the loyal forces really was, but a little progress towards
staying the rebels was being made.

The truth of the matter was that behind the numerous threats of
overwhelming force, the Crown was finding it difficult to raise an
adequate army.[46] Few loyal men could be found within the county of
Lincoln; lord Hussey and lord Burgh could only raise a quarter of the
forces expected of them;[47] the prior of Spalding refused to furnish men
to the king;[48] Norfolk had insufficient horses, and Suffolk was clamour-
ing for 'ordnance, artillery and a thousand or two of harness'.[49] As
Suffolk's letter of 9 October shows, his scheme was to avoid fighting in
order to gain time for larger forces to assemble. The rebels, however,
had begun to desert and return to their own houses. But on Sunday
messengers came from Beverley and Halifax pledging support for the
rebels and reporting that Yorkshire was also rising.[50] On Monday and

[41] LP XI, 534.   [42] LP XI, 536.   [43] LP XI, 568.   [44] LP XI, 571.
[45] LP XI, 615.   [46] LP XI, 808.   [47] LP XI, 576.   [48] LP XI, 567.
[49] LP XI, 615.   [50] LP XI, 971.

Tuesday rebels began to leave but many were still there to hear the king's answer which was brought to the gentlemen assembled in the Chapter House on Tuesday afternoon. Some of the commons wanted to go forward but the gentlemen persuaded them to wait in Lincoln where, the following evening, Lancaster Herald arrived. Early on Thursday 12 October[51] the herald induced the mob to disperse and most of them had left by Friday 13 October when the gentlemen and some of the rebels offered their submission to the duke of Suffolk at Stamford.[52] And so the Lincolnshire rebellion was over just as Yorkshire was beginning to rise; on Tuesday 17 October Suffolk went to Lincoln to overawe the populace.[53]

What interpretation are we to put on the events of these early October days?[54] The Lincolnshire rebellion has attracted the attention of many scholars and there has been considerable disagreement as to the motivation of the revolt, the role of the gentry, the degree of organization, the extent of the people's devotion to the old religion, the part played by social and economic forces and so on—nearly every aspect of it has been hotly debated. As to motives, there is little doubt that the causes of the rising were mainly if not entirely religious, and the rebels' demands support such an interpretation. The six demands of the rebels were: that no more religious houses should be suppressed; that the subsidy should be remitted; that the clergy be released from the payment of first fruits and tenths to the Crown; that the statute of uses be repealed; that villein blood be removed from the privy council, and that five heretic bishops, of whom Longland was one, should be deprived and punished.[55] The demands point to clerical influence and also reflect the interest of the gentry, for few of the commons understood, let alone would be affected by, the statute of uses.[56]

The Misses Dodds in their book *The Pilgrimage of Grace and the Exeter Conspiracy* published in 1915 sorted out the events of the Lincolnshire rebellion so well that their account still stands as a masterly narration of what took place in those days in early October 1536, and their work has recently been praised by a leading historian of the period, Professor A. G. Dickens.[57] Sir Francis Hill in 1956 gave an eminently clear description of the rebellion especially as it affected the city of Lincoln.[58] Thus the details are well known but, like so much in human affairs, different

---

[51] LP XII, i, 380.   [52] LP XI, 672.   [53] LP XI, 728, 756.   [54] LP XI, 789.

[55] J. W. F. Hill, *Tudor & Stuart Lincoln*, Cambridge, 1956, p. 43; SP, *Hy.* VIII, I, pt. ii, pp. 463–6.

[56] 27 Hy. VIII, c. 10 in SR III, pp. 539–42.

[57] In 'Religious and Secular Motivation in the Pilgrimage of Grace', G. J. Cumming (ed.), *Studies in Church History*, IV, Leiden, 1968, pp. 39–54.

[58] J. W. F. Hill, *op. cit.*, pp. 41–9.

constructions can be put upon ascertained and agreed facts. Many writers[59] have thought of the Lincolnshire movement as 'unplanned', 'confused and incoherent' or as 'characterized by mob law and meaningless violence' but recently M. E. James has attempted a revaluation of this view.[60] It seems clear that, although the rebellion started by a spontaneous movement of common people who had probably been egged on by certain clerics, by Tuesday night or Wednesday morning gentlemen were beginning to take over its control. Nicholas Melton, probably the ringleader at Louth was a shoemaker, and there were in addition a cobbler, a tailor, a butcher, a weaver, and two carpenters who were instigators.[61] At Horncastle, William Leech, though a more substantial man than Nicholas Melton, was a yeoman who stirred up the 'poor men', and who paid them 1s. each for their services,[62] while at Louth disbursements out of the parish funds were given to the rioters. At Caistor, George Hadswell appears to have belonged to the upper levels of the yeomanry which used the title gentleman[63] but one of the ringleaders, Brian Stone of Miningsby, was described as a labourer. So the movement started among the yeomen and craftsmen of the small market towns who paid men to riot, for many men would join if they were paid, and, to judge by the dispatches of Suffolk and others to the Court, few would join 'the forces of law and order' until they saw the colour of the king's money.[64]

The view that the gentlemen 'feared the commons quite as much as the troops who opposed them' and that they would remember the German Peasant Revolt of 1525 can hardly be accepted.[65] There are no signs of a *jacquerie* in Lincolnshire in the autumn of 1536, and for the most part the commons were glad to submit to the leadership of the gentry. The commons and certain clerics, both parish clergy and religious, had to pay the penalty but the fiction that the gentlemen had been coerced was accepted. This fiction has been accepted also by most twentieth-century writers, but M. E. James has advanced some convincing arguments that throw doubt on this interpretation.[66] Of the gentlemen who were with the rebels, Sir William Ayscough, Sir Edward Maddison, Henry Booth, Sir Robert Tyrwhit, Thomas Portington, Thomas Moigne, Guy Kyme, Sir Andrew Billesby, Sir Robert Dymoke, his son Edward Dymoke the sheriff, a younger son Arthur, Robert Dighton, Nicholas Saunderson, Thomas Littlebury, Sir John Copledyke, Sir John Sutton, Robert Sutton, the Disneys, probably

[59] Dodds, op. cit.; Dickens, op. cit.; D. Knowles, *The Religious Orders in England*, III, Cambridge, 1961.
[60] In James, op. cit.   [61] LP XI, 975 (p. 402).   [62] LP XI, 967.
[63] James, op. cit., p. 25.   [64] LP XI, 587.   [65] Dodds, op. cit., i, p. 126.
[66] James, op. cit., passim.

most had been brought in and compelled to take the oath; but were they so unwilling as they later pretended? Certainly the king had his doubts about this excuse.[67] Instructions were given that the ringleaders were to be examined as to how the gentlemen really used themselves and it was wondered whether 'the gentlemen did wink at the rebellion'.[68] No gentleman apparently initiated the disturbances but, at Horncastle, Leech was a friend of the Dymoke family[69] which supplied victuals and money to the insurgents.[70] Moreover, the resistance which the gentlemen put up seems like a token resistance and Henry certainly thought it was.[71] None of the gentry was maltreated and even Bellow and Milisent, the agents of the hated Cromwell, suffered no more than the stocks and a fortnight's imprisonment. These gentlemen brought their tenants with them, well harnessed, and they activated the machinery of the musters to raise the countryside in such a way that many of the insurgents must have thought they were not rebelling against the king but going through the normal process of mustering. The gentry were able to keep a certain degree of order,[72] and the killing of Dr Rayne and Wolsey was an isolated incident in a movement that was not entirely one of mob law and meaningless violence.

The gentlemen played throughout a somewhat ambivalent role: they kept open an escape route by pretending to the Crown that they were being coerced but at the same time they helped the rebellion along because they had a number of grievances which they wished to have redressed. The gentlemen were not "the asses, so unlike gentlemen" as John Williams described them.[73] Sir Robert Dymoke and Sir Christopher Willoughby had been knights of the body, the former having been treasurer of Tournai and chancellor of Queen Katherine. Sir William Ayscough attended Henry VIII at the Field of the Cloth of Gold and Sir William Skipwith had been a knight attendant at the coronation of Anne Boleyn and had represented the shire in parliament. John Heneage was the brother of Sir Thomas Heneage of Hainton, the keeper of the king's privy purse, and Sir Robert Tyrwhit and Sir Edward Maddison had both been M.P.s.[74] They were not a group of backwoods gentry. They knew what they were doing and they must have known that Henry would regard their actions as treasonable— hence the 'coercion theory'. On the other hand perhaps their continued protestation of loyalty to the Crown, a protestation which the commons shared to the full and constantly repeated, was not mere delusion or deceit but a legitimate means of bringing grievances to the notice of the Crown and seeking redress. This view[75] rests on the thesis that the

[67] LP XI, 569, 843.   [68] LP XI, 764.   [69] LP XII, i, 70 (xiii).
[70] *Ibid.*, (vii) and (ix).   [71] LP XI, 569.   [72] LP XI, 853.   [73] LP XI, 888.
[74] James, *op. cit.*, p. 4 fn. 10.   [75] *Ibid.*, p. 6.

rebels were not aiming at a return to the feudal anarchy of the fifteenth century, which century was not perhaps as anarchic as Tudor Englishmen supposed. This view is opposed by most scholars[76] but yet may have something to commend it. These gentry had respect for established authority, above all for the authority of the Crown, since their entire position depended upon such respect but some protest against misgovernment was allowable and such protest should lead to the correction of injustice and the re-adjustment of governmental policy.

What were the grievances of the Lincolnshire gentry? They were, in part, those which applied to gentry throughout the country, in particular, they entailed opposition to the statute of uses but also specific local problems clearly affected them.[77] Smaller gentry such as Robert Carr of Sleaford, Philip Trotter, and Guy Kyme were prepared in the interests of the acquisition of property or for ideological reasons to risk more than established gentlemen would, but even the established families seem to have been upset by developments in the shire in the decade before the rebellion. As we have seen[78] in the early Tudor period a decline had occurred in the baronial families which had provided the gentry with leadership. As a result there emerged in Lincolnshire a gentry polity where no great family dominated the scene and the gentry consequently acquired the stewardships and bailiwicks of the lands of the defunct peers, of the duchy of Lancaster estates, and of many monastic manors. But, from 1525, with the advent of Charles Brandon, duke of Suffolk into the county and with his control over thirty Lincolnshire manors, acquired first by the wardship of, and then by his marriage with, Katherine, lady Willoughby d'Eresby, he became the dominant magnate in the shire.[79] The Lincolnshire landed establishment might not welcome this since a great landowner would tend to aggregate offices to himself and to his nominees. Moreover, Suffolk had had an acrimonious controversy with his wife's uncle, Sir Christopher Willoughby, that ended only when the power of the Court, which the duke could count upon, put him in possession of two manors that the court of Chancery had awarded to Sir Christopher. This was achieved by an act of parliament of February 1536 (27 Henry VIII c.40),[80] and the Percy lands in Lincolnshire also came to him by another act, 27 Henry VIII c.38.[81]

---

[76] A. G. Dickens, *Thomas Cromwell and the English Reformation*, London, 1964, p. 125; G. R. Elton, *England under the Tudors*, London, 1955, pp. 147–8.

[77] For the way in which the statute was pushed through both houses, see E. W. Ives, 'The genesis of the Statute of Uses', EHR LXXXII, 1967, p. 673 *et seq.*

[78] See *ante* p. 5.   [79] James, *op. cit.*, p. 41.   [80] SR III, pp. 596–7.
[81] *Ibid.*, p. 591.

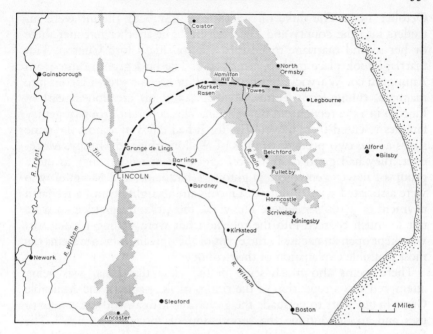

Fig. 1. Sketch map of Lincolnshire Rising, 1536

It is difficult to obtain precise evidence that families such as the Tyrwhits, Skipwiths, Thimblebies, Ayscoughs, Dymokes resented the intrusion of this Court favourite but it is highly probable that the wealthier gentry would have sympathized with Sir Christopher Willoughby in his misfortunes and with his Tailboys relations. The Willoughby family had undoubted grievances and support for the rebellion came from their estates, notably from Belchford and Fulletby, the home of the Leaches, and Sir Christopher's son William was accused of being the 'grand captain of the whole host'.[82] So the Willoughbies had little love for the king, and it was the same with some of the Tailboys family for a struggle had broken out between Gilbert, lord Tailboys and his mother over the size of the marriage portion granted to his wife Elizabeth Blount, Henry VIII's discarded mistress. Lady Tailboys senior refused to hand over some of the lands assigned to her daughter-in-law and the dispute reached its height in 1528-9 at the time when Suffolk acquired the wardship of young Katherine Willoughby. Sir Christopher was married to Lady Tailboys's daughter Elizabeth, and another daughter Anne was the wife of Edward Dymoke the sheriff who played a leading part in the events of

[82] LP xi, 805, 828 (vii).

October 1536. The duke of Suffolk and Elizabeth Blount were in-truders into the county and Elizabeth brought another intruder there by her second marriage to Edward Clinton ninth lord Clinton. This marriage took place probably in 1531-2. The bridegroom came from Amington co. Warwick, but he finished his life as a great Lincolnshire magnate, ruling from Tattershall castle, and his creation as earl of Lincoln in 1572 recognized his position. This coherent group of gentry families resented these newcomers for it had enjoyed almost the same status as the two peerage families of Willoughby and Hussey. More-over, they had good cause to feel aggrieved at royal policy as did a group of newer gentry the Dightons, Granthams, and Moignes who were associated with the city of Lincoln and its fight against a fee farm payment of £100 *per annum*. The view, then, that the gentlemen were not so much coerced into the rebellion but were willing participants who kept open an excuse in the event of the uprising's failure seems the most plausible explanation of their conduct.

There seems also much sense in the view that what was being attempted was a repetition of the risings of 1525 against the Amicable Grant in an effort to persuade the government to amend the statute of uses and to discontinue the suppression of monastic houses.[83] The former policy was revised by the statute of wills of 1540 (32 Henry VIII c.1) but the latter remained unaltered and was even enlarged to encompass the suppression of all houses. In 1525, the gentlemen had been able to achieve their aim—the withdrawal of the Amicable Grant—because their policy had been supported in high places at Court by those who disliked Wolsey and so, eleven years later the Lincolnshire gentry tried to play the same game.

Lord Hussey was the obvious man, with his influence at Court, to undertake the role that the dukes of Norfolk and Suffolk had played in 1525 but Hussey in fact was out of favour at Court and his wife was suspect on account of her sympathy for the Lady Mary. Anne Hussey was no help to her husband and he certainly knew it:[84] she was either too outspoken or too forgetful for the Kremlinesque intrigues of Henry's court. Hussey was much connected with the reformed Catholic piety,[85] and John Fewterer's 'The Mirrour or Glasse of Christes Passion' had been dedicated to him in 1534. Sir Robert Dy-moke was obviously the other man with Court influence upon whom the gentry relied, but his Court connections had also been much with queen Katherine as chancellor of her household from 1527 to 1533. Dymoke also was connected with the *devotio moderna* since his sister-in-law was prioress of the Dominican convent of Dartford in Kent which was a centre of religious revival. It was when the gentlemen realized

[83] James, *op. cit.*, p. 51.   [84] LP XI, 852.   [85] See chap. II p. 14.

that no help was forthcoming from the Court magnates that they surrendered rather than wage all-out war against their sovereign liege.

Hussey had refused to commit himself. He said he would not be false to his prince but that he could not be against the rebels because none of his tenants would support him.[86] But on Saturday 7 October he fled from Sleaford to Nottingham where the earl of Shrewsbury was gathering his forces. When this news reached Lincoln the following day, the gentry knew that all was over and determined to abandon the commons and make what terms they could with the representatives of royal law and order. But Hussey had probably decided to go to Nottingham, thinking that Shrewsbury might be persuaded to influence many lords to whom he was related to put pressure on the king to modify the government's policies and jettison some of his ministers; the lord steward was known to be conservative in his religious views.[87] Shrewsbury, however, chose to remain loyal,[88] and when Hussey knew this, he stopped wavering and joined him in Nottingham: both were men indoctrinated by a lifetime of service to the Tudor dynasty who could not see themselves as rebels and traitors.

The motivation for the beginning of the rebellion differed considerably from the motivation which led the gentlemen to assume leadership—despite the plea of coercion. The statute of uses and royal taxation were perhaps primarily what the gentry objected to, and the insertion of these items into the Lincoln and Boston demands was an invitation to the gentry in other shires to support them. But, as has been seen, the commons had not heard of the statute of uses, still less did they know of its implications. Their complaints were religious rather than economic. A correct analysis of the outbreak of the rebellion would appear to be that the commons rose as a result of discontent at the king's religious policy and were joined on the third day by the gentry who had other grounds for opposition to Henry or at least to his chief minister. Some of the gentry, however, also shared the commons' conservative religious outlook although, already, the prizes of the acquisition of monastic property were beginning to allure them. The *fons et origo* of the rebellion, then, on 1st and 2nd October was opposition to the imposition of the Ten Articles[89] and to the dissolution of the monasteries. The prominent part played by clerics is sufficient proof of this. The Ten Articles really brought home to the clergy the protestant character of the changes that parliament had enacted which they had to pass on to the laity. The abolition of papal authority, of pilgrimages, and of superstitious practices were to be rammed home to the people, and the

[86] LP xii, i, 70 (iii).   [87] LP xi, 561.   [88] LP xi, 589.
[89] Burnet's History of the Reformation, iv, pp. 308–13.

closing of the monastic houses reinforced the general message. Little wonder that parsons like Dr Kendall of Louth, Nicholas Leech of Belchford, William Johnson vicar of Alford, Thomas Yoell parson of Sotby, Thomas Retford vicar of Snelland, John Fisher of Scartho, William Smith of Donington, John Lyon of Biscathorpe and William Holton vicar of Cockerington, to say nothing of the abbots of Kirkstead and Barlings and six monks of Bardney, were, if not 'stirrers' of the revolt, then certainly early supporters of it.[90] The three houses were deeply implicated, for the abbot and three monks of Kirkstead, Reginald Wade, William Swale, and Henry Jenkinson, together with the abbot and four monks of Barlings, Thomas Bradley, Richard Warin, William Holme, and James Hodgson, and from Bardney John Tennant, William Coy, John Frances, William Cowper, Richard Phelip, and Hugh Lonsdale played a part and suffered for their involvement.[91]

The clergy had multiple reasons for suspicion of the government's intentions. Most of them were not influenced by the new thought that had spread in the southern part of the diocese and probably most found it difficult to assume a preaching–teaching role instead of the liturgical–pastoral role to which they were accustomed. The visitation of the clergy of 1536 was of a different sort from the episcopal visitations that Longland had so diligently carried out. Some of the clergy may have feared that they would lose their benefices if they were found insufficiently educated to preach or lacking in enthusiasm to expound the new doctrines of the Ten Articles.[92] Others thought that they might be deprived so that incoming clergy would be liable for 'first fruits', and it would seem that the act of first fruits and tenths (26 Henry VIII c.3)[93] might lead to a sort of clerical 'musical chairs' for the benefit of the royal coffers. These fears rather than passionate fervour for the old religion may have been the main-spring of the clergy's opposition, but perhaps one should not separate the two elements. Certainly Dr Kendall of Louth showed a firm religious commitment and urged the rebels to repress heresy and to maintain the faith.[94] He declared later that the common people 'grudged' at the new opinions concerning Our Lady and purgatory,[95] and at the abrogation of holy days, although in his sermon on Sunday he stressed that the crosses might be taken away. Many also heeded the rumour that a number of parish churches were going to be suppressed. After the rebellion, however, it was declared that Lincolnshire had risen 'for maintaining of Christ's Faith, Holy Church, honour of our native crown, realm, nobility and commonwealth.'[96] The religious were alarmed that the government was going to dissolve the larger monasteries after it had finished with those having an income

---

[90] LP XII, i, 581.   [91] LP XI, 805.   [92] LP XII, i, 481.   [93] SR III, pp. 493–9.
[94] LP XII, i, 70.   [95] LP XI, 828 (i) and (iii).   [96] LP XVIII, i, 26(5).

of under £200 a year.[97] Naturally they feared for their future and supported a movement that was dedicated to stopping further monastic dissolutions.

The idea that the rising was for the maintenance of the old faith and for the 'native crown' demands further attention.[98] Undoubtedly, Kendall was in favour of the old religion, and perhaps he is the only parson of whom this can unequivocally be said, although Simon Maltby, rector of Farforth, prayed for the pope and college of cardinals on 8 October.[99] Some who said they had preached up the royal supremacy may in fact have had discussions on it.[100] One of the clerical leaders, Nicholas Leech, was guilty of several misdemeanors.[100] But the striking thing is that, throughout, the rebels thought of themselves as loyal to the Crown.[101] The gentlemen and peers had no thought of resorting to *diffidatio*, the renunciation of their allegiance to their feudal overlord the king, and in this sense no thought of a return to feudal anarchy, but they were concerned as to how they could make their dissidence known at a time when parliament had been unable to check the onrush of royal power and to present an effective opposition to it. The revolt was a movement which sought to rid the king of evil counsellors, as did the Peasants' revolt of 1381 and Cade's rebellion of 1450, and like them some association between commons and gentlemen occurred. Like them also the revolt terminated when the gentlemen abandoned the 'common people'. The gentry were saved from denying their obedience to the king because the oaths had been forced upon them by the common rabble. But 'rebels and rebellions though the devil raised them,'[102] could be used to bring a prince to his senses and make him rule justly for he was ultimately responsible. This is what the Lincolnshire rebels had in mind.

Perhaps the gentlemen secretly stirred matters up, for the convention seems to have been that revolt must start among the common people, be joined by the gentry, and then receive the backing of a great nobleman who could influence the sovereign to change his policy.[103] When the 'countenance' failed the gentlemen abandoned the cause and left the commons in the lurch. In 1537, nineteen of the commons were executed along with twenty-six priests, both secular and religious, but only one gentleman and one peer suffered the death penalty while, in addition, a few commoners had probably been killed earlier. The remaining

---

[97] LP XII, i, 702.   [98] See W. G. Zeeveld, *Foundations of Tudor Policy*, Harvard, 1948.
[99] LP XI, 975.   [100] *Ex inf.* Mrs M. Bowker.
[101] LP XI, 534, 853; XII, i, 70(xi).
[102] L. B. Campbell (ed.), *The Mirror for Magistrates*, Cambridge, 1938, p. 178.
[103] James, *op. cit.*, p. 75.

gentlemen escaped and most of them flourished. The family tensions grew less and some of the gentlemen's demands were achieved in and after 1540.

The rebellion was the one occasion in the whole of the Tudor period when the shire was in the forefront of national history. From 1st to 12 October 1536 the county shook Henry VIII's throne as it had not been shaken before and yet it was only part of the shire that rebelled. The movement did not apparently spread much to the west of a line drawn between Stamford, Sleaford, Lincoln, and Alkborough, and lord Burgh had a steadying influence in the north-west of the county. It is clear that the power of the noblemen or gentlemen with his tenants who were 'raised' in almost the same way as 'retainers' had been recruited in the previous century was of enormous significance. Most of the tenants were prepared to follow their landlords and undoubtedly if clergy and gentlemen had taken a firm line the rebellion would almost certainly have been checked. But grievances were widespread, and all social classes combined to make Lincolnshire a focus of national attention at the beginning of a period of several months that were crucial for the Tudor monarchy.

CHAPTER IV

THE EFFECTS OF THE DISSOLUTION

(a) UPON THE EX-RELIGIOUS

IN the main, the effects of the Dissolution were twofold. We must look at the effect upon the ex-religious and the effect upon the social structure of the shire. The first study involves an examination of the pensions and promotions of the ex-religious in order to ascertain their living standards and their way of life, while the second requires a review of what monastic land there was, how much of it was sold and to whom, in order to determine how great a contribution the Dissolution made to the establishment or expansion of landed families. But before attempting such analyses, we must narrate in outline the dissolution of the thirty or so houses which still remained in Lincolnshire after the revolt had been suppressed. Whether or not Henry VIII or Cromwell had determined upon the dissolution of all the monasteries at an early date is open to question. Some scholars[1] hold to the view that this was not the government's intention from the first; others,[2] that perhaps only 'policy' prevented Cromwell from dissolving all at once but that such an intention may have been and probably was present from 1535–6. The rebellion in Lincolnshire and the Pilgrimage of Grace, although they were both suppressed by the government, left large areas of the country in an unsettled state, and it would have been suicidal to launch a major attack on the monasteries immediately. Nevertheless, those two rebellions may well have persuaded the government to make an end of the rest of the monasteries which were possible centres of loyalty to Rome, and which were immensely wealthy. Governmental expenses were rising and the temptation was great.[3] In the end the greatest act of nationalization without compensation was completed by 1540.

At first, some of the smaller monasteries were allowed to continue. We have already seen how Kyme paid a large sum to do so, and Heynings was permitted to continue on 27 November 1536.[4] Exemption was

---

[1] J. Youings, *The Dissolution of the Monasteries*, London, 1971, pp. 61–3.
[2] G. R. Elton, *England under the Tudors*, London, 1955, pp. 144, 148.
[3] F. C. Dietz, *English Government Finance, 1485–1558*, Illinois U., 1920, pp. 131–2.
[4] LP XI, g. 1217 (26).

usually obtained only by those houses that could secure the good offices of someone with influence at Court and pay a high fee. Kyme paid £300,[5] and Stixwold a fine of 900 marks and first fruits of £150. But it was not long before the work of suppression continued and the men active in it may be divided into two classes. Firstly there were the 'civil servants', the direct representatives of the court of Augmentations, such as John Freeman and Robert Gowge, who were receivers of the court in Lincolnshire, John Wiseman the auditor, and John Bellow, a personal representative of Cromwell. But these 'civil servants' were not able to deal with all the monastic property themselves, and so commissions were given to the county gentry. Such well known Lincolnshire names as the Heneages, Tyrwhits, Skipwiths, Dymokes, Carrs, and Halls, and even yeomen such as the Broxholmes and Brocklesbys gave assistance in the work of suppression.[6]

The attention of the commissioners was turned to the attainted houses of Kirkstead and Barlings. On 12 March 1537 Sir William Parr received orders from Cromwell to make inventories of the possessions of the two houses.[7] He began work on Tuesday 13 March and continued until Saturday, putting Edward Dymoke and John Heneage in charge at Kirkstead—one wonders whether they recalled what they had been doing less than six months previously—and Thomas Dymoke and Robert Dighton at Barlings. On 18 March Mr Richard Pollard commanded Mr Thomas Hall to 'pluck down' the lead, have it melted and cast into fodders.[8] The lead at Kirkstead which had been valued at 1,000 marks was supposed to be worth £1,000 and that at Barlings £400.[9] Plate was worth relatively little, at Kirkstead only 20s. and at Barlings only 20 nobles, but the question of how much the monks had 'salted away' for their enforced retirement will have to be considered in any examination of the living standards of the ex-religious.

Throughout 1537 and the early months of 1538 it was firmly and frequently denied that there was any intention on the part of the government of dissolving all monastic houses.[10] But the Crown was ever ready to accept surrenders. However, between the suppression of the attainted monasteries and the final phase of the Dissolution from late 1538 onwards only two Lincolnshire houses had surrendered, the Carthusian house at Epworth in the isle of Axholme in June 1538[11] and the Gilbertine priory of St Katherine's Lincoln in July.[12] By July 1538, twenty-three houses had been dissolved[13] and in September, John Freeman was given a commission to accept the surrender of all Gilbertine houses in the county. By this time houses were willing to surrender to

[5] LP xi, g. 519(2).   [6] LP xi–xv, *passim*.   [7] LP xii, i, 639.
[8] LP xii, i, 676.   [9] *Ibid.*, 677.   [10] *Ibid.*, 573.   [11] VCH *Lincs.*, ii, p. 160.
[12] PRO *DK's 8th Report*, App. ii, p. 27.   [13] LP xiii, ii, 1195.

the Crown; the religious could clearly see that there was no future for them in the cloister and were anxious for a negotiated surrender that would secure them a pension. Between 18 September and 2 October 1538, Sempringham,[14] Haverholme,[15] Catley,[16] Bullington,[17] Sixhills,[18] Alvingham,[19] Nunormsby,[20] and Newstead-on-Ancholme[21] surrendered to Freeman. The receiver surveyed the houses. The value of the plate was £2,000; ready money obtained for 'stuff sold' with the revenues in Lincolnshire, £5,600 and the bells; lead brought in £8,277 and the annual rents reached £8,100.[22] This figure for rents was an improvement of £800 on the 1535 valuation. By 20 October, only eleven monasteries remained standing in Lincolnshire[23] and before the end of the month Dr Legh had a commission to dissolve Bardney which surrendered on 1 November.[24] All houses by this time realized that surrender was the only possible course. Judging by the lack of protest public opinion had probably swung against the abbeys so that they were not the objects of pity that they had been two years previously.

On 21 February 1539, a warrant under the privy seal was addressed to Dr Richard Layton, Dr John Layton, Dr John London, Robert Cotton, John Freeman, and John Wiseman to take surrender of the Lincolnshire houses.[25] Dr London took the surrender of Kyme,[26] Irford,[27] Nuncoton,[28] Fosse,[29] and Heynings[30] between 6 and 11 July 1539. Crowland was probably the last of the houses to 'go down' on 4 December 1539.[31] Small cells usually survived until 1539, being dissolved with their parent houses.

What happened to the ex-religious? The old stories, advanced by cardinal Gasquet,[32] of the monks and nuns being turned adrift to wander the roads almost as beggars have long been disproved. Perhaps, in reviewing the evidence which proves that the religious were not turned out without any means of support, some writers may have overdone the contrast and hence painted too rosy a picture of the provisions made for the ex-religious.[33] The act of 1536 (27 Henry VIII c.28) did not provide for pensions for the rank and file of the religious but only for the heads of houses, since they could not be expected to enter religion elsewhere and to become other than 'governors'. If they were in orders,

[14] LP XIII, ii, 375.   [15] Ibid., 411.   [16] Ibid., 423.   [17] Ibid., 432.
[18] Ibid., 440.   [19] Ibid., 449.   [20] Ibid., 470.   [21] Ibid., 517.
[22] Ibid., 459.   [23] Ibid., 649.   [24] Ibid., 737.   [25] LP XIV, i, 328.
[26] Ibid., 1222.   [27] Ibid., 1235.   [28] Ibid., 1242.   [29] Ibid., 1250.
[30] Ibid., 1251.   [31] VCH Lincs., II, p. 117.
[32] F. A. Gasquet, Henry VIII and the English Monasteries, London, edn. 1906, pp. 435 et seq.
[33] G. Baskerville, English Monks and the Suppression of the Monasteries, London, 1937; EHR XLVIII, 1933, pp. 199 et seq.; 'The dispossessed religious after the suppression of the monasteries', in Essays in History presented to R. L. Poole, Oxford, 1927, pp. 436–65

two courses were open to the monks of smaller houses suppressed in 1536: they could either accept 'capacities', thereby becoming capable of holding benefices as secular clergy, or they could continue in religion in another house of their order. The nuns had the choice of leaving religion altogether or being transferred to another house. The monk who chose to change his regular for a secular garb on the dissolution of his house, applied for a capacity and it seems that the suppression commissioners sent the application to Cromwell, but it must be assumed that these capacities were in fact granted by the Faculty Office of the archbishop of Canterbury.[34]

There must have been some practical problems as to how the documents reached those who had applied for capacities. Moreland, one of the ringleaders of the revolt and an ex-monk of Louth Park, distributed twenty-six[35] of these capacities which he delivered to monks of the dissolved houses of Markby, Hagnaby, and Wellow. These he had received from an ex-canon of Bourne. Did these two distributors of capacities demand a fee for their services? We do not know. Frequently it would appear that the process of obtaining a capacity took some time since for an ex-monk entitled to a pension, a warrant for his free capacity had to be secured through the court of Augmentations. The pension also had to be validated by the same court.

The standard of living of the ex-religious depended on two factors: their pension and their preferment. Until the negotiated surrenders, which did not occur in Lincolnshire until June 1538, none of the ex-monks and nuns, apart from the 'governors', received a pension, and when the friaries were abolished no friar obtained a pension either. In the post-1541 diocese of Lincoln some 277 un-pensioned ex-religious and friars have been counted, while 429 were pensioned because they left from houses that were dissolved after June 1538.[36] From the same area only twenty-eight nuns were un-pensioned as against 221 who received some award, but the women's pensions were usually rather meagre. We must therefore postulate a considerable degree of hardship among many men and women who had been in religion, and especially among those who obtained neither pension nor preferment. By the year 1554 only eleven out of the 277 un-pensioned male ex-religious and chantry priests can, with any degree of assurance, be said to have obtained preferment as secular priests, whereas 52 per cent of the 429 pensioned ex-religious men secured similar promotion.[37] The total, eleven out of

[34] D. S. Chambers (ed.), *Faculty Office Registers 1534–1549*, Oxford, 1966, p. li.

[35] Chambers, *op. cit.*, p. li has 76.

[36] G. A. J. Hodgett, 'The un-pensioned Ex-Religious in Tudor England', *Jnl Eccles. Hist.*, 13, 1962, p. 201.

[37] Hodgett, art. *cit.*, p. 202.

277, roughly 4 per cent, seems very low and it may well be that many of these men were employed in the parishes in a minor capacity, as minor chaplains, sacristans, almoners, or doorkeepers.[38] But until more research is done, we cannot be certain and it may well be that they were absorbed into lay society.[39] William Newton, a canon of Bourne, eventually became the town clerk and organist at Edenham, and we know that some pensioned ex-religious became schoolmasters, weavers, tanners, and yeomen;[40] so why should those without a pension not have done the same? The after-careers of the un-pensioned can still only be sketched in.

Of the pensioners and of those who secured promotion to benefices more can be said. Preferment was often more important than the pension in determining the living standard of an ex-religious. Some pensions were granted on condition that they ceased if the grantee was promoted to a living of an equivalent or greater value, although it is clear that pensioners retained their pensions when they were promoted to livings by patrons other than the Crown.[41] A number of ex-religious eventually held more than one pension, as they had become chantry priests or entered one of Henry VIII's collegiate foundations, and, upon their dissolution in 1547, such men acquired a second pension. Of the ex-monks and regular canons resident in the county in 1554, some 55 per cent had incomes from benefices in addition to their pensions. A few fortunate ones were holding two benefices while retaining their pensions.[42] After 1547, pensioned chantry priests come into the picture, and by 1554 nearly 51 per cent of them had incomes from benefices as well as their pensions. Of these 204 ex-monks and chantry priests[43] residing in Lincolnshire in 1554, four pensioners were holding two benefices and of these William Coke was the wealthiest. He had a pension of £4 10s. as an ex-chantry priest, was rector of Fulbeck at £20 per annum and also of Halton at £12.[44] On the other hand fourteen pensioners, nearly 7 per cent of the total, held two pensions, one as an ex-monk and one as a former chantry priest. Roger Dalison, a nabob among pensioners, was the former dean of and professor of theology in Thornton college with a pension of £50 a year, but that did not prevent him from acquiring the benefice at Haxey in the isle of Axholme worth

[38] Chambers, *op. cit.*, p. xlix.   [39] Hodgett, art. *cit.*, p. 202.
[40] G. A. J. Hodgett (ed.), 'The State of the Ex-Religious and Former Chantry Priests in the Diocese of Lincoln', LRS 53, 1959, p. xxi.
[41] LRS 53, p. xvi.
[42] G. A. J. Hodgett, 'The Dissolution of the Monasteries in Lincolnshire', unpublished London M.A. thesis, 1947, chap. iv.
[43] This figure includes 40 residents within the county who had been in religion outside it.
[44] Hodgett, thesis, chap. iv.

£13 6s. 8d. a year, the vicarage of Laceby, four miles south-west of Grimsby, with the same income, and that of Stondon in Bedfordshire at £2; so his total income reached £78 13s. 4d. a year.[45] The other ex-religious who acquired three livings was Thomas Gurnart, formerly a Durham monk: he increased his annual pension of £10 to a total of £39 6s. 8d. by the benefices he held.

Apart from the ability, or lack of it, to obtain benefices, living standards of the ex-religious were affected by the value of the pensions themselves which varied widely. At the top of the scale were the pensions of £133 6s. 8d. paid to the former abbot of Crowland[46] and the former prior of Spalding,[47] while at the bottom were those of £2 *per annum* paid to the nuns of Alvingham and of 16s. 8d. a year allotted to the nuns of Fosse. The wealth of the house and the time spent in religion were apparently the criteria that affected the rate of pension paid.[48] Some disagreement has occurred between historians as to what was an adequate income on which to sustain life in the post-dissolution period.[49] It would appear that £5 a year was a low, but not unreasonably low, subsistence wage for a single man. The majority of male pensioners in Lincolnshire, therefore, who had between £5 and £6 13s. 4d. a year would have been able to survive fairly comfortably although the inflation of the 1540s and early 1550s would have caused them hardship. Moreover, the pensions were subject to the ecclesiastical tenth and to a statutory fee of 4d. in the pound. But if the men were able to manage at a reasonable standard, most women pensioners were below the subsistence level since their income was, on average, £3.[50] But for the male pensioners, both ex-monks and ex-chantry priests, it was the combined pension plus income from a benefice which established the standard of living. In the lowest income range, up to £2 *per annum*, only 1 per cent of the male pensioners are to be found.[51] Those with combined incomes of over £2 but under £5 totalled 29½ per cent, those with £5 to £6 13s. 4d. comprised 15 per cent and those with over £6 13s. 4d. but under £10 formed 14½ per cent. Nearly 29 per cent enjoyed total emoluments of between £10 and £20 *per annum* while 11 per cent were wealthy with £20 a year or over. Only 30 per cent of the ex-religious were, then, in real hardship and most of them were those who had for some reason or other failed to obtain ecclesiastical preferment.

The women pensioners, however, were often receiving pensions on which they could not have lived without support from their relations

---

[45] LRS 53, p. xvii.   [46] VCH *Lincs.*, ii, p. 117.   [47] *Ibid.*, p. 122.
[48] LP xiv, ii, 631, 652.   [49] Summed up in D. Knowles, *op. cit.*, vol. iii, p. 407.
[50] *Ibid.*   [51] These figures refer to the whole diocese.

or recourse to marriage, when, after the spring of 1549, it was allowed.[52] Admittedly nearly all the women, unlike 53 per cent of the male ex-religious (including friars) had pensions but they were woefully small.[53] Sixty per cent of them had £2 a year or less, and 28 per cent of them over £2 but under £5 so that, in rough figures, 88 per cent of the women were below the reasonable £5 to £6 13s. 4d. income range, while only 30 per cent of the men failed to reach this modest affluence. And in the higher income brackets only 6 per cent of the women had between £5 and £6 13s. 4d., 4 per cent between £6 13s. 4d. but under £10, and only 2 per cent had over £10 but under £20.[54] There is some evidence of joint housekeeping, possibly in order to reduce expenses, although acquaintance in the cloister would often carry over after the Dissolution into friendship outside it. Cecilia Steward and Grace Wyse, for example, were doubtless trying to eke out a living at Torksey, near their former monastery of Fosse, on two pensions of 16s. 8d. each; some additional assistance would have been necessary but we do not know who provided it.[55] Similarly Agnes Grey and Dorothy Fishbury of Bullington were both living in Ingham.

Marriage was one way of solving the financial problem, but it was nearly ten years before marriage was permitted. However, within five years after 1549 about 31½ per cent of the nuns still living within the county had married.[56] The nuns of Sixhills appear to have had a propensity for marriage for five of them were no longer spinsters by 1554 as against two unmarried survivors. Those who married brought with them a useful addition to the family income. Few heads of houses married, only the prioress of Gokewell, Anne Castleforth and the prioress of Legbourne, Joan Mussenden. The latter, a member of the well-known Healing family, was married to a gentleman, William Ottbie, and living with him at Croxby near Grimsby. A marriage of two ex-religious, both Gilbertines, occurred when Joan Astley, a former nun of Sempringham, married Christopher Hudson, previously a canon of Catley. In 1554, they were living together at Dorrington near Sleaford where Christopher was vicar and Joan's pension of £2 6s. 8d., which was larger than her husband's of £2, would have helped to raise their standard of living: their combined income with the vicarage came to £10 6s. 8d. Married clergy were forced to leave their wives during Mary's reign so we may assume that the lot of Mrs Hudson, Mrs Stainton (née Castleforth), Mrs Lane (née Lowesdale), and Mrs Field (née Bones) cannot have been pleasant between 1554 and 1558.

[52] By 2 and 3 Ed. VI, c. 21, SR IV, p. 67.   [53] Hodgett, art. cit., p. 201.
[54] LRS 53, p. xvii.   [55] Ibid., p. xxi.
[56] Eighteen married; thirty-nine unmarried and three not stated—LRS 53, passim.

Having looked at the part played by preferment and pensions in establishing the living standards of those formerly in religion, we must turn to a factor far more difficult to determine. The extent to which monks and nuns were able to make provisions for themselves before the dissolution of their houses is a subject upon which more research needs to be done. The extent to which assets were 'salted away' certainly varied from one monastic house to another and probably between different regions of the county. In Lincolnshire the evidence of large scale misappropriation of assets is hard to come by and, by the very nature of the operation, this is to be expected. The degree to which previous provisions were made depended upon the perspicacity with which the ex-religious divined what might happen, and there is a division of opinion between those historians who think that the religious were soothed by the assurances of the government, and those who believe that many monks feared from the beginning that their turn might come.

It seems that the two houses, the Premonstratensian Barlings and the Cistercian Kirkstead, which were so deeply implicated in the rebellion as to be attainted of treason probably had taken measures to safeguard the future of their inhabitants. Sir William Parr found plate worth only 20s. at Kirkstead and less than twenty nobles at Barlings although here he managed to unearth more that had been given to 'five or six simple men'.[57] Sir William also reported that three weeks or a month before the insurrection the abbot had sent plate worth £100 and other ornaments out of the monastery and that a canon named Burton who was lodged in the Tower could say where it had been hidden.[58] At Axholme the monks complained that the prior had gone away leaving only £3 in the house,[59] and by 1539 Dr John London was complaining that everywhere religious people 'makith ther hondes'.[60] By that date none could have mistaken that the government's intention was a total dissolution but many must have believed from the beginning of 1537, if not even earlier, that all houses would be dissolved and it is clear that the government thought it was faced by an attempt, perhaps well organized, on the part of the monks to secure their future. Whatever the analysis of scholars may be, the government met the threat in two ways. Throughout 1537 and early 1538 firm denials were given that any intention of dissolving all monastic houses existed;[61] on the other hand severe threats were made against those who misused monastic property.

[57] LP XII, i, 677.
[58] Ibid., 702; Mrs M. Bowker is of the opinion that the goods were sent to a church in Lincoln.
[59] Ibid., 693.   [60] LP XIV, i, 1321.   [61] LP XIII, i, 573.

The 'salting away' of cash and ornaments, plate and vestments was perhaps of secondary importance to the arrangements that the religious might make to help themselves by leasing monastic lands on beneficial terms. In October 1538 John Freeman made a general charge that the monasteries were leasing their demesnes and diminishing their stocks and stores,[62] and Dr London made a similar complaint.[63] How far did Lincolnshire monks and nuns take such measures? The act of 1539 (31 Henry VIII c.13) provided for the annulment of all leases made within one year prior to the surrender or suppression of a house, and in practice all leases made were examined by officials of the court of Augmentations: yet remarkably few of them were disallowed. Joan Thompson, the prioress of Irford, certainly advantaged her relations and doubtless helped to safeguard her own future by the sixty-year lease of lands in Goulceby and Ranby to Thomas Thompson for an annual rent of £1 13s. 4d.[64] The former prioress was living at Irby-on-Humber in 1554 on a pension of £5, but it may be that her relations remembered with tangible gratitude her generosity in former years. Another Joan (or Jane) Thompson, prioress of Nuncoton, was admonished by the bishop of Lincoln not to grant further corrodies or long leases of monastic property to her brother George.[65] It would appear that she was preparing for some eventuality by favouring her relations.

Another way in which the religious did not perhaps directly prepare to ease their own way into extra-cloistral life, but a way in which they sought rather to reward their servants and relations, was to grant them corrodies and pensions. Only four months before the surrender the abbot and convent of Crowland granted a corrody of 20s. *per annum* to Geoffrey Pinchbeck to be paid from lands in Baston.[66] He was thus rewarded for his services in 'negotiations' *i.e.* in the business affairs of the house. On the back of the indenture granting the corrody, Robert Wingfield, the auditor of the court of Augmentations, affirmed that it was a true concession and Geoffrey was still being paid in 1552.[67] On 7 October 1539, less than two months before their surrender, the monks of Crowland made Robert Littlebury bailiff of their manor of Langtoft with a pension of 15 marks. He was also an annuitant of the house with an annual payment of £1 13s. 4d. which was paid until his death on 8 January 1558.[68] But on the whole there is no evidence that widespread provisions to secure their future were made by the monks leasing land,

[62] LP XIII, ii, 528.   [63] LP XIV, i, 1321.
[64] PRO Exch. Augmentations Office, Conventual Leases (E 303), Lincoln 10, 11.
[65] *Archaeologia* XLVII, 1882, p. 58.
[66] PRO Exch. Aug. Off., Conventual Leases (E 303), Lincoln 7.
[67] LRS 53, pp. 43, 70.   [68] *Ibid.*, p. 129.

since only five late leases drawn up by monastic houses in and after 1536 are extant.[69]

From the official file of conventual leases it would appear that no widespread alienation of monastic property occurred in Lincolnshire, but J. Nichols[70] printed a list of some forty-six annuitants who were granted payments secured on various Crowland estates. Not all the estates were in Lincolnshire nor were all the grants made to Lincolnshire men, but some grantees belonged to well known county families. Thomas Heneage had 40s. a year secured on Bucknall manor (7 miles S.W. of Horncastle), and Adelard Welby of Gedney, 33s. 4d. secured on monastic lands in Gedney itself. These grants were made on 16 September 1536 and 31 January 1539 respectively, the latter grant being quite late in Crowland's existence. Robert Littlebury had 33s. 4d. in Claxby and 5 marks in Langtoft and the second grant was perhaps the last made by the dying house. John Wendon of Boston, an expert in music and medicine, received an annuity of 26s. out of the cell of Freiston on 8 October 1538. John Bellow obtained an annuity of 40s. secured on Hallington and Legbourne, Anthony Orby, 20s. in Holbeach, George St Paul, 20s. in Langtoft and Baston, and Richard Ogle of Pinchbeck, £3. The last named, a lawyer of the Middle Temple, had also 20s. from Spalding priory, 13s. 4d. from Thorney abbey (Cambs.) and another 40s. from Crowland secured on land in Gedney. He had been the official of Crowland's courts in Kesteven and Holland. In addition to annuities, the house also granted leases. Robert Thakker, a yeoman of Holbeach, took a lease of the grange and house there for forty years at £41 per annum in October 1538. William and Thomas Bogge leased the site of the manor called Dow Dyke Hall in Sutterton, the parsonage of the church, the tithes of corn, wool, hay, flax, lambs, etc. together with a windmill for forty-six years at an annual payment of £30. The abbey, however, kept the advowson but William and Thomas were not to be responsible for dyking the moat or repairing the chancel. But advowsons were sold since on 18 October 1538 the abbot granted to John Frysnay of 'Dennington' (rectius Benington), John Davy of Leake and merchant of the staple of Calais, William Dawne and Richard Frysnay of Crowland the advowson of Freiston church. How far these were purely normal business transactions or how far they were operations designed to 'feather the nests' of those who were soon to be ex-monks, it is difficult to say.

[69] PRO Exch. Aug. Off., Conventual Leases (E 303) Lincoln.
[70] In his 'Appendix to the History of Crowland', pp. 121–3 in *Bibliotheca Topographica Britannica*, III, London, 1783: Kraus Reprint, N.Y., 1968.

(b) UPON THE SOCIAL STRUCTURE OF THE COUNTY

The expropriation of monastic lands by the Crown between 1536 and 1540 and the subsequent re-granting of many of them to laymen had a profound effect upon the structure of society in Lincolnshire. It has been stated that in the country as a whole, 'very few new or appreciably enlarged estates were built up, by 1558, entirely or even principally out of monastic lands',[71] with the implication that the Dissolution made rather less impact on society than might have been thought. But this is a generalized judgement, and in a county that had so much monastic land as did Lincolnshire we would expect its alienation by the Crown to have a far reaching effect. It is true that most of the purchasers of monastic lands were already prominent in county society and that few were parvenus who obtained their position in that society because of their acquisitions of monastic property, but it is also true that many who had been 'on the fringe of the county establishment' became firmly members of it as a consequence of their increased landed wealth.[72] It would be erroneous to give the impression that the structure of society had not been changing before the Dissolution; indeed, a change had been effected gradually from the later fourteenth and fifteenth centuries. Families such as the Custs of Pinchbeck[73] and the Skipwiths of Ormsby[74] were adding to their estates in the late fourteenth and fifteenth centuries and there were several other families like them,[75] but their holdings at that time were often small compared with those of people of similar status in the later sixteenth century. Undoubtedly the expanding land market resulting from the Crown's decision to alienate monastic estates played a prominent part in the rise of some gentry and in the increased prosperity of the yeomanry in Tudor Lincolnshire.

It is impossible to provide a completely accurate figure of the acreage of monastic land[76] in the county. The figure of 208,442 acres given by W. O. Massingberd cannot be accepted[77] because so many difficulties stand in the way of assessing the acreage of the land owned by the monastic houses that we cannot assert that it amounted, even approximately, to one eighth of the total land in the county. The value of monastic property is easier to assess than its acreage and the best assessment can be made by comparing its value with that of other properties. The annual net income from monastic property was about six times that derived by the duchy of Lancaster from its estates in

---

[71] Youings, op. cit., p. 130.   [72] James, op. cit., p. 26.
[73] Cust, Lady Elizabeth, Records of the Cust Family, 1970, I, pp. 2, 30.
[74] W. O. Massingberd, History of Ormsby, 1893, p. 69.
[75] VCH Lincs., ii, pp. 326-7.   [76] Savine, op. cit., pp. 76-100.
[77] VCH Lincs., ii, p. 325.

Lincolnshire, and about eighty times that obtained from the county by the bishop of Lincoln.

Three great noblemen benefited from the acquisition of vast acres of Lincolnshire monastic property; Charles Brandon, duke of Suffolk, Edward Fiennes, lord Clinton and Saye, and Thomas Manners twelfth baron Ros of Hamlake, created first earl of Rutland. Acquisition of monastic lands by these three noblemen certainly affected the structure of the top echelon of Lincolnshire society since, although it did not exactly introduce these strangers into the county—custodial and matrimonial causes had done that—it enormously consolidated their power. The circumstances that brought the duke of Suffolk into Lincolnshire have been previously mentioned,[78] as have those which introduced Edward Fiennes to the county,[79] but it is undeniable that the position of both was strengthened by the acquisition of former monastic property. These noblemen belonged to the group that obtained lands before the first commission to sell monastic lands was issued in December 1539,[80] and some of this group did obtain property either as a gift or on beneficial terms.

The duke of Suffolk made his largest acquisition of Lincolnshire monastic properties by a deed dated 30 September 1538 by means of which he exchanged his manor of Eye in Suffolk for monastic sites, manors, and granges.[81] Lands belonging to the dissolved houses of Thornholme, Louth Park, St Katherine's Lincoln, Bullington, Barlings, Kirkstead, Greenfield, Markby, Nocton Park, Vaudey, and Newhouse, together with the sites of those houses, were granted to him and, in addition, lands of Bourne, Stixwold, Elsham, and Sixhills. A supplementary deed of 20 June 1540 made adjustments to secure that the exchanged properties were of equivalent value.[82] Most of the lands were held by knight service and an annual rent to the Crown was reserved upon them. It is unnecessary here to enter into the details of Charles Brandon's career of loyal service to his sovereign but he was one of Henry's closest *confidants* and also his brother-in-law. The question as to whether he acquired the lands as a gift or at the market price does not arise, since this was an exchange which was obviously intended to build up his power in Lincolnshire, where he had played the major role in suppressing the rebellion two years previously.

Suffolk's position in the county in which he controlled thirty Willoughby manors *iure uxoris* was still further strengthened by this acquisition of monastic lands, so that no doubt could any longer exist as to the person who was the leading man in the shire. Some of this

---

[78] See *ante* p. 32.   [79] See *ante* p. 34.   [80] Youings, *op. cit.*, p. 117.
[81] PRO Exch. Aug. Off., Deeds of Purchase and Exchange (E 305) E 94.
[82] PRO Exch. Aug. Off., Deeds of Purchase and Exchange (E 305), A 51.

land he sold: Grange de Lings which was a grange of the abbey of Barlings was disposed of by the duke on 24 June 1544 to George St Paul,[83] and he had previously, in February 1541, alienated the manor of Legsby, formerly belonging to the priory of Sixhills, to George's uncle, Matthew St Paul, who had married Margery, daughter of Sir Robert Tyrwhit of Kettleby. George St Paul of Snarford had married Jane, daughter of Sir William Ayscough of South Kelsey; he was recorder of Lincoln in 1542, represented the city in parliament from 1547 to 1557, and died in 1559. The St Paul family is typical of a number of gentry families that increased their holdings of land, and which, by so doing, brought them more prominently into the administrative system of the shire. Not only did George St Paul acquire Grange de Lings just outside Lincoln, but he had previously, on 29 March 1539, purchased Westlaby grange, formerly Kirkstead property, from the duke whose servant he was said to be.[84] The word 'servant' undoubtedly here means legal adviser to the duke of Suffolk. In June 1540, the duke alienated the priory of St Katherine's Lincoln to Vincent Grantham. He did not therefore keep his vast holding of Lincolnshire lands entirely intact since, within six months of its acquisition, he had begun to relinquish some of it for ready cash, but, nevertheless, his holdings at his death were vast.[85] However, on the death of his two sons in 1551[86] most of the estates were widely dispersed among distant relations.[86] William Sidney, grandfather of Sir Philip, succeeded to part of the Revesby estate as one of the heirs general of the duke of Suffolk, but in June 1572 it was sold to Archibald Barnard.[87]

Edward Fiennes or Clinton, ninth lord Clinton, was brought into the county by his marriage to the widowed lady Tailboys, and for a time his Lincolnshire interests were largely limited to his wife's estates that her former husband had settled upon her. But he buttressed his position in the county by the acquisition of two adjacent manors, Horbling and Billingborough, which had previously belonged to Sempringham priory.[88] These he obtained in 1539 but much of this land was re-sold to the Crown in 1542.[89] He did, however, retain some former monastic lands in the county for in May 1543 he acquired property that had formerly belonged to the priory of Catley and the abbey of Swineshead.[90]

---

[83] PRO Chancery, Close Roll, 36 Hy. VIII, pt. 4, m. 7.
[84] PRO Ct. of Common Pleas, Plea Roll, Trinity 31 Hy. VIII.
[85] 'Wills from Doctors Commons', Camden Soc., 83, 1863, pp. 27–42.
[86] GEC, *Complete Peerage*, *sub* Suffolk. And *Ibid.*, the estates devolved on the descendants of the numerous daughters of their great-grandfather, Sir William Brandon *i.e.* the aunts of the first duke.
[87] LAO *Archivists' Report*, 19, 1967–8, p. 9.
[88] PRO Exch. Aug. Off., Particulars for Grants, C 43.   [89] *Ibid.*
[90] LP XVIII, i, g. 475(3).

After the tragic death of the duke's two sons, Henry and Charles Brandon, on 14 July 1551, lord Clinton clearly became the most prominent man in the county. He was lord lieutenant of Lincolnshire from 1552 until his death in 1585, and although his post of lord high admiral, which he held during that same period, must have kept him away from the county quite frequently, he was attached to it by his creation as earl of Lincoln in 1572, and by the fact that he resided at Sempringham.

The third peer to acquire monastic lands in the county was Thomas Manners, twelfth baron Ros of Hamlake and first earl of Rutland. He had some connection with the county for his father, George Manners, was from Belvoir, although he had inherited Helmsley (Yorks.) as the heir of his uncle, the tenth lord Ros. The twelfth baron's mother was Anne a sister of Edward IV, and Thomas became a great favourite of Henry VIII who bestowed upon him many honours and offices. In 1525 he was created a knight of the garter and earl of Rutland. The earl was actively engaged in suppressing the rebellion of 1536 when he held a joint command with the earls of Huntingdon and Shrewsbury: after assembling at Nottingham he marched to Newark, Southwell, and Doncaster. Rutland had acted as steward for a number of monasteries; especially, in Lincolnshire, of Crowland and Neubo,[91] and it was on account of his knowledge of monastic property, his favour with Henry, and his services to the Crown that he secured much monastic land. He obtained the site of Belvoir priory and many of its lands, some of which were in Lincolnshire, the site and lands of the Templars' preceptory at Eagle, about eight miles south-west of Lincoln, and lands belonging to the abbey of Kyme.[92] Belvoir on the border of the county became, and remains, the principal seat of the Manners family. He received his Lincolnshire lands in exchange for his manor of Chingford (Essex) plus a payment of £289 10s. to the Crown in June 1541.[93] The estates were granted in tail male to help support the dignity of his earldom.[94]

Although the holdings of these three great noblemen influenced their standing in the shire, and transformed Lincolnshire from a county in which there was no outstanding landowner into one where three or four landowners dominated it, the acquisitions of lesser men had, in some ways, a deeper effect upon its social structure. Between January 1538 and July 1540 seven of the local gentry and six royal officials or royal servants received grants of land. Sir Thomas Heneage of the privy chamber, who was born at Hainton in 1480, and married Katherine

[91] Savine, op. cit., p. 255.   [92] LP XVI, g. 1056 (78).   [93] Ibid.
[94] S. B. Liljegren, 'The Fall of the Monasteries and the Social Changes up to the Great Revolution', Lunds Universitets Årskrift, 1924, p. 29.

daughter of Sir John Skipwith of South Ormsby,[95] had held several offices at Court, and was well established when he still further enhanced his position in the shire by the acquisition of various monastic properties. Heneage requires special notice because he falls into two categories of grantees: he was one of the group of courtiers and servants in government departments and, at the same time, one of the group of county gentry who purchased land. Robert Tyrwhit of the king's household falls, like Heneage, into the same two categories, although later in his life he transferred his interests from Lincolnshire to Huntingdonshire.[96] Thomas Heneage's youngest brother Robert may also be regarded, in a sense, as falling into both categories for, although he was not a courtier in the sense of being in immediate attendance upon the king, he was an auditor of the duchy of Lancaster who was appointed master of the woods in the court of General Surveyors in January 1543.[97] He had, moreover, made a good second marriage with Margaret, sister of the first earl of Rutland.

The Heneage family well illustrates the thesis that it was for the most part men who had some standing in the shire who bought ex-monastic lands but that by their purchases they raised their position in the county hierarchy. A John Heneage who had died in 1435 had acquired the manor of Hainton, on the edge of the Wolds nine miles west of Louth, and by the end of the fifteenth century the family had risen to the ranks of the more important gentry.[98] But the sixteenth century witnessed a further rise in their prominence. At the time of the dissolution of the monasteries there were four surviving sons of John Heneage of Hainton[99] who had been born in 1452 and who had married Katherine, daughter of Thomas Wymbish of Nocton. John had died in 1530 leaving Sir Thomas, already a man of fifty, well established at Court; John about whom rather less is known; George, dean of Lincoln;[100] and Robert already in the court of the duchy of Lancaster. In the county, they were J.P.s, commissioners for sewers, and members of the commission for gaol delivery.[101] In May 1538, Sir Thomas acquired lands formerly belonging to Tupholme abbey, and in March of the following year, the site and lands of Sixhills priory which were adjacent to Hainton.[102] Premises at Barton-on-Humber belonging to Nunormsby were granted to him in April 1540,[103] part of which he sold in November. In December 1540, he obtained lands formerly of Legbourne,

[95] Massingberd, op. cit., p. 92.
[96] A. R. Maddison (ed.), Lincolnshire Pedigrees, Harleian Soc., 52, p. 1020.
[97] DNB sub nomine and Harl. Soc., 51, p. 481.
[98] A. R. Maddison, Lincs. Wills 1500–1600, pp. xxix et seq.
[99] Harl. Soc., 51, pp. 480–5.   [100] J. Le Neve, Fasti, says he was dean 1528–38.
[101] LP passim.   [102] LP xiv, i, g. 651 (49).   [103] PRO MS. Index.

which he alienated to his brother-in-law Sir William Skipwith.[104]
Lands belonging to the former houses of Wellow, Sixhills, and Thorn-
ton he secured in May 1544,[105] and he also took a lease at £12 5s.
per annum of the rectory of Edlington that had belonged to Bardney
abbey.[106] Sir Thomas Heneage's holdings also included the manor and
lordship of Clee and the site of Wellow abbey,[107] all acquired in
December 1543, the manor of Fauxfleet in Blaketoft, formerly of
Thornton Abbey, demesne lands at Grimsby, and the parsonage of St
James's Grimsby and the manor and lands at Sixhills. Robert, the other
Heneage, who was also a government official spending most of his
time in London and who was buried in the church of St Katherine Cree
in 1556, acquired monastic property nevertheless. He turned to monastic
lands in his native county. It may be that he wished to provide some
land for his four sons, Thomas, and Robert, and two others whose
names appear as Michael and William or George and John;[108] or it may
be that he was attracted by the idea of investing part of the fees, that he
obtained from his offices, in real estate in his native county. For whatever reason, he obtained, in September 1539, rents and reversions of
leases of lands formerly belonging to the houses of Nunormsby,
Newstead-on-Ancholme, Sixhills, and Bullington.[109] He alienated
Tealby to John Clerk in October 1539,[110] who in turn sold it to Thomas
Bard in January 1541;[111] the site of Newstead-on-Ancholme he got rid
of to John Bellow. John, who apparently held no office, paid £99 10s. 10d.
for property of the suppressed houses of Haverholme, Nunormsby,
Sixhills, and Bullington in July 1540.[112] Part of this land he sold the
following November. John Heneage also acquired premises at Barton-
on-Humber on 26 April 1540 that had belonged to Nunormsby, as well
as a little close at Panton formerly the property of Bullington priory.[113]

Although not all the lands acquired by the three brothers remained in
their hands—we have no record that the dean of Lincoln obtained any
such properties—the Heneages obviously bought for investment purposes. The prominence of the family grew, and it provided high
sheriffs for the county in 1576, 1585, and 1598. John's sons George
(d. 1595) and William (d. 1610) were both knighted and both served the
shrieval office. This increased prominence was the consequence, in some
measure, of their increased estates in the county, and the view cannot
seriously be advanced that the placing of monastic lands on the market

[104] LP xviii, i, g. 226 (72).   [105] LP xix, i, g. 610 (78).
[106] PRO Exch. Aug. Off., Misc. Books (E 315), vol. 190 p. 28.
[107] PRO Deeds of Purchase etc., (E 305), D 21.
[108] Harl. Soc., 51, pp. 481-2.   [109] LP xiv, ii, g. 264 (5).
[110] PRO Chancery, Pat. Roll 31 Hy. viii (C 66), pt. 6, m. 15.
[111] Ibid., 32 Hy. viii, pt. 2, m. 36.   [112] LP xv, g. 942 (118).
[113] PRO Exch. Aug. Off., Deeds of Purchase and Exchange (E 305), H. 38.

made little difference to the position of the Heneage family. There were several other Lincolnshire families like them.

Sir Robert Tyrwhit of the king's household belonged to the Kettleby family of that name. The Tyrwhits were a slightly more prestigious family than the Heneages for they had been established at Kettleby, three miles east of Brigg, since the fourteenth century, and the head of the family in most generations was knighted. Robert was not the eldest son of Sir William Tyrwhit, and thus he had probably entered royal service to obtain, or at least to augment, his livelihood. Being near the king he was in a position to pick up information about the disposal of monastic property, and he obtained lands belonging to Stainfield priory in February 1538,[114] and to Irford, Bardney, Stainfield, and Markby in December 1539.[115] On 24 June 1541 he obtained the site of Kyme priory, the rectory and the advowson of the vicarage there, premises at Metheringham that had belonged to Kyme, and two annuities payable to monasteries.[116] Robert Tyrwhit shared in grants made to others. In the same grant made on 24 June 1541 he secured jointly with the earl of Rutland the site and demesne lands of Belvoir priory, lands and premises around Belvoir just outside the shire boundary, and premises at Woolsthorpe just within it. With lord Clinton in May 1543 he received lands that had belonged to Swineshead and to Catley,[117] and lands formerly of Irford were granted to him and Thomas Kiddall of South Ferriby in September 1544.[118] What Tyrwhit's role in these grants was, cannot easily be determined but in at least in one instance it would appear that he put up part of the purchase price.[119]

Other royal officials obtained lands in Lincolnshire soon after the Dissolution. Members of the court of Augmentations were obviously in a favoured position both to ascertain what lands might be acquired and to make an accurate evaluation of them. John Freeman, the receiver of the court in the county, obtained, in August 1539, lands belonging to the dissolved priories of Markby, Nunormsby, Bullington, and Hagnaby abbey. William Riggs, said to be of Clerkenwell London, but probably one of the Rigges of Stragglethorpe, was auditor of the court of Augmentations,[120] and he acquired in May 1540 lands, mostly granges, of the dissolved houses of Sempringham, Haverholme, Heynings, and St Katherine's Lincoln.[121] In July 1544 along with Richard Disney, who was to become M.P. for Grantham ten years later

---

[114] LP XII, i, g. 384 (93).   [115] LP XIV, ii, g. 780 (12).
[116] PRO Exch. Aug. Off., Deeds of Purchase and Exchange (E 305), C. 30.
[117] LP XVIII, i, g. 475 (3).   [118] LP XIX, ii, g. 340 (29).
[119] He supplied part of the purchase price with Lord Clinton.
[120] His signature appears on Particulars for Grants PRO E 318.
[121] LP XV, g. 733 (54).

and subsequently high sheriff of Lincolnshire, he took possession of further lands of Sempringham and St Katherine's,[122] and in August of that year he co-operated with Leonard Browne in the purchase of more lands of these two monasteries.[123] David Clayton, an official of Augmentations, purchased lands which had been of Sempringham priory in November 1544. Philip Hobby, one of Cromwell's servants and a gentleman of the privy chamber, secured the site and lands of Torksey priory in March 1539,[124] and more lands of the same house in April 1544. The land from this latter grant he alienated three months later to Ralph Parker of Fulham.[125] John Wiseman, auditor of the court of Augmentations in Lincolnshire, obtained lands formerly belonging to Bardney; and Robert Gowge,[126] a receiver of the court, was one of a trio who, in August 1544, purchased lands of Wellow, Alvingham and Irford.[127] It would seem that these officials who had no roots in Lincolnshire made very little permanent impression on county society since none of them established families that continued to play a significant role in the shire.

So far we have reviewed the purchases of the gentry who had official connections, and of officials some of whom had no Lincolnshire affiliations, but there were gentry who, if they were not solely 'local men', had fewer links with the Court and with royal administration. Such were the Skipwiths of which there were at the beginning of the sixteenth century three branches, one at South Ormsby, another at Utterby, and a third at Habrough. Sir William Skipwith who had married firstly Elizabeth, daughter of Sir William Tyrwhit, and secondly Alice, daughter of Sir Lionel Dymoke, obtained lands formerly of Kirkstead abbey in July 1538.[128] Edward Skipwith junior of Habrough, whose mother was the daughter of John Heneage of Hainton, paid 400 marks in May 1540 for the house and site of Nuncoton,[129] and Thomas Skipwith of the Utterby branch of the family took a lease of Utterby grange which had formerly belonged to Nunormsby priory.[130] Moreover, Sir William Skipwith or his son William purchased properties from others, some of which had belonged to monasteries. In 1543, he acquired from William Stamford the manor of Asserby (two miles north-east of Bilsby) and lands in Ingoldmells, Skegness, Winthorpe, and Bilsby, and from William White lands in Louth.[131] The following year he obtained lands in Manby, Saltfleetby, North and South Somer-

[122] LP XIX, i, g. 1035 (130). [123] Ibid., ii, g. 166 (21).
[124] LP XIV, i, g. 651 (21). [125] LP XIX, i, g. 812 p. 507.
[126] Their signatures appear on Particulars for Grants. [127] LP XIX, ii, g. 166 (61).
[128] LP XIII, i, g. 1519 (59). [129] LP XV, g. 733 (19).
[130] PRO Exch. Aug. Off., Misc. Books (E 315), vol. 190, p. 3.
[131] PRO Ct. of Common Pleas, Feet of Fines, Linc., Easter 35 Hy. VIII (C.P. 25 (2)), m. 198d.

cotes, and Horncastle from Nicholas Spertes[132] and, in 1545, lands at Cockerington some of which were re-sold.[133] Here again it can be asserted that the Skipwiths were no parvenu family in the shire, but neither can it be denied that their standing in the county was advanced by the increased size of their estates.

The Dymoke family whose influence in the county may have been underrated, perhaps because too much attention has been focused on its role as king's champion, apparently added little land to its estates at this time. In November 1538, Sir Robert Dymoke[134] purchased a life interest from Sir William Tyrwhit in lands at Glentworth and Fillingham, formerly of Gokewell nunnery, which the latter had acquired in July of that same year.[135] But these were two small tofts of land worth only 15s. and 12s. *per annum* respectively.[136] On the other hand the Carr family of Sleaford although not unknown before the Dissolution made such considerable purchases of monastic land that it might be said that its fortunes were based upon them. Robert Carr has been described as 'on the fringe of the county establishment.'[137] It is true that his father was a merchant of the Staple and left him lands in Kirkby-la-Thorpe, Evedon, and Holdingham,[138] but the acquisition of the site and lands of Catley priory as well as lands of Haverholme, Sempringham, Bullington, and Sixhills was the real foundation of the family fortunes. Robert might have lost his head for the part he played in the Lincolnshire rebellion, but he testified against lord Hussey and was released on Cromwell's own orders.[139] It may be that the opportunity to purchase monastic property was presented to him as a reward for his Judas-like services. For whatever reason, he was able in December 1539 to purchase these properties for £400.[140] Moreover in June 1542 Robert Carr purchased from lord Clinton former monastic lands in Haverholme, Anwick, and Ruskington, so that he achieved a considerable estate in the district around Sleaford.[141] The fine, dated 12 June 1542, records that for a consideration, said to be £440,[141] Carr obtained four fishponds, 120 messuages, thirty tofts, thirty cottages, 560 acres of arable, 315 acres of meadow, 400 acres of pasture, four watermills, four dovecotes, thirty gardens, twenty acres of wood, and forty acres of heath in Haverholme, Anwick, and Ruskington.[142] Here was a family whose

---

[132] *Ibid.*, Mich. 36 Hy. VIII, m. 254d.   [133] *Ibid.*, Mich. 37 Hy. VIII, m. 8d.
[134] LP xiii, ii, g. 967 (29) and PRO Chancery, Pat. Roll 30 Hy. VIII, pt. 1, m. 20.
[135] *Ibid.*, i, g. 1519 (59).   [136] W. Dugdale, *Monasticon*, edn. 1817–30, v, p. 721.
[137] James, *op. cit.*, pp. 26–7.   [138] *Ibid.*, p. 27, fn. 134.   [139] LP xii, i, 591.
[140] LP xiv, ii, g. 780 (38).
[141] PRO Ct. of Common Pleas, Feet of Fines, Linc., Trinity 34 Hy. VIII (C.P. 25 (2)), bundle 26, file 172, m. 25. The consideration is not necessarily or even probably the total sum paid.
[142] *Ibid.*

estate was enlarged appreciably by the acquisition of monastic property: an estate was created which the Carrs held until the death of the fourth baronet in 1684.

Thomas Hall of Huntingdon may have been related to some Lincolnshire Halls for he secured the lease of Lynghowe grange in Ashby-de-la-Launde (formerly Haverholme) in June 1540,[143] and in September he acquired lands of the former priory of St Katherine's Lincoln. The Grantham family of St Katherine's Lincoln and Goltho was one which had prospered in trade and city office but it was only just 'arriving' among the gentry. Their standing was doubtless increased by Vincent Grantham's acquisition of the site of St Katherine's in June 1540 when the Crown allowed the duke of Suffolk to alienate it to him and to Thomas his son.[144] But there were other families whose position between the gentry and the yeomanry was even more marginal. The Dightons of Lincoln and Great Sturton might be classed as gentry, but the Broxholmes of Owersby, the Bellows, and the Brocklesbies were almost certainly yeomen at the beginning of the sixteenth century. Thomas Hutton, Francis Leke, Robert Dyson, and William Smith probably belonged to the class of wealthier yeomen which purchased land directly from the court of Augmentations as did the Disneys of Norton Disney,[145] but many yeomen bought small parcels of monastic land from 'land-agents'.

These 'land-agents' who were once described by economic historians as 'speculators',[146] are now perhaps more correctly looked upon as agents who performed a useful and indeed necessary function for the small men who wished to acquire some monastic land.[147] Perhaps some were both speculator and agent. London merchants were certainly an important set of purchasers of monastic lands and, although more involved in counties nearer the capital, their activities extended into Lincolnshire. In July 1544 Roger and Robert Taverner paid £481 3s. 10d for lands formerly belonging to St Katherine's Lincoln, Humberstone, and Louth Park and to monastic houses in other counties.[148] 'Land-jobbers' were not active in Lincolnshire before 1544 and until then most grants of monastic lands had been made direct to well known grantees,

[143] LP xv, 1032 (p. 556).

[144] PRO Chancery, Pat. Roll 32 Hy. VIII (C66), pt. 7, m. 28 & LP, xv, g. 831 (19).

[145] Richard Disney, although described as a yeoman, was treasurer of the earl of Rutland—LP xv, 998.

[146] R. H. Tawney, *The Agrarian Problem in the Sixteenth Century*, London, 1912, p. 381 and *passim*; Hodgett, 'The Dissolution of the Religious Houses in Lincolnshire and the Changing Structure of Society', LAAS IV pt. 1, n.s. 1951, pp. 91-3.

[147] H. J. Habakkuk, 'The Market for Monastic Property 1539–1603', EcHR ser. 2, X, 1958, pp. 377–80; Youings, *op. cit.*, pp. 126–8.

[148] LP XIX, i, g. 1035 (68).

but the rapid alienation of monastic property by the Crown in that year brought agents into the market in our county. In August 1544, thirty-two citizens of London paid £2,136 13s. 4d. for monastic lands in widely scattered counties and some lands formerly of Kyme priory were part of the grant.[149] In the same month, twenty citizens combined to pay £1,753 6s. 8d. for lands some of which belonged to the houses of Hagnaby and St Katherine's Lincoln.[150] At the same time, £566 13s. 4d. was paid by seven salters, a plumber, a cordwainer, a girdler, a brewer, a beer brewer, and a poulterer for lands belonging to the dissolved monastery of Crowland.[151] The grants made in the summer of 1544 frequently had attached to them the proviso that, if the money was not paid within a year, the grants would be void: also the purchasers frequently received within a few days licences to alienate, so that in such instances they were most probably acting as agents. Such men may indeed have already received payment from small men who themselves did not have the courage or the knowledge to apply to the court of Augmentations directly.

In Lincolnshire, John Bellow and John Broxholme played a prominent part in the purchase and re-sale of monastic lands. As we have seen, they were men of Lincolnshire stock; John Broxhome was possibly an unsuccessful candidate for election to parliament in 1547. The two men, on 12 February 1545, requested permission to purchase monastic lands belonging to twenty-two Lincolnshire houses.[152] The particulars for the grant show the clear annual value of the property to have been £120 19s. 8d.[153] On 15 July, the lands asked for were granted by letters patent to Bellow and Broxholme for a payment of £790.[154] This is an unusual price at only six and a half times the annual value and we shall perhaps never know why it deviated from the norm of the 'twenty years' purchase' formula. The nature of the property might[155] have been such as to induce the commissioners to reduce the price from £800 by £10 to £790 for it would appear that all the property was leased out. It may well be that Bellow and Broxholme were simply buying the reversions to leases but still the price appears to be rather a low one. The lands were to be held of the Crown in socage, and they were to be freed of all encumbrances except the leases and the charges to be made by the lessees according to their indentures: it may well be that much of the land was leased for fairly long periods. Also in July 1545 the two purchasers made a joint purchase for £2,370 19s. 0½d. of lands formerly of Humberstone, Barlings, Newstead, Heynings, Nunormsby, Kyme,

---

[149] LP xix, ii, g. 166 (54).   [150] Ibid., (57).   [151] Ibid., (58).
[152] PRO DK's 9th Report, App. ii, p. 169.
[153] PRO Exch. Aug. Off., Particulars for Grants (E 318), file 124.
[154] LP xx, i, g. 1335 (12).   [155] Youings, op. cit., p. 125.

Hagnaby, Sixhills, Bullington, Wellow, Nuncoton, Gokewell, Sempringham, Stixwold, St Katherine's Lincoln, Neubo, Thornholme, and Newstead-on-Ancholme, and of a few monasteries in other counties.[156] In September of the same year, a further request was made by the two 'agent-speculators' for Lincolnshire and other monastic properties to the clear annual value of £233 8s. 11½d. and the Crown granted these to them in December for a consideration of £3,338 13s. 3d.[157] A fourth purchase occurred in November 1546 when these same two men paid £1,301 4s. 6¼d. for monastic lands mostly not in the county but some of which had belonged to Bardney, St Katherine's and Crowland.[158] Thus, between July 1545 and November 1546, these two men of Lincolnshire yeoman stock paid £7,800 16s. 9¾d. to the Crown; perhaps the equivalent of about £3½ m. in modern money.

Nor were these the only purchases of land by these yeomen. John Broxholme on his own paid £1,222 15s. 6d. in August 1544 for monastic property most of it in Lincolnshire.[159] The Broxholmes were obviously acting as agents for had they retained all their acquisitions they would have become one of the leading families in the county: such a position they did not achieve. In fact all they did was to strengthen their territorial position in Owersby and its neighbourhood by the purchase of lands there and in Osgodby, Usselby, Normanby-le-Wold, and Walesby.[160] Here, John and Robert Broxholme acquired compact estates, not necessarily all out of monastic property; the one of four houses, three gardens, and 260 acres; and the other of one house, four tofts, two gardens, and 242 acres. John Bellow had co-operated in October 1543 with Robert Brocklesby of Glentworth, a village ten miles north of Lincoln, to pay £946 16s. 8¼d. for monastic lands.[161] In August 1544, with Robert Gowge of the court of Augmentations and Robert Lawrence he bought lands, mostly in Lincolnshire, for £560 16s. 6d.[162] With Edward Bales, in March 1545, he bought lands for £1,386 1s. 1d.[163] and with Robert Bigott in November 1546 he paid £1,456 8s. 7½d. for monastic property.[164] Most of these lands were re-sold since John Bellow, like the Broxholmes, did not build up a large estate in the county. He probably came from Great Grimsby—although he is described on one occasion as 'of Legbourne'[165]—and he took leases of the Newstead-on-Ancholme grange of Sturton and of land at Blyborough: he also acquired the manors of Clee, Utterby, 'Hole',

---

[156] LP xx, i, 1335 (11).   [157] LP xx, ii, g. 1068 (19).
[158] LP xxi, ii, g. 476 (96).   [159] LP xix, ii, g. 166 (40).
[160] PRO Ct. of Common Pleas, Feet of Fines, Linc., bundle 26, file 172, m. 5 and 17.
[161] LP xviii, ii, g. 327 (17).   [162] LP xix, ii, g. 166 (61).
[163] LP xx, i, g. 465 (22).   [164] LP xxi, ii, g. 476 (85).
[165] PRO Exch. Aug. Off., Misc. Books (E 315), Particulars for Leases, vol. 190, f. 97.

'Frunescowgh' and 'Elkington Stowe' in 1546.[166] But he sold the site of Haverholme early in 1545,[167] and other properties, whether acquired as speculations or not is difficult to say, were also alienated.

Robert Dighton, another agent, was a London goldsmith[168] but he was, almost certainly, one of the Dighton family of Lincoln and Great Sturton, for his father Christopher was probably a nephew of Robert Dighton who was mayor of Lincoln in 1494, 1506, and 1510 and who died in 1520.[169] The Londoner, Robert Dighton, in August 1540, paid £1,178 19s. 11d. for lands which had belonged to Stixwold, Haverholme, Catley, Bourne, Alvingham, Kyme, and Spalding.[170] Lands in Pinchbeck, formerly of Spalding, he sold to Thomas Hill in January 1541;[171] lands previously of Bourne in Spanby, Threckington, and Billingborough to Lawrence Sturtibant in November of the same year;[172] and lands of Catley to Sir Robert Hussey of Linwood in Blankney, brother of the executed lord Hussey, in May 1545.[173] George Welles purchased from him in April 1543 Catley lands in Billinghay and Kyme lands in Coningsby.[174] Dighton might therefore have been something of a speculator if we are to accept that such a term should be applied to one who, when he purchased the properties, 'had only a hope but not a certainty of sale'.[175] Unlike others who had licences to alienate, often granted on the day of the purchase, Dighton would appear not to have been acting as an agent as he gradually sold off properties over a period of nearly five years. Unfortunately, as the Crown was not interested in the considerations given, the documentation is insufficiently detailed to allow us to estimate the profit which he undoubtedly made.

Several of the purchasers had been connected with monastic lands before the Dissolution either as monastic officers or as lessees of abbey lands. Among purchasers who had been monastic officers we find Sir John Heneage who had been a steward of Bardney abbey and also at Revesby and Thornton,[176] Sir Robert Tyrwhit and his brother Sir William, who had both held office at Thornton, George St Paul, a steward of Thornton, and Edward Skipwith who had also served that house. The earl of Rutland's offices have already been noted.[177] Richard Disney's father William had a long-standing connection with Belvoir

---

[166] PRO Ct. of Common Pleas, Plea Roll, Easter 38 Hy. VIII (C.P. 40).
[167] PRO Exch., Index to the L.T.R. rolls 6922, Hilary 36 Hy. VIII.
[168] Maddison, *Lincs. Pedigrees sub* Dighton.
[169] Linc. Public Lib., A List of Mayors etc., compiled by J. B. King in 1945.
[170] LP xv, g. 942 (99).   [171] LP xvi, g. 503 (54).   [172] *Ibid.*, g. 1391 (29).
[173] LP xx, g. 846 (93).
[174] PRO Chancery, Pat. Roll 35 Hy. VIII (C 66), pt. 2, m. 18.
[175] Youings, *op. cit.*, p. 126.   [176] Savine, *op. cit.*, p. 258.
[177] See *ante* p. 52.

prior since he held a lease of Auborn parsonage from that house from 3 May 1531.[178] Anthony Mussenden and Thomas Moigne, who was executed, had connections with Bardney, Crowland, and Thornton although no record exists of them or their families as purchasers of monastic land. A pattern therefore emerges which demonstrates that the alienation of monastic property by the Crown had a profound effect in enhancing the position of a number of gentry families in the shire and in founding the fortunes of a number of yeoman families. The effects of the expansion of the land market by the alienation of these lands and buildings were far reaching and long lasting.

[178] PRO Exch. Aug. Off., Conventual Leases (E 303) Lincoln, 18.

I Charles, duke of Suffolk (died 1545) who married as his fourth wife the young Katherine baroness Willoughby de Eresby.

II Dr. Thomas Wilson, of Strubby, author, lawyer, tutor to the dukes of Suffolk, M.P. for Lincoln, Privy Councillor, ambassador and Secretary of State to queen Elizabeth; he became Dean of Durham, and died 1581. (The ascription to Nicholas Bacon is an error.)

III Portrait of a city father: Peter Euer, second son of Robert Euer of Belton, Isle of Axholme, born 1549, died 1612. Freeman of Lincoln, 1531, M.P for the city, 1581–89 (and for Derby, 1601); knighted 1603. He was buried at Washingborough.

IV Doddington Hall: entrance porch. One of two major late Elizabethan houses in Lincolnshire which were apparently designed by Robert Smithson, it was built between 1593 and 1600 at the order of Thomas Taylor, Recorder of the Bishop of Lincoln. The house is plain, with elaborate details only on the porch. The exterior has survived relatively unaltered since the sixteenth century.

V Irnham Hall. Home of the Thimbleby family, it was built between 1510 and 1531. Although altered in 1745 and severely damaged by fire in 1887, much of the original building survives. (a) The Elizabethan porch (with its unusual openings on two sides) leads to (b) the cross passage at the lower end of the great hall; a gallery surrounds the hall on two sides.

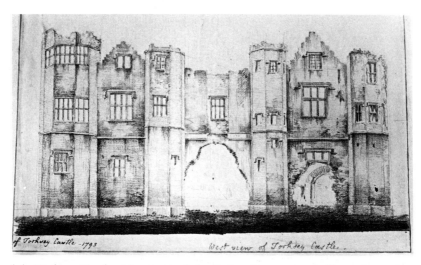

(a) *Torksey Castle. Mansion built by Robert Jermyn, probably in the 1560s. The lower stage is of stone, the upper of brick, with stone quoins and windows. The house was captured and destroyed by Royalists in 1645. This drawing by Charles Nattes shows that all the house except the west front had vanished by 1793.*

(b) *Sleaford Vicarage. One of the few late fifteenth or early sixteenth century half-timbered and jettied houses surviving in Lincolnshire, it has apparently always been the vicarage house. Most of the windows have, however, been altered, and the eaves, as also the brick extension, are of course Victorian.*

VI Rural housing.

VII Urban housing. Tudor shops on the High Bridge, Lincoln. The building of houses and shops over bridges was a common feature of late medieval towns, but few survive. These have been heavily restored, but their general outline and some details are original.

VIII Page from Lincoln Corporation Minute Book. Note the counting of 'voices' given for each of the candidates for mayor of the city in 1518 – Thomas Norton (24), William Fox (40 voices, plus 10 from 'the [aldermanic] bench'), John Halton (19) and Robert Smyth (30 voices, plus 2 from 'the bench'). Fox was thus elected.

CHAPTER V

LAND AND RURAL SOCIETY
c. 1550 TO 1603

WE have already seen that the consequences of the Reformation and the introduction of new men into the landed aristocracy of the shire had brought about considerable changes in some respects in Lincolnshire rural society. These changes introduced a number of aristocratic families who dominated some regions of the shire, and the increased acreage of most landed families—many of them of knightly status—enabled them also to have a greater hold over a district than had been possible fifty years previously. The paucity of dominant families in parts of Lincolnshire has been noted earlier and it is true that some regions, notably the fens, continued to have few prominent landed families.

A list of Lincolnshire landowners, called a list of 'inheritors', which dates from just before 1558,[1] gives us perhaps the best guide to the important gentry families in the second half of the sixteenth century but many compilations of gentry families exist. A. R. Maddison in an article entitled 'Lincolnshire gentry in the sixteenth century' covered many of the sources, one of which was the visitation by heralds.[2] There was a visitation in 1562, and another in 1592, and the records of the former were printed by W. C. Metcalfe in 1881.[3] Manuscript copies of this visitation are to be found in the Lincolnshire Archives Office, at least one of which was written some sixty to seventy years after the visitation.[4] Yet another list of landowners, in effect, is the list of 'those persons who subscribed towards the defence of this country at the time of the Spanish Armada'.[5] The 'Burton Hall list' of *c.* 1557 contains 133 names[6] as against 136 in Harleian Manuscript 2145. Both lists note not

[1] Lincs NQ, x, 1908–9, pp. 56–62, where it is stated that this list was then in the Library of Burton Hall and that it is a copy of BM Harleian MS. 2145.

[2] LAAS, XXII, pt. 1, 1894, pp. 174–222.

[3] W. C. Metcalfe (ed.), *The Visitation of the County of Lincoln in 1562–4*, London, 1881.

[4] LAO, Cragg, 1, 2/6/1 and 2/6/2.

[5] T. C. Noble (ed.), *The names of those persons etc.*, London, 1886, a reprint of a tract of 1798 which owed much to BM Lansdowne MS. 81 (55).

[6] Although A. R. Maddison prints only 129 names in the list, omitting Cetton,

the name of the 'inheritor's' wife but whose daughter and heir she was, and also the annual value of the inherited estates of those recorded. The list in BM Harleian Ms. 2145 contains the names of Mr Haughstede (£30), Ambrose Sutton (£100), Mr Sandon (£80) and John Brothlin (£80) which do not appear in the printed version of the 'Burton Hall list', while the latter contains the name of Mr 'Hanshfelde', identified as John Angevine, which name does not appear in Harley 2145. This Mr Hanshfelde could be the same as Mr Haughstede as their estates are both assessed at an annual value of £30. Neither of these lists includes the estates of the aristocracy and, as has been noted, some families have been inexplicably omitted.[7] Nevertheless, these lists give a reasonably full compendium of the landed families of the decade 1550–60 which could not have numbered more than about 150 in all. The list of those who subscribed to the defence of the country at the time of the Armada is not *per se* a roll of county gentry but most, if not all, of the 129 names on it belonged to that rank of society. In fact the 129 names were reduced to 115 by the lord treasurer discharging fourteen of those originally listed, mostly on grounds of insufficiency to make a contribution, and some evidence exists that various people refused to pay.[8] Many new names that had not been listed thirty years previously appear on the record: indeed, only about forty to forty-five names on the 1588 list bear surnames which unquestionably belong to established Lincolnshire landed families of the 1550s. This difference adds point to what is already known in general terms that an active land market existed in the second half of the sixteenth century, and that some families were rising and some falling. The Friskneys, Kymes, Busheys, Billesbys, Asfordbys and Angevines had given ground to the rising Skipwiths, Tyrwhits, Ayscoughs, and Dymokes in the fifteenth century, and they in turn were to lose pre-eminence to the Heneages and Monsons in the later sixteenth century.

What clearly emerges from the mid-century survey is the considerable difference between the wealthiest gentry and the poorest. At the top were three gentlemen, the annual value of whose estates reached £333 6s. 8d.: Sir Francis Ayscough of Stallingborough and South Kelsey, Sir Edward Dymoke of Scrivelsby, and Sir Robert Tyrwhit of Kettleby. At the bottom were three gentlemen of Holland worth only £10 a year in rents: Anthony Cony, Thomas Flete, and Thomas Pulvertoft. In Lindsey, one landholder, Sir William Skipwith of South

---

[7] Lincs NQ, x, p. 61.   [8] Noble, *op. cit.*, p. xxxiii.

Wyne, and Scameton, whom he cannot identify (NQ, x, p. 61), these names appear in BM Harl. MS. 2145 as Cotton, Wryne, and ? Staineton. He also omits from the list Richard Thimbleby because his estate is not valued.

Ormsby, had lands worth £266 13s. 4d. a year, four were worth £200, six worth £133 6s. 8d. and eleven worth £100 annually. Also in that part of the county fourteen gentlemen held lands worth £80 a year, one £70, and one £66 13s. 4d. This last figure denoted the annual value of the lands of the two richest gentlemen in Holland, William Adams and Thomas Holland, while only four men were worth that amount in Kesteven where two landholders had £100 each and Richard Disney, the wealthiest in that part of the county, was worth £133 6s. 8d. In Lindsey, if we take the Burton Hall list of ninety-seven landholders and add the three names from the Harleian manuscript, the arithmetic becomes simple. Of these gentlemen, 3 per cent had lands worth £333 6s. 8d.; 1 per cent, £266 13s. 4d.; 4 per cent, £200; 6 per cent, £133 6s. 8d.; 12 per cent, £100; 16 per cent, £80 and 1 per cent, £70. Thus, 43 per cent of the landholders had lands worth £70 a year and more. The remaining 57 per cent were divided as follows: 1 per cent, £66 13s. 4d.; 6 per cent, £60; 3 per cent, £50; 13 per cent, £40; 16 per cent, £30 and 18 per cent, £20. In Kesteven, with only twenty-one gentlemen, percentages in each category are less meaning-ful but 33 per cent held land worth £66 13s. 4d. or more, while 43 per cent were worth £20. In the parts of Holland, with only eleven listed 'inheritors', nearly half of them were worth either £10 or £20, four £40, and two £66 13s. 4d.

These landed families were, of course, a tiny proportion of the total population. An ecclesiastical census that recorded, among other things, the number of families in each parish was taken in 1563.[9] Although there are no returns extant for the archdeaconry of Stow, the total number of households in the county in that year (apart from Stow) was 22,505.[10] Returns for Stow exist for 1603[11] which tell us the number of com-municants in the four rural deaneries of the archdeaconry: the total (including non-communicants) was 16,222.[12] The difficulties of turning these records into population figures for the county are enormous but, if we take a multiplier of four, the population of the shire in 1563, apart from the area to the north and west of Lincoln bounded roughly by Torksey, Gainsborough, Crowle, Winteringham, Brigg, and Barlings, was 91,192. What multiplier to employ is always a difficult decision to take but the allowance to be made for non-communicants in the 1603 returns is equally difficult. Although we cannot be certain at what age

[9] BM Harl. MS. 618, ff. 2–14v and ff. 38–38v.

[10] These figures fall short of the 22,589 given in LRS 23, p. 442.

[11] LRS 23, 1926, pp. 337–53.

[12] These figures include 13 recusants and fall just short of the 16,226 in LRS 23, p. 443. My figures for the rural deaneries of Corringham are 5,270 (5,306) and for Lawres 4,023 (3,991).

they began to take holy communion, children under ten years of age should probably be regarded as non-communicants: to add a fifth to the Stow returns of 16,209 to allow for them cannot be much more than a guess. Moreover, some allowance must be made for the thirteen recusants and their families and perhaps for a few non-conforming lay-men and their children who slipped through the count. Also the Stow returns are unsatisfactory because the large numbers of round figures strongly indicate that the number of communicants was estimated rather than correctly counted in most parishes. The total population of the archdeaconry of Stow in 1603 would then have been, if we make the suggested allowances, 19,450. To add this figure to the 91,192 would be unjustifiable because, although it cannot be quantified, some increase in population occurred between 1563 and 1603. We have, however, the figure of 80,225 communicants in the archdeaconry of Lincoln in 1603.[13] To this figure we must add thirty-nine recusants, so making a population of 80,264. If we again add a fifth for children who were not old enough to take communion, the total population within the arch-deaconry of Lincoln in 1603 might have been 96,317 and in Stow 19,450; a total of 115,767 for the whole county as against an estimated total for 1563 of 109,400. These figures can only be speculative and they certainly appear to underestimate the population growth in the country generally of the last forty years of the sixteenth century, but they have been essayed solely to show how small, in relation to the total popula-tion, the percentage of people belonging to considerable landed families was. If these 150 wealthy families are allowed ten members each, they still comprise only about one in every seventy-two people; 1·4 per cent of the population.

The county comprised four agricultural regions. Arable farming, in which sheep rearing played a prominent part but where much corn was produced, occurred on the wolds and on the heath which extended in a narrow belt north and south of the county town. Another system of arable farming based on corn and cattle was found in the clay vales between the cliff and the wolds and in the west of the county bordering Nottinghamshire and Leicestershire. A third type of mixed farming comprising corn growing, especially wheat, and the fattening of stock for the market occurred in the marshland. The fourth agricultural region was the fenland. Here stock fattening and dairy-farming were import-ant, with fishing and fowling playing a significant part in what was essentially a pastoral economy.

As to cultivation methods and crops grown, little change appears to have taken place in the Tudor period. In most parts of the shire, the method of exploitation of the land in the 1590s was the same as it had

[13] LRS 23, p. 443.

been in the 1520s or in the 1480s. The county was overall little affected by enclosure as an abstract of the returns of the commissioners appointed in 1607 to investigate the extent of depopulation shows.[14] They found twelve villages in Kesteven and seventeen in Lindsey either completely or largely depopulated by reason of enclosure and conversion to pasture. In Lindsey at least 4,000 acres had been converted, and the destruction of most of the villages was the work of Henry, earl of Lincoln, from 1585 to 1616; he destroyed Thorpe Tilney in Kesteven and caused some depopulation at Tattershall in Lindsey. The earl was an unpleasant tyrant who was afraid of no man—the privy council had to reprimand him on more than one occasion—and it is not likely that he would hesitate to offend his tenants. Sir Christopher Wray of Glentworth, lord chief justice from 1574, and his son William between them destroyed three Lindsey townships. Depopulation did not always follow enclosure but as enclosed land was frequently used for pasture, the tendency was for a reduction in population to ensue. In the parts of Kesteven there was a tendency for larger enclosures to be more readily accompanied by depopulation than for smaller ones where depopulation was less marked.[15] Very few enclosures resulting in depopulation occurred in Holland because the areas of land enclosed there were all small. But enclosures and conversion to pasture were not the sole cause of depopulation and, in fact, the causes of half the decay of farmhouses were 'ingrossing', that is the joining together of two or more holdings, which inevitably meant the decay of one farmhouse, and the loss of one farmer's livelihood.

Despite the fact that husbandry remained overall the same, sheep farming had become more important by 1607 than it had been in 1517 for, in 1607, Lincolnshire was first among counties in the amount of acreage that had been converted to sheep pasture. Upwards of 13,000 acres had been converted to sheep farming as against 10,746 in Northamptonshire, but in terms of the proportion of converted land to the total acreage of the county,[16] Lincolnshire suffered less conversion to sheep farming than Northamptonshire, Leicestershire, and Huntingdonshire, and possibly than Bedfordshire. It is true that the number of farmhouses either 'decayed' or abandoned was much greater than in the counties of Warwick, Leicester, Northampton, Buckingham, Bedford, and Huntingdon and that the number of villages wholly or largely depopulated was also high. However, the average number of dwellings in these townships was small, and probably most of them had 'passed

[14] J. D. Gould, 'The Inquisition of Depopulation of 1607 in Lincolnshire', EHR, 67, 1952, pp. 393 et seq. quoting the abstract, BM Add. MS, 11,574, ff. 70–98.
[15] Gould, loc. cit., p. 394.   [16] Modern acreage 1,705,293 acres.

a fair way along the road to destruction'.[17] In most villages only one or two farmhouses were decayed or, deprived of lands, became cottages.[18] By depopulation and decay of husbandry resulting therefrom, about 4,000 acres in Lindsey were made over to pasture, but 5,500 acres were deliberately converted from arable to pasture. However, a total of around 9,500 acres out of 972,796 acres[19] is not a very high proportion. In Kesteven 3,163 acres out of 469,377 acres[19] was converted from arable to pasture for sheep and cattle and in Holland only 502 acres.[20] The number of farmhouses decayed, abandoned, or turned into cottages was also recorded by the commissioners in 1607. Four categories were defined; farmhouses that were abandoned by wasting and decay of husbandry; by taking in lands from houses of husbandry and thus turning them into cottages; by the engrossing of farms and letting farmhouses stand empty and, lastly, by great depopulation and decay of husbandry. In Kesteven there fell into the four categories, 36, 85, 50, and an estimated 80; in Lindsey 130, 313, 39, and an estimated 160, and in Holland 35 and 28 in the first two categories. The totals over the three parts of the county were 201, 426, 440 and an estimated 240 or, in all, an estimate of some 1,292 farmhouses decayed, abandoned, or turned into cottages in the whole shire; 1,292 was a relatively small number and so Lincolnshire remained predominantly a county of arable production in large open fields.

A remarkable survey of the manor of Kirkby Underwood drawn up on 1 August 1595 provides one example that manorial lands were still being cultivated as they had been 100 years previously.[21] Kirkby Underwood on the clay lands, five miles NNW of Bourne, was in well wooded country and the arable was cultivated in three open fields, the North, the East, and the South Field. At the time of the survey the lord of the manor was Richard Brownlow, a London-born lawyer who had become chief prothonotary in the court of Common Pleas in 1591.[22] He bought the more important estate at Belton near Grantham but in 1595, when he had Kirkby Underwood surveyed, he was already a prosperous man 42 years of age. The North Field contained 15 furlongs held in several, all of which are described in detail: *e.g.* 'the Clay Pits furlong lying east and west beginning at the land of John Buckstones on the south and ending at a land of Thomas Chamberlens at the north'.[23] Each of these furlongs—one cannot presume that they are all strips of

[17] Gould, *loc. cit.*, p. 395.   [18] BM Add. MS. 1 1,574, ff. 73–4, 84–8, 97.
[19] Figure of 1961.
[20] The 1961 acreage of Holland, 263,120 is not relevant to the sixteenth-century acreage.
[21] LAO Ancaster, VI/B/10.   [22] DNB *sub nomine.*
[23] LAO Anc. VI/B/10, f. 1.

10 acres—is named.[24] The East Field held 9 furlongs, and contained as part of it Whitecross field of 5 furlongs and the Haile field of 6 furlongs, so in all it contained 20 furlongs. The South Field possessed 9 furlongs and two wongs called Swallow wong and Simon's wong.

The site of the manor house of Kirkby Underwood, which was called Kallends, was 7 acres and 19 perches with a little close of 1 acre, 2 roods, 10 perches; and meadow land of 1 acre and 33 perches. Other meadows and closes brought the total acreage of the manor site to 10 ac 3 r 12 p. The site of the rectory with its abutments was 1 ac, and 6 p to which there were added two little crofts and a cottage. The glebe land consisting of 21 different parcels in the North Field, 29 in the East and 35 in the South gave James Griffethe the rector a total holding of 38 ac 3 r 23 p. The tenants are listed with a full record of their holdings. Thomas Chamberlaine is the first, who, like so many more, was a tenant-at-will with a dwelling-house that had attached to it a back-side (*i.e.* backyard and outhouses) and a little close. The scattered nature of such a tenant's holding is clearly demonstrated for he holds 65 parcels in the North Field totalling 37 ac and 9 p; 95 in the East Field with 28 ac 2 r 22 p; 101 in the South Field comprising 31 ac and 20 p. Also in the East Field in Short Haile furlong he held 33 parcels totalling 11 ac and 17 p and in South Field in Over Throwell, 28, containing 9 ac and 22 p. The sum of all his lands including the tenement and close was 51 ac 1 r 19 p. There were sixteen other such tenants-at-will holding between Chamberlain's 51 acres and John Ellsey's 4 ac 2 r 19 p, and four cottagers holding 1 ac 3 r 20 p, 1 ac 2 r 11 p, 1 ac 1 r 7 p, and 2 r 20 p respectively. Three of the tenants who had about 30 acres each shared another 4 acres of pasture between them.

Adding up all the waste and the land used for streets and lanes the sum total of the lord's land within the manor was 485 ac 2 r 15 p and what he held plus his tenants' and cottagers' holdings amounted to 1,076 acres. The enclosures were also noted. In the North Field were ten enclosures, the largest, known as Long Close, contained 36 ac 2 r 2 p and the smallest 3 r 3 p; in all, 224 ac and 15 p were enclosed in that field. In South Field, nine enclosures had been made, ranging in area from 70 ac 2 r 0 p to 1 ac and 9 p, and comprising in all 225 ac 1 r 4 p. Thus in the manor there were 449 ac 1 r 19 p of enclosed pasture. Nor must the woody nature of this part of the shire be overlooked, for five woods, the largest of 43 acres and the smallest of 16 ac and 12 p, totalled 141 ac and 2 p and more woodland was bought after the making of the

[24] Whitecross; Runsyke; Harden Leas; Greendikes; The Marsh; Long Leas; Persons Hurne; Four Acre; Henn Hill; Newgate; Deerleap; Glogate; Decke; Briar Bush.

survey.[25] In all, 590 ac 1 r 21 p consisted of enclosed pasture and woodland out of the 1,076 acres of the lord's land although the latter figure
includes a few additional small closes adjacent to houses.

Free tenants also lived in Kirkby Underwood. Nine of them held a
total of 96 ac and 12 p of land. The largest holder was William Damme
who had 32 ac 3 r 37 p, and Robert Sawle followed him closely with
30 ac 2 r 12 p. One of the free tenants was the rector of the adjacent
parish of Rippingale who owned 4 ac, three of them in the East Field.
The total acreage of the lord's as well as of the freeholders' several
grounds was 1,172 ac 0 r 12 p. The 1961 returns give 1,094 acres to
Kirkby Underwood with a population of 129: some alteration of
boundaries may have taken place but the population in 1595 was perhaps about 100 souls—no great change in nearly 400 years. Finally, the
survey notes that a number of tenants of the lord held arable lands lying
within the manor of Rippingale. Thomas Chamberlaine, in addition to
his 51 acres in Kirkby, had another 10 ac 2 r 5 p in the adjacent manor,
and his four holdings, like those of others, were all in Rippingale Hill
Field. At the end of the survey a list drawn up on 23 September 1636
notes the changes that had taken place in the intervening forty years.
The terrier is, of course, a document that gives a static picture of the
manor at one point in time, and it is regrettable that no accounts exist
of the same period from which some impression of the estate's profita-
bility might be obtained.

Much of the richest land in the county was in the parts of Holland
and for this to be cultivated properly it had to be drained. Drainage was
one of the great problems of the fens and much is known of the work
of the commissioners of sewers whose responsibility it was to maintain
it. Just because the significant advances in the history of drainage came
in the post-Tudor period, drainage must not be thought unimportant
in the sixteenth century. But as the late Dr Mary Kirkus wrote, "the
aim was not the drainage of great areas of marsh and swamp but the
maintenance of the *status quo*".[26] Some advance on that policy of
maintenance was attempted, even if little was achieved, in the years after
1585 when schemes were put forward for the recovery of drowned and
surrounded grounds.[27] The work of the commissioners of sewers had a
double importance: it was critical both for the continuation of husbandry and for the maintenance of transport facilities. We are here concerned with the contribution which those connected with drainage

[25] LAO Anc. VI/B/10, f. 57v.
[26] '*The Records of the Commissioners of the Sewers* ... *1547–1603*', LRS 54, 1959,
p. xxxvii.
[27] H. C. Darby, *The Draining of the Fens*, London, 2nd edn., 1956, p. 14 *et
seq.*

made to the prosperity of the agrarian economy of those low-lying parts of the county.

Of the Isle of Axholme's drainage little is known in the sixteenth century[28] but about the fen area, mostly in the parts of Holland, we have much information.[29] The district bounded by Friskney near Wainfleet, through Stickney, Dogdyke, Kyme, Heckington, Helpringham, Swaton, Horbling, Bourne, Stamford, the Deepings, Crowland, Gedney, Tydd St Mary, Long Sutton, and Lutton contained land that was at most a few feet above sea level. Drainage had to be undertaken in considerable measure in order to make the land available, sometimes for arable, but mostly for pasture and meadow. In most years, the drainage was adequate but occasionally, as in 1571 which was a very wet year, the rivers overflowed or the sea broke in and consequently much damage occurred. That the fenland farmers on the whole were prosperous was the result of constant vigilance in freeing the land from excessive water, and as a result many villages were enabled to maintain a high density of population.[30]

The work of drainage was effected by a fairly complex administrative control which to some degree originated in the fifteenth century. Of course, measures of drainage had been undertaken earlier but the act of 1427 (6 Hy. VI c.5)[31] appointed commissioners of sewers for a period of ten years. Their duties were to inspect the defences against flooding, to enquire who was to blame for any damage, to call juries which could testify to the facts, to order repairs to be done and distrain upon the goods of those who failed to carry out their orders, and to make statutes concerning drainage. Subsequent acts appointed commissioners for differing periods, but the system was overhauled by an act of 1532 (23 Hy. VIII c.5) which remained the law on sewers until 1930.[32] Each commission was to last for three years, although this was raised to five years from 1552, and to ten years in the 1590s. The commissioners were to be men with at least £26 13s. 4d. a year in freehold land and tenements, which qualification was raised to £40 in 1571, or else be resident in a corporate town with a capital of £100 or else be a barrister. The commissioners of the sewers were named by the lord chancellor, the lord treasurer, and the chief justices of the two benches or by three of these of whom one had to be the lord chancellor. The commissioners

[28] J. Thirsk, *Fenland Farming in the Sixteenth Century* (Univ. of Leicester, Dept. of English Local History, Occasional Paper, no. 3), p. 20 mentions a survey of 1633 and E. Peacock, 'Notes from the court rolls of the manor of Scotter', *Archaeologia*, XLVI, 1881, p. 371 *et seq.*

[29] LRS 54 and 63, 1968.

[30] J. Thirsk, 'Fenland Farming in the 16th century', *op. cit.*, p. 11.

[31] SR II, pp. 236–8.   [32] SR III, pp. 368–72.

apparently split into groups, each commissioner receiving 4s. for every day he spent on sewers' business.³³ The clerk, paid 2s. a day, soon became an important person: John Burton probably held that office as early as 1552 but between 1574 and 1582 Richard Coventry had succeeded him, and in 1586 John Jackson, the earl of Lincoln's servant, assumed office.

The commissioners mostly belonged to those Lincolnshire families which were serving in other capacities, as justices of the peace, on the commissions for gaol delivery, as collectors of subsidies, and so on. The Irbys of Gosberton, Whaplode, and Moulton, the Ogles of Pinchbeck, the Welbys of Moulton and Gedney, the Ayscoughs of Stallingborough and South Kelsey, the Quadrings of Irby, Thomas Massingberd of the Burgh, the Gunbys of Gunby, the Bolles family of Haugh, the Copledykes of Harrington—all performed service as commissioners. Sir Edward Dymoke and his second son Charles, William Heneage of Hainton, and two Thorolds acted during the sixteenth century, and the mayor of Boston was often added *ex officio* to the commission.

The commissioners sat in various places in the fenland; at Spalding and Boston most frequently, but also at Bourne, Stamford, Sleaford, Swineshead, Market Deeping, and elsewhere. Also the number of commissioners at a sitting varied from one to twenty, and at a session they heard the verdicts as the presentments of the jurors were called. The jurors offered evidence of sewers in ruin for lack of scouring and of banks that were defective because they were not high or broad enough, and of gotes (sluices) that did not work properly because the gates had rotted. Other verdicts declared that those liable for sewer maintenance had not paid their dues. Maintenance was secured by a variety of methods. Direct labour, the so-called menework, unpopular though it was, remained as a burden on some communities and the inhabitants of Moulton in 1563 were presented by the dikereeves as not having maintained the bank to the correct height and breadth which should have been done by 'commen meynworkes'.³⁴ This duty often placed the community under an obligation to turn out for two days a year. But other obligations for repair arose. Certain individuals and corporations were obliged to keep up the banks by 'joycement' and their names were entered in the 'joyce books'. Joycement or agistment, meaning a stint or limit by arrangement, described the limits which certain landholders had to repair, namely, a prescribed stint or length of the bank. Yet another way in which obligation for repair was decided was a calculation made on the acreage which a landholder possessed; when this was commuted to cash it became an obligation to pay 'acre silver'. Sometimes

³³ LRS 54, p. xxiii.   ³⁴ *Ibid.*, p. 127.

the burden was assessed according to the value placed upon a man's fishing rights or his homestead and another method of securing repair was by 'dozenage' *i.e.* by a tithing group of ten households.

If the commissioners were important men, the dikereeves were probably more important. They first appear as manorial officers in the fifteenth century but they were possibly parish or village officials in origin. By the later sixteenth century dikereeves were parochial officers along with the churchwardens, constables, overseers of the poor, and surveyors of highways, and they were often elected in south Lincolnshire. The dikereeve was a man of some substance having to possess freehold or copyhold land to the value of 40s. *per annum.* But the office was not sought after as the fairly heavy fine of £3 6s. 8d. for refusal of the dikereeveship demonstrates. The dikereeve had to keep the joyce book, organize repair work, and levy acre silver and other dues. When landholders would not pay, he, along with others, often formed the jury and presented the defaulter to the court of the sewers, having to distrain the guilty party according to the commissioners' orders. Each parish had two surveyors who examined the dikes but they were less important officers than the dikereeve. Perhaps the thing that lightened the dikereeve's burden was a clear appreciation on the part of the landholders of the fens that it was in their own best interests to keep the drainage system in good order and, that being so, he would have had the support of the community against the recalcitrant few. The fact that the court of sewers did not meet every year until after 1571 is perhaps a tribute to the way in which the dikereeves kept the water flowing in the first three-quarters of the century. Alternatively, after 1571, the year of the great flood, the commissioners appear to have become far more diligent in their duties and between that date and 1602 they failed to sit only in 1573 and 1593, and in some years they held a number of sessions. In 1571, seven sessions were held between 23 March and some date after 21 September; six were held in 1575 and 1576, and five in 1595.

This intensified interest in drainage emerged in the 1570s for under the 1531 act the view was taken that the commissioners had no authority to make new drains or to erect and maintain new banks.[35] Moreover, some neglect may have resulted from the selling off of monastic lands, thus sub-dividing the liability for maintenance among a number of new landholders. Views as to whether the Dissolution led to neglect in the cleansing of drains and the repairing of banks have differed, but if the new owners neglected their duties, so had some monasteries.[36] In general between the 1530s and the 1570s the policy was to maintain the existing dikes and other works, and in 1549 a code of fen laws for the

[35] Darby, *op. cit.,* p. 6.   [36] Thirsk, *English Peasant Farming,* p. 27.

general management of the fens was drawn up by the council of the duchy of Lancaster at a Great Inquest of the soke of Bolingbroke.[37] The orders deal with the marking of animals pastured on the fen by those who were entitled to do so and restricted the fishing and fowling rights. The code was confirmed and added to in 1573 and remained in force until the early nineteenth century. But even in the late 1560s some people must have been thinking not only of maintaining but of improving conditions for the cutting of the Maud Foster drain to the north of Boston in 1568 certainly drained more land. It may have been that the disastrous floods of 1570–71 stimulated men's minds to a consideration of how the land might be better protected and the acreage of dry land extended.[38]

In 1575 a request was made for the granting of a patent for the sole right of making and employing certain hydraulic engines for the draining of marshes,[39] and three years later Sir Thomas Golding applied for a 21-year patent for a method of draining marshes by newly invented machines.[40] Letters patent were granted on 26 June 1580 to Peter Morris to drain certain fens,[41] and the following March the privy council was considering how certain lands in Lincolnshire might be drained. A summary of an act entitled 'an act for the recovery and inning of drowned and surrounded grounds and the draining dry of watery marshes' appears among the State Papers Domestic of 1585,[42] but there were many delays in pushing forward a more vigorous policy. A dispute arose between a Mr Carleton and others with liability for the drains and it was put before lord Burghley on 16 March 1585.[43] Earlier, more drastic measures had been taken to raise the height of the banks of the Glen and to dyke the river to a width of forty feet from Baston Spout to 'Dove Horne' and from there to the sea at the accustomed width.[44] Men's minds were turning to the possibility of extending the cultivable area: Dr John Dee wrote his 'Questions and Observations about Draining the Fens',[45] and other proposals signed by a man named Latreille on behalf of some Frenchmen were drawn up in 1584.[46]

As early as 1577, Barnaby Googe who was closely associated with the Cecils had translated a German writer's agricultural textbook, Konrad Heresbach's *Four Books of Husbandry*, from the original Latin into English. This translation, in all probability, demonstrates the interest

[37] Lincs NQ, xx, pp. 58–64, 74–77.
[38] Darby, *op. cit.*, p. 12, and for the effect of the flood on Bourne, J. D. Birkbeck, *A History of Bourne*, p. 32.
[39] SP Dom. Eliz., cvi, p. 62.   [40] *Ibid.*, cxxv, 49 and cvi.
[41] APC xii, p. 68–9.   [42] SP Dom. Eliz. clxxvi, p. 74.
[43] BM Lansdowne MS. 46 (56).   [44] BM Lansdowne MS. 41 (45).
[45] Bodl. Lib., Ashmolean MS. 242/45.   [46] BM Lansdowne MS. 42/31.

which the gentry had in improving the land and it can be assumed that, since Googe was a native of the county, some Lincolnshire gentry shared those interests. In the fens improvement of this sort could only be achieved by drainage.

However, some of the fen dwellers, probably the majority of them, opposed vast drainage schemes for they were afraid that they might lose valuable fishing and fowling rights. The fenlanders had what was to them a satisfactory system of farming, producing, as they did, butter, cheese, fat sheep, and cattle, while the drainers wanted to introduce an arable-farming system. This would have completely transformed the economy since it would have necessitated the creation of large farms suitable for growing coleseed, then grain and other crops, and this in turn would have wrought a complete transformation of society. Since the structure of society in arable regions with its large farmers and agricultural wage labourers is different from that of pastoral regions with its larger number of small, often freeholding, tenants, a wide drainage scheme demanded a transformation of society and the fenlanders fully appreciated the situation. Moreover, they did not relish being pushed by outsiders. The local commissioners complained that they were being overruled by strangers and foreigners and disputes arose over the methods of draining. So tangled had issues become that on 21 March 1589 the privy council reviewed the whole situation and recommended Humphrey Bradley of Bergen-op-Zoom, John Hexhame, and Ralph Agas to the commissioners of sewers because the latter's efforts had achieved such slender results.[47]

Humphrey Bradley drew up 'A Treatise concerning the state of the marshes or inundated lands (commonly called fens) in the Counties of Norfolk, Huntingdonshire, Cambridgeshire, Northamptonshire, and Lincolnshire' dated 3 December 1589.[48] In it he expressed the view that the only way to drain the land was to dig canals to carry the waters out into the sea, and four years later Bradley was again writing to lord Burghley. In fact, perhaps not so much would have been heard of these schemes if the queen's first minister had not been a Lincolnshire man who was ever willing to listen to matters that closely affected his native county. Bradley recognized the difficulties created by vested interests and proposed an act of parliament to overcome them[49] and when the bill was introduced it promised, according to lord Willoughby, to 'raise a tempest'. His letter[50] contained the nub of the argument against draining which was that a man could make more in a week by cutting reeds, essential for thatch and fuel, and catching and selling fish and

[47] APC n.s. XVII, pp. 112-3.   [48] BM Lansdowne MS. 60 (34).
[49] SP Dom. Eliz., ccxliv, p. 97.
[50] HMC Report, earl of Ancaster, 1907, pp. 337-8.

wildfowl than he could in some months by using the land as pasture
because of the high rents that would have to be paid to cover the costs
of the improvements.

He wrote "but a pore man will easelye gett 16s. a weeke by cutting
down of three or four loads of reede for thacke and fewell to bake and
brew withall, whearof that countrye hath greate wante, every load of
the same being worth four or five shillings at the least, and likewise
three or four shillings a weeke in fishe and foule, serving the next
marketts, where it will be some moneths ether by kyne, milke or
grasing, paying such a rent as the Lord and engineer must let his land
for, eer he can recover so good means and commodities as it is sade he
hathe weeklye by the other, which I speake not of hear say butt of
myne owne knowledge." The reaction of many men lord Willoughby
had heard in the courts of Sewers and he expressed it in these words:
"I have heard many cry out 'that thear could be nothing more unhappye
for them then [than] to have a beast fedd where a gouse or ducke did
grase, and whensoever that should happen unto them they would
thinke themselves, their families and the most part of that country over-
throwne'." He concluded "I wishe the end of the bill such as it pre-
tends."

Nevertheless, in 1600 an act for the recovery of the marshes was
passed which permitted the lords of the soil, with the agreement of the
majority of the commoners to alienate part of the commons to
those who paid for the drainage of the lands.[51] As the Elizabethan era
drew to its close a great deal of talk and planning and even legislation
occurred which prepared the way for the great drainage schemes of the
next half-century. And yet activity was not entirely limited to theo-
retical discussion for some piecemeal draining was going on in the
1590s: although Ralph Agas complained to lord Burghley that "almost
as many errors are committed as operations undertaken",[52] his mere
complaint shows that something was being done. The notorious wet
summers of that decade may have helped to stimulate the putting into
practice of the theorists' recommendations. As Samuel Hartlib wrote in
his *Legacie* about half a century after the queen's death, 'in Queen Elizabeth's dayes, ingenuities, curiosities and Good Husbandry began to
take place and then salt marshes began to be fenced from the Seas'.[53]
Beginnings had been made in the Tudor period which were to result in
the addition of many thousands of acres to the county, particularly in
the parts of Holland. The proof of this is to be seen in the growing of
coleseed. The export of coleseed from Boston in 1602 clearly demonstrates that this crop was being grown in the area for the Dutch grew it

[51] Eliz. c. II, SR, IV, pp. 977–8.   [52] BM Lansdowne MS. 84 (32).
[53] Darby, *op. cit.*, p. II.

on newly drained land: the exports are a sign that already the drainage was successful enough in some places to allow coleseed to be raised.

The rich lands of Holland enabled families to obtain a living from a small acreage; elsewhere, as we have seen at Kirkby Underwood, for example, it was necessary to have 30 to 50 acres on which to maintain a family's livelihood. An idea of the social structure can be obtained not only from the amount of land that a man held but also from the taxation he paid and from the goods he possessed at his death. Probate inventories which were taken between ten days and two to three months after the deceased's funeral give a clear picture of the distribution of wealth.[54] At the 'Cliff' village of Welbourn, of fifty-three men and women whose inventories survive for the years 1530 to 1600, 19 per cent died leaving goods valued at under £10. Fifteen per cent of the deceased left goods and chattels valued at between £10 and £20; 17 per cent, £20 to 30; 7½ per cent, £30 to £40; 5·7 per cent, £40 to £50; 7½ per cent, £50 to £60; 7½ per cent, £60 to £70; 5·7 per cent, £70 to £80; 3·8 per cent, £80 to £90; 1·9 per cent, £90 to £100, and 9·4 per cent, over £100. In the sixteenth century a landholder might in one region have had sufficient wealth to place him high in the social structure of his village, in so far as that ranking was attributable to worldly possessions, while in another a man with similar resources might have been low in the list. Some difficulty arises over the criteria by which a landholder's wealth ought to be judged. The value of goods and chattels as recorded in inventories is only one criterion; the size of a man's arable holding, the total of his stock are others and they are fairly easily measurable. The size and complexity of his house might be taken, but that is much more difficult to evaluate. The median flock of sheep of the fifty men and women in Welbourn was twenty-three, while in the fens the median was seventeen in 1530, twenty in 1560, and twenty-five to six in 1590. These inhabitants of Welbourn had more cattle and pigs but fewer horses than their counterparts in the fens. The recorded arable area of the median farms in Welbourn was seventeen acres as opposed to seven to ten acres in the fens, but those figures tell us more about the fertility of the soil than the wealth of Welbourn farmers. Nevertheless, the social structure of different parts of the county varied considerably.

From a survey of the thirty or so prominent landed families out of some 130 mentioned in the returns of c.1557, it would appear that the majority were either in or just outside the Wolds. One concentration of large landed families lay between Scrivelsby and Hogsthorpe with wealthy families at Stainsby, Harrington, South Ormsby, Haugh, Tothby, and Bilsby, mostly in the southern part of the Wolds. Fairly

[54] F. W. East, 'Welbourne in the Sixteenth Century', Lincs. Hist., 2, no. 5, 1958, p. 1.

near that group were large landowners at Edlington, Tattershall, and
Bratoft. Another group was in the north Wolds inland from Great
Grimsby where large landed families were to be found at Healing,
Stallingborough, Elsham, Kettleby, Croxby, Osgodby, Fonaby, and
Hatcliffe. Along a line running from north-east to north-west of the
county town, large landed families are to be found at Sturton, Aisthorpe,
Snarford, and Hainton, and nearer to Lincoln at South Carleton, and
Burton. North of Grantham such families were established at Norton
Disney, Hougham, Marston, and south of it at Barrowby, Harlaxton,
Denton, and Belvoir. Around Bourne large estates were to be found
at Witham-on-the-Hill, Grimsthorpe, and Irnham.[55] These observations, using only those families whose landed wealth was mostly valued
at over £100 a year, and with only two with a valuation as low as £40,
are possibly too narrowly based to tell the full story—all 136 should be
mapped. However, even if a complete survey had been attempted, it
would not alter the picture for Holland where large land-owners were
to be found only in Pinchbeck, Gosberton, Swineshead, Benington,
Sutton and Tydd St Mary, and where only six of them had £40 a year or
more. It would appear that few landed families of any prominence had
settled in the poor clay lands between the Lincoln Edge and the fens to
the west of the river Witham, and few in the Isle of Axholme. It is
clear, even on a limited survey, that rural society in the parts of Holland
was more egalitarian than in the other two divisions of the county.
While in Lindsey and Kesteven the tax-payers paying at the lowest rate
to the subsidy of 1524 formed between 35 per cent and 46 per cent of
the total tax-payers known to us, in the wapentake of Elloe they were
only 32 per cent and in Kirton only 22 per cent of all those paying the
tax.[56] Such indicators clearly show the differing social structures of the
different farming regions of the county.

[55] See map.   [56] Thirsk, *English Peasant Farming*, p. 46.

CHAPTER VI

INDUSTRY, TRANSPORT, AND TRADE

LINCOLNSHIRE was an overwhelmingly agricultural county. It contained no area, like that around Robertsbridge, the centre of the Wealden iron industry, or like parts of Cornwall, of the Forest of Dean, or of Derbyshire, where whole communities lived by non-agrarian pursuits. No coal or iron was exploited within the county. Such industry as existed was scattered and almost entirely urban and, moreover, it was closely tied with agriculture. We shall leave till later some aspects of industrial organization in general, and of apprenticeship in urban areas and especially in Lincoln itself. But the major centres of population, Boston, Grantham, Stamford, Grimsby, Spalding, Bourne, Horncastle, and Louth, as well as Lincoln itself and the numerous market towns all had victualling industries, such as brewing, and leather-using industries. The great era of cloth making in Lincoln, and perhaps in a few other towns of the shire, had passed long before the opening of the Tudor period, but an agricultural community created a demand for metal goods. Ploughshares, forks, spades, rakes, harrows, horseshoes, scythes, cartwheel rims, and nails as well as the household requirements such as pots, pans, kettles, spits and fire irons, all necessitated for their manufacture various small scale industries. The smiths forged iron implements and were, to some extent, specialized, the farriers, for example, making the metal accoutrements for horses and, above all, shoeing horses. The braziers made brass objects, mostly pots and pans for the household, and the pewterers finer vessels of lead and tin often with an admixture of some silver. Another industry was the making of baskets of reeds or osiers necessary on the farm—the skeps or hampers made by the skeppers. At least one skepper in Lincoln took on an apprentice. In the sea ports of Boston and Great Grimsby a boat repairing industry probably existed although no proof, rather the contrary, exists of any large scale shipbuilding.[1]

Apart from the towns, some industry flourished in the countryside. Not all industry was urban but much of it used labour that was part-time employed in agriculture. On a farm, in addition to skeps, need

[1] R. W. K. Hinton (ed.), 'The Port Books of Boston 1601-40', LRS 50, 1956, p. xxxv.

would arise for other containers such as sacks and the isle of Axholme was noted for the weaving of sackcloth.[2] The hemp fibres from which sackcloth was woven was also used in the making of ropes, another essential on the farm. The people of the fens also wove hemp and flax into sackcloth and linen cloth. This work was a by-employment for the farmers of the fenland, many of whom were principally engaged, not in arable farming, but in rearing cattle, breeding horses, fattening beef and mutton, keeping geese and in fishing, all occupations which at certain times of the year left them with considerable spare time for industrial work. Rush plaiting was also a frequently found occupation in the fens. This domestic industry was more common in the Lincolnshire fens than in many other counties for it was an area of much enclosed pasture land where neither the hamlet nor the village but the family was the co-operative working unit. The family supplemented its income by this domestic industry.

Lincolnshire, however, did not in general send out manufactured goods to the rest of the country. Its exports were the products of its rural husbandry, butter, cheese, cattle, poultry, fish, some wool, grain, malt, a little beer, calfskins, beans, and linseed. The routes along which goods were sent and people travelled were the roads and rivers or canalized rivers. Some of the main roads of the twentieth century existed in Tudor times. The main artery between south and north, the Great North Road, has already been referred to,[3] and other important roads, some of them of great antiquity crossed the shire. Part of the Roman road from Lincoln north to the Humber was much used, although it diverted to Barton-on-Humber, while to the south Ermine Street was probably less heavily trafficked although the road that diverged from it to Sleaford was important. From the Humber through Louth and Spilsby to Boston, and from Boston to Spalding, ran roads that carried much wool to the port. From Boston also went roads to Spalding, Crowland, and Market Deeping. Another route ran from Doncaster to Lincoln through Gainsborough, and frequent ferries crossed the Trent as bridges were few, while the Fosse Way may have served as a direct link between the county town and the Trent at Newark.

Water transport was, in theory at least, more economical than road transport, but keeping rivers open to free passage was a problem as they were frequently beset with devices for netting fish. One of the tasks of the commissioners of sewers, whose work has been discussed earlier,[4] was to keep waterways free so that boats could pass freely up and down them. They ordered the removal of such impediments as

[2] J. Thirsk, 'Industries in the Countryside' in *Essays in the Economic and Social History of Tudor & Stuart England*, ed. F. J. Fisher, London, 1961, p. 85.
[3] See *ante* p. 2.   [4] See *ante* p. 71.

piles of wood, stakes, leaps, nets, and reeds[5] and by their efforts they kept the Witham between Lincoln and Boston as a navigable river in the Tudor period. They did the same for the Welland at least from Spalding to the sea, and probably parts of the Glen from Baston to its junction with the river Welland were navigable. But the link which had given direct connection between the Trent and Boston by providing a navigable watercourse between Torksey and Lincoln was in a perilous condition in the sixteenth century. The Foss dyke which effected this connection had fallen into disrepair in the Tudor period: a neglect that was the result rather than the cause of the decline of trade in Lincoln and Boston. The corporation of Lincoln was not prepared to accept the closing of the Foss dyke as a navigable channel, and in 1521 scouring work was undertaken since in that year William Merying complained that the mayor and aldermen had dyked Foss dyke upon his ground.[6] Moreover, they had felled his wood growing on the bank, and he alleged that when the dyke overflowed it drowned his pasture and that the siting of it blocked the way to the pasture that his tenants had normally taken. Some considerable work was on hand for the mayor laid out £17 of his own money to keep the men on work,[7] and men were ordered to ride to Hull and York to gather money for the repair of the Foss Dyke.[8] Merchants of both these cities might be expected to benefit from the upkeep of the waterlink and, therefore, it was hoped that they might contribute: it is not known whether they did. The following year further provision was made for work on Foss dyke,[9] and in 1529–30 the landholders were compelled to cut the sedges yearly and maintain the banks so that they retained the water.[10] But the improvements were not permanent and in the middle years of the century the cut was perhaps little used, since in 1571 complaint was made that the city could not be cheaply supplied with timber, turf, and thatch.[11] These commodities, scarce in Lincolnshire so it was said, were more plentiful in Nottinghamshire, Derbyshire, and Yorkshire and city supplies would have been reasonable if importation by water had been possible. Therefore, the corporation proposed an act of parliament to appoint a commission that would assess all persons living within seven miles of the city for a payment to dyke, cleanse, and scour the Foss dyke so that sufficient water might flow from the Trent to allow boats to navigate it.

What type of boats used these navigable rivers and canals we do not know but they must have been of shallow draught. Similarly the types of vehicles that used the roads cannot be clearly described. Most people

[5] LRS 54, p. xxviii.　[6] LAO Li/1/1/1, f. 104.　[7] Ibid., f. 115v.
[8] Ibid., f. 117.　[9] Ibid., f. 142.　[10] Ibid., f. 209v.
[11] HMC, 14th Rep., App., pt. VIII, p. 65.

who went on journeys of any length went on horseback, for the coach only came into England during Elizabeth I's reign and very few even of the noblemen owned one before about 1605–10. Goods might be carried on carts for considerable distances, but here too the pack-animal, either horse or mule, probably carried more goods than did carts. Water transport of goods was slower but also it was less costly, although the fact that economies were achieved by large scale consignments meant that delays were frequent until a cargo of sufficient size could be accumulated to fill a ship. This waiting might also put up the cost of water transport as in the meantime storage would be necessary until a cargo could be made up.

Apart from local trade, however, from the villages to the nearest market town, important trade links existed with the two ports of Grimsby and Boston. The Lincolnshire coast was not well favoured with good havens, and the coasting trade recognized that between Yarmouth and Hull few refuges in a storm existed. But the Wash had other ports besides Boston and Lynn; there were several between Boston and Wainfleet; in fact until the early sixteenth century Wainfleet remained of some importance. Also, coal and other cargoes were discharged at small harbours such as Kirton, Frampton, Fleet, Leake, Fishtoft, and Fosdyke as late as the 1570s.[12] But one of the difficulties for trade from the Lincolnshire ports was the changing coastline where the sea encroached in some regions and receded in others. Wainfleet, Grimsby, and Boston all suffered from the silting up of their harbours. At Grimsby the haven continued to deteriorate but up to the middle of the century trade played a significant part in the life of the town and of the villages for fifteen to twenty miles around it.[13] Here the silting up was only gradual, and maintenance work was put in hand in 1519 when thirty-eight men promised donations up to a total of £12 2s. 4d. for a pair of 'cloughs' to amend the haven: these were built at Simwhite bridge and a custodian paid 4s. a year to look after them. As with Foss dyke, the merchants of other towns who might have had an interest in maintaining the viability of the port were asked to contribute; and in 1537 alderman Michael Mason obtained money from Newcastle towards the improvement of the haven. Ordinances affecting the use of the haven were made each year at the Easter and Michaelmas courts. In 1514 the mayor had agreed to forgo part of his pension as a contribution towards the upkeep of the bridge which was not to be used by vessels as a mooring post. The town built common staithes or jetties and orders were promulgated that refuse was not to be thrown into the West haven by butchers or fishmongers except on a falling tide. Also,

---

[12] Thirsk, *English Peasant Farming*, p. 12.
[13] E. Gillett, *A History of Grimsby*, 1970, p. 98.

above the watermill near the stonebridge it was decreed that clothes and tripe were not to be washed, because the West haven provided most of the town's water supply. But from the middle of the century the haven was less and less frequently used by shipping, and by 1571–2, two keels, a crayer, and four hoys, and the occasional Scottish ship appear to have been the only vessels berthing there.[14] In 1592, London merchants made attempts to use the port, but nothing came of them, and an act of the privy council laid it down that no merchant was to use any port between Boston and Hartlepool unless he had first been admitted to the incorporation of Hull. The rising influence of Hull caused Grimsby to decline to such a degree that its sea-borne trade became insignificant.

In many ways the history of Boston was similar to that of Grimsby. Boston was, and remained a much more important port than Grimsby, but its decline was equally marked. It had been the second port of the realm in the early thirteenth century, and its prosperity continued throughout the fourteenth century as a great wool exporting port. But when cloth replaced wool as the principal English export, as it did in the later fourteenth century, Boston was not well placed in relation to the principal cloth producing areas to act as an export centre. Boston's hinterland had been a great wool-producing region, especially of the long wools for which there was so much demand on the Continent, and Lincolnshire was a county studded with monastic houses that had wool for sale. When that wool, however, was diverted to the home market to be used by the English clothiers, the cloth that they produced principally in the west of England, in East Anglia, and Yorkshire was exported from other and more convenient ports. The result of this trade revolution left Boston in severe decline long before the opening of the Tudor period. In addition to the diminution in trade, the town had to deal with some deterioration in the haven. The sluice gate needed attention in 1499 when Mayhave or Matthew Hake of Gravelines did the work,[15] and in 1575 the harbour was said to be in a bad state. The trouble, it was asserted, was due to an alteration in the course of the river Witham through the Deeps, and Elizabeth granted a charter to enable the town to raise money for necessary repairs and to mark the channel into the port.[16] Complaints of the sanding up of creeks were common in the later years of Elizabeth's reign. In 1592, the queen discharged the borough from the payment of fifteenths and tenths because of its 'poor estate'.[17]

[14] Ibid., p. 104.
[15] T. Allen, The History of the County of Lincoln, 1834, p. 67 et seq.
[16] Pishey Thompson, The History and Antiquities of Boston, 1856, p. 72.
[17] LAC, Archivists' Report, 15, 1963–4, p. 48.

Neither Boston nor Grimsby were helped by the interference in their affairs of the court of Admiralty. The lord high admiral's authority in Grimsby seriously curtailed that of the borough court and the municipality sought to limit his authority as much as possible in commercial matters, particularly by regulating the weights and measures to be used at the haven. Apparently the borough regarded anyone who co-operated with the Admiralty as potentially disloyal, for in 1579 the mayor and burgesses disfranchised Richard Holmes who had been acting for the Admiralty. Lord Clinton wrote from Tattershall castle signifying his displeasure at this action but the borough put up a strong resistance and wrote a spirited reply.[18] In addition to the meddling of the Admiralty, the borough opposed what it regarded as the interference of customs officers, and tried to cite them before the borough courts. The fact that the lord high admiral from 1552 to 1585 was a Lincolnshire magnate with influence in the two major ports made it more difficult to ignore the Admiralty's jurisdiction. At Boston until the incorporation of the borough, the jurisdiction of the Admiralty could be little checked, but from the 1550s similar opposition grew between the two authorities. However, by a charter of 10 February 1573, the queen exempted the borough from the lord high admiral's jurisdiction and granted it an Admiralty court of its own.[19] It is unfortunate that we have no records of this jurisdiction before the eighteenth century,[20] so that how the borough exercised its privilege cannot for certain be known. But it may be assumed that all matters justiciable before the Admiralty courts, such as wrecks, salvage, ownership of vessels, and maritime contracts were brought before the municipal authorities.

The business of the port was run by three bodies, the Admiralty, the borough council, and the customs officers. The government had re-organized the latter group to some extent at the beginning of Elizabeth I's reign. It initiated a full scale enquiry into places where goods were shipped to and landed from foreign countries, and legislation resulted which ordered that loading and unloading were only to be done in daylight at quays where customs men were present.[21] This was a continuation of the tightening up that had occurred under Philip and Mary, and that had resulted in a new book of rates. Another enquiry followed in 1565 and there ensued further reforms which inaugurated the port books. From this series of documents we can form a complete picture of the different customs officials' duties in the later Tudor period. On arrival the shipmaster went to the customs house, which incidentally at Boston was rented from the municipality, and gave the

---

[18] Gillett, op. cit., p. 102.   [19] LAC, Archivists' Report, 15, p. 47.
[20] Ibid., p. 52.   [21] LRS 50, p. xiv, quoting 1 Eliz. c. 11.

officers, either by bill of lading or verbally, certain information. He told them the ship's name, its home port, the port it had come from, its tonnage, his own name and nationality, the names and nationalities of the owners of the cargo, and a general description of the shipment. All this information was entered in the shippers' book inwards. Then the owners of the cargo or their representatives came to the customs house and declared the goods in full. The collector of customs, known also as the customer, assessed the duty payable with the knowledge of the comptroller, and each official kept a book which the importer signed as a token that he acknowledged the correctness of the entry. The officers then made out a warrant in duplicate, copied from the entry in the port books, and gave one part to the owner and the other to the searcher. When goods were being exported, for dues were payable on exports as well as on imports, the shipmaster declared his intention to take goods out and his ship was entered in the shippers' book outwards. The merchant declared his goods and the officers entered the merchant's goods with the duty payable in their original books, and issued a cocket in the same form as the warrant, and the searcher examined the exports to see if they tallied with the document. The exporter signed the original books in the same manner as the importer. In the early seventeenth century a surveyor was appointed, supposedly to check the searcher passing through more goods than appeared on the warrant or cocket, but in fact it may be that the surveyor was a substitute for the searcher.

Different sets of books were kept for coastal traffic, but more research needs to be done on coastal traffic pre-1600 before the full picture of that very important trade will emerge. However, from the material that has already been sifted by historians much information on ships, their tonnage and nationality, the nature of imports and exports, the merchants, and their nationality can be assembled. But the documents afford much information about Boston itself. In 1558 there were four legal quays, of which the principal one was Packhouse quay on the east bank of the Witham opposite Spain Lane and the Guildhall. It was sixty yards long and the ships using it and the three other quays came in on the tide and would be stranded at low tide. Few vessels appear to have overturned since between 1601 and 1618 it is known that only three ships were damaged or wrecked in the port. Farther down river between the Haven and the sea on the west side was Goat quay (named after Skirbeck Goat) and on the east side Stillyard quay. These were well sited for taking heavy goods inland without having to cross the bridge in the town. A fourth quay was beside a tavern called the 'White Fleece'. Commissioners reporting on the Lincolnshire coast in 1565 declared that Boston had few ships of any considerable size, only one of

100 tons, two of 40 tons, one of 30 tons, and four between 10 and 20 tons.[22] The port books of the years 1601–5, however, show that the port then had eight vessels of 35 to 40 tons, and two or three of 30 tons, while by 1610–18 there were seventeen ships; four of about 60 tons, four of 35 to 40 tons, and at least four of 30 tons. These statistics raise doubts as to how far the port of Boston was decayed; indeed, a report of 1565 said that it was not,[23] but the government's action in 1592 suggests the contrary. Certainly after the 1620s signs are evident of some degree of recovery at the port and the average tonnage of the ships entering rose, which would indicate that the harbour and its approaches were being kept in good order.

Imports paid the subsidy of tonnage or poundage; the former on wine, the latter on dry goods. Poundage was either at a fixed rate on the quantity of the imports or at 5 per cent *ad valorem* while, in addition, aliens paid a custom at a quarter of the rate of the subsidy—that is an extra payment of 3*d.* in the pound. Some goods bore impositions that were already related to the subsidy and, for aliens, to the custom also. In the early Tudor period, before the revision of duties in Mary's reign, the duties on wool exported were heavy: 40*s.* on a sack of 364 lb. being paid by denizens, and 76*s.* 8*d.* by aliens.[24] Cloth exports on the other hand were lightly taxed, 1*s.* 2*d.* per cloth of assize being paid by denizens, 2*s.* 9*d.* by aliens, and 1*s.* by the Hansards.[25] In certain circumstances goods were allowed through duty-free: the practice of portage allowed a small quantity of goods to the ship's master and to the mariners. Personal baggage was not liable to duty, and goods that had been exported and returned to the country because unsold, were not charged import duties. Leccage allowed for wastage of wine in transit, and with leccage something was deducted from the duty. The necessity to keep a record of these differing duties enables us to ascertain what goods and their quantities were being imported and exported and by whom. At the beginning of the Tudor period, although exports of wool were negligible compared with those of the thirteenth and four-teenth centuries, they still provided some customs revenue in the port of Boston. Throughout Henry VII's reign the sums collected varied between a high of £4,675 19*s.* 9*d.* in 1489–90 and a low of £379 12*s.* 2¾*d.* in 1499–1500.[26] If we ignore the two years 1490–92 when

[22] *Ibid.*, p. xxxv.   [23] *Ibid.*, p. xxxvi quoting PRO E178/1273.

[24] E. M. Carus-Wilson and O. Coleman (eds.), *England's Export Trade, 1275–1547*, Oxford, 1963, p. 194 *et seq.*

[25] Denizens paid 1*s.* 9*d.* for cloth in half grain, and 2*s.* 4*d.* for cloth in full grain; aliens paid 2*s.* 7*d.* and 3*s.* 6*d.*, and Hansards 1*s.* 6*d.* and 2*s.*—*England's Export Trade*, p. 194, fns., 2, 3, 4.

[26] All figures are from G. Schanz, *Englische Handelspolitik gegen Ende des Mittelalters*, Leipzig, 1881, vol. 2, pp. 45, 57.

no wool was recorded as exported, the average collection for Henry VII's reign was £2,558 3s. 7d., and the median £2,361 0s. 3½d. In the following reign the high came in 1518–19 with £2,754 7s. 7¾d. and the low in 1546–7 was £139 11s. 8¼d. Ignoring the three years 1524–5, 1542–3, and 1544–5, when apparently there were no wool exports, the average was £1,347 10s. 7d. and the median £1,266 0s. 5½d. But a closer look at the figures shows a distinct change in the pattern of wool exports after 1520–21, since up to that date the highest payment was £2,754 7s. 7¾d. and the lowest £1,060 8s. 9d. in one isolated year 1512–13, while for all the remaining twenty-six years of Henry VIII's reign the highest figure was only £922 1s. 6¼d. (1541–2) and the average only about £864 11s. The last Hanse cloth export from Boston was in 1501–02,[27] but other aliens exported a little cloth through the port from 1496–7 onwards.

Deprived of virtually any wool exports, what goods passed through Boston in the greater part of the sixteenth century? A few cloths went out through the port in Henry VIII's reign: of undyed cloths exported by denizens, the largest number in any one year was sixty and a half (1533–4), and the lowest ten (1541–2), while foreigners took out between sixty-one (1517–18) and a half cloth (1521–2). The number of worsted cloths exported was negligible since in only three out of the thirty-eight years of Henry's reign, 1511–12, 1535–6, and 1544–5 did any natives export worsteds, and in thirteen years foreigners exported between half a worsted cloth and seven worsteds in any one year. Similarly the port had a minute trade in skins, although, as the figures were joined with those of King's Lynn, the total amount of leather exported cannot be stated. Some wine, small in comparison with the amount imported into Bristol, Southampton, or London, was brought into Boston. Compared with London's imports in Henry VIII's reign of 5,000 to 10,000 tuns a year, the Wash ports' quantities were small indeed. Native importers in most years between 1509 and 1547 brought in between 38 and 90 tuns; the largest amount of 222 tuns was in 1543–5, and the smallest of 4 tuns in 1509–10.[28] In five years of the reign there were no native importers. Foreign importers only brought in wine in seven out of the thirty-eight years, and then only in minute quantities: the year with their largest import was 1511–12, when 26 tuns were imported, while in 1539–40 only half a tun was landed. The ton or tun of 252 gallons is the only measure that has been here noted, but butts or pipes of 126 gallons, tercyans or punches of 84 gallons, and barrels of 31½ gallons formed part of the landed cargoes. In addition, between 1509 and 1547, 18 tuns of sweet wine were landed by natives, and 19 tuns

[27] *England's Export Trade*, p. 112.
[28] Schanz, *op. cit.*, p. 145.

by foreigners, and in 1542–3 foreigners imported 2 pipes of Malvoisie (Malmsey), and the following year 12 pipes. Gascon wine was still being landed at the end of Elizabeth I's reign for, on 16 October and 2 December 1601, 2 tuns and 35 tuns were imported.[29]

In the later part of the sixteenth century Boston and Grimsby were probably more important in the coasting traffic than in foreign trade. However, from abroad came vinegar as well as wine, prunes, timber in the form of fir spars and deal boards, starch, and rosin, while white salt was also landed, some of which originated abroad. Lead, calfskins, linseed, malt, beer, beans, and barley were the principal commodities exported. The export of victuals demands further notice. Coal was also brought into Boston from the mines around Newcastle which handled the output of the Durham field. Grimsby also had an important trade in coal, most of it shipped by Newcastle owners, but there were some Grimsby men in the trade. At that port Scottish vessels played a prominent and sometimes a threatening part. In 1571–2, four hoys laden with coal used the port.[30] The more northerly Lincolnshire port also had a growing trade in fish; here too the Scottish ships were much involved. Stockfish was imported, and a few Grimsby men developed an interest in the herring fisheries. Thomas Chalender, who died in 1541, left a third share in a ship called 'God's Grace' with the herring nets. Grimsby's trade was probably more hindered than Boston's by the Scots, for in 1523 so many Scottish ships were at the mouth of the Humber that no shipmaster dared venture out without assistance, while twenty years later French and Scottish ships threatened the transport of corn from Hull and Grimsby to the Scottish border. Flare-ups arose from time to time as when, in 1549, 'The Rose' of Grimsby and 'The Michael' of Hull attacked a ship of Amsterdam and thirty years later a ship that had been attacked by pirates, 'The Boyer' by name, was brought into Grimsby, and the merchants of the Steelyard were awarded restitution of their goods, mostly pitch and stockfish.[31]

The export of victuals requires special notice for it was supposedly licensed according to the plenty or lack of various foodstuffs in the neighbourhood of the port. Both Boston and Grimsby were considerable exporters of food and drink. Wheat, barley, oats, beans, beef, and bacon were exported from time to time. Boston was well placed to attract surplus produce from its rich agricultural hinterland, some of which produce could be transported down the navigable Witham. Grimsby also was prominent in the exporting of grain, much of which went north, presumably to pay for coal imports from Newcastle, rather than south to feed the capital.[32] Robert Butler of Immingham con-

[29] LRS 50, p. 4.   [30] Gillett, op. cit., p. 104.
[31] APC, n.s. XI, 1578–80, p. 65.   [32] Gillett, op. cit., p. 99.

tracted in March 1500 to deliver 120 quarters of barley to John Scott of Newcastle at 7 groats a quarter, and he received 5 marks as God's penny (earnest money) to confirm the contract. In 1532, a toll was levied at Grimsby on twenty voyages made by ships and keels that had taken a total of 3,078 quarters of corn from the haven: the mayor had licensed its export. Some disagreement had arisen over the shipping of corn for the king's use in 1522. Richard Powell, the king's purveyor, had directed the mayor, William Hatcliffe, that 80 quarters of wheat belonging to John Allen and Richard Lucas should be loaded on a vessel 'The Magdalene'. The price was to be 7s. a quarter but Lucas said that he had been offered 8s. and that the mayor had no authority in the county. The mayor replied that he held the king's commission to value the corn, and the mayor's sergeant arrested Lucas. The port exported large amounts of corn for the king in 1524, sending consignments to Berwick, Calais, and Sandwich. The export of victuals was closely linked to their price in the port, and at Grimsby the usual measures were taken to ensure fair competition. Only the mayor and his servants could buy food before it came into the market, and in times of scarcity corn suffered special restrictions. In 1550 no corn was to be sold before 11 a.m. in summer or noon in winter, to allow time for all the country farmers to get into the town, and before 2 p.m. the amount of purchases was restricted to what a family needed for a week's supply. Central government kept its eye upon the export of corn for it well knew what complaints were likely to arise, if, in times of high prices, the populace saw grain being sent out of the area. On 26 December 1580, letters were sent by the privy council to the sheriff and justices of Lincolnshire restraining the export of grain,[33] and again similar instructions went out on 14 October 1591.[34] Earlier, at a meeting of the privy council on 27 December 1589,[35] transport of grain out of the realm was stopped from twelve counties of which Lincoln was one, because of rising prices and because some 'not regarding the publicque benefytt, doe transport the same by stealth to make their private lucre.' Commissioners were told to watch the harbours because some who said they were taking part in coasting traffic were in fact sending corn overseas. The provisioning of the capital was a continuing anxiety for Elizabeth I's government, and in November 1595 it gave orders to ship 700 quarters of grain from the ports of York, Hull, and Lincoln to London while a month later the county was asked to provide 300 quarters of wheat, the same of malt, 100 quarters of peas, 150 oxen, and 400 flitches of bacon for the navy. Considerations of overall policy made it necessary for strict control of the export of victuals, but Boston and Grimsby were

[33] APC n.s. XII, 1580–81, p. 296.   [34] Ibid., XX, 1590, p. 31.
[35] Ibid., XVIII, 1589–90, pp. 280–1.

involved in the trade and it may have been the most important part of their commerce at some times during the Tudor period.

Evidence as to the degree of decline in the two ports is conflicting. In Boston perhaps a noticeable decline emerged about 1520 and continued until the 1590s with some upturn about the end of Elizabeth's reign: in Grimsby, trade probably drifted on at a fairly low level until the 1550s; thereafter the town declined into a port that dealt only in coal, fish, and grain. As we have seen, attempts to revive Grimsby were not successful but at Boston it was thought that a settlement of foreigners might effect an improvement. On 10 February 1573, Boston had licence to retain forty households of Dutchmen within the borough, and permission to export, at a reduced customs rate of 8d. a quarter, 20,000 qrs. of grain spread over a period of five years.[36] Some years earlier in 1569 the corporation had sent two persons to Norwich to enquire how the Flemings were dealt with there, and had asked Burghley's permission for foreigners to dwell in Boston, so that the settlement was a calculated one. It is impossible to estimate accurately what effect these Dutchmen with their families and servants made to Boston's prosperity, but it was seemingly not an immediate one for complaints about the borough's poverty continue into the 1590s: only after the queen's death did some recovery begin.

[36] LAC, *Archivists' Report*, 15, p. 48; Pishey Thompson, *op. cit.*, p. 69.

CHAPTER VII

THE GOVERNMENT OF THE SHIRE

ALREADY much of what we have written about the county has dealt with problems not of Lincolnshire alone but with problems common to the whole country in the Tudor period. The dissolution of the monasteries was a Lincolnshire problem but it was one imposed on the men and women of the shire by central government. In seeking to establish how far the writ of Tudor monarchs was enforceable in Lincolnshire it will be necessary to look both at the ways in which the king's government could influence the county, and how the influence of the shire was exerted centrally through officials and also through members of parliament. Dr R. B. Smith in his book on the West Riding[1] has stressed the strength of the medieval liberties which, with their privileged jurisdictions, might hinder royal intervention in the effective carrying out of justice. Only one great liberty existed in Lincolnshire, the honour of Bolingbroke, but, as that was in the hands of the duchy of Lancaster, and as the duchy had been controlled by the Crown since 1399, no opposition to the royal will could arise in that privileged area. Other areas such as the soke of Caistor,[2] the soke of Grantham,[3] and the soke of the manor of Crowle[4] were little more than areas which had their own sessions, while the liberty of Scotter belonging to Peterborough abbey[5] enjoyed the immunities which that monastery's lands possessed.[6] Practically nothing then is heard of powerful men diverting the course of justice by maintaining their *protégés* before royal courts, either by packing juries or by other means, as apparently occurred in Yorkshire. George St Paul was accused of trying to bribe a witness in 1599,[7] and the controversy between Sir Edward Dymoke and his uncle the second earl of Lincoln led almost to a private war with much rowdyism and many affrays.[8] In 1519, William Sammes had been accused of attempting to bribe and of threatening one of the

---

[1] R. B. Smith, *Land and Politics in the England of Henry VIII*, Oxford, 1970.
[2] LAC *Archivists' Report*, 1951–2, p. 12.   [3] *Ibid.*, 1953–4, p. 8.
[4] *Ibid.*, 1965–6, p. 15.   [5] *Ibid.*, 1966–7, p. 35.
[6] Dugdale, *Monasticon Anglicanum*, I, p. 400.
[7] APC xxx, pp. 140–1 and History of Parliament Trust; PRO Star Chamber, 5/429/16.
[8] HMC Hatfield, xII, pp. 410 *et seq.*

sheriffs of the city of Lincoln.[9] But such instances were rare. How then did the Crown ensure that its policies were carried out in Tudor Lincolnshire?

Most important of all in this regard were the justices of the peace for upon their loyalty and enthusiasm the Crown depended not only for the enforcement of the law but for the gathering of information and for the putting into effect of royal policy. But in the shire other more prestigious officers existed who were instruments of the royal will and who in some degree controlled and exhorted the justices. The lord lieutenant of the county was the sovereign's representative there and hence the first man in the shire: he acted as the agent and informant of the privy council.[10] Lords lieutenant were first appointed in Henry VIII's reign on an *ad hoc* basis to deal with specific issues which involved mustering men either for the king's service in time of war or for the suppression of rebellion.[11] Their existence and military authority was given a statutory basis in 1550,[12] but they remained temporary representatives until 1585, although the appointment of assistants known as deputy-lieutenants, indicates that they had been growing in importance.

The lord lieutenant was usually a nobleman but sometimes knights were chosen: the main consideration, however, was that he should be a local man with a considerable stake in the county. In the earlier part of the century lord Hussey is said to have been lord lieutenant of the county,[13] but in May 1559 Elizabeth gave commissions of lieutenancy to three Lincolnshire men, lord Willoughby of Parham[14] Sir Robert Tyrwhit the younger, and Sir Edward Dymoke.[15] When three men were appointed they were jointly responsible since the three parts of the shire were never given a separate lieutenant. Lord Willoughby had previously been lord lieutenant of Lincolnshire between August 1557 and October 1558.[16] Ten years later, in 1569, lord Clinton[17] was made lieutenant with similar orders to keep the peace, to punish tale-tellers, and to supervise the justices of the peace. In 1585, Edward Manners, third earl of Rutland became lord lieutenant until his death in April 1587.[18] The lord treasurer, the first lord Burghley received the queen's com-

[9] LAO Li/1/1/1, f. 103v.
[10] W. S. Holdsworth, *A History of the English Law*, IV, London, 2nd edn. 1937, p. 75.
[11] G. Scott Thomson, *Lord Lieutenants in the Sixteenth Century*, London, 1923, pp. 1 *et seq.*; Holdsworth, *op. cit.*, IV, pp. 76–7.
[12] By 4 Ed. VI c. 5.
[13] A. R. Maddison, 'Lincolnshire Gentry during the 16th Century', LAAS XXII, pt. i, 1894, p. 175.
[14] GEC, *Complete Peerage, sub nomine*.   [15] Scott Thomson, *op. cit.*, p. 47.
[16] GEC, *Complete Peerage, sub nomine*.   [17] Scott Thomson, *op. cit.*, p. 50.
[18] J. C. Sainty, (Comp.), *Lieutenants of Counties 1585–1642*, London, 1970, *sub* Lincolnshire.

mission in 1587 and he remained in office until his death in 1598.[18] His main estate lay just outside the county boundary, but his mother had come from Bourne, and he had been educated at Stamford and Grantham, so he can be accounted a Lincolnshire man. He was, however, a privy councillor and the queen's first minister and he could rarely leave court; moreover, he was, as he admitted in a letter to lord Willoughby of Parham, not so well acquainted with the state of the three different parts of the shire.[19] Burghley therefore had to exercise his powers through deputies, and he appointed lord Willoughby and Sir Edward Dymoke to act for him in Lindsey, and his son, Sir Thomas Cecil, and Sir Anthony Thorold of Marston in the parts of Kesteven and Holland. They were asked to apportion horse and foot to the different parts of the shire in preparation for the threatened Spanish attack. After Burghley's death, the county was without a lord lieutenant until Roger Manners, fifth earl of Rutland was appointed to serve on 20 September 1603. By this time it had become customary for lords lieutenant to serve for life and so the earl held the commission till his death in June 1612.

The lord lieutenant's duties proliferated at the end of Elizabeth's reign. True, their primary duties were still connected with defence and therefore with the musters, but they also had thrust upon them administrative and economic duties. They had, at times, to oversee the enforcement of regulations concerning the eating of meat in Lent and were responsible for purveyance for the Navy.[20] The functions which the lord lieutenant performed were usually carried out during a vacancy by commissioners who were former deputy lieutenants with the addition of the sheriff. But the most important duty of the lord lieutenant was to act as a two-way channel. He held conferences with his deputies and other gentry on the condition of the shire and on how peace could be preserved, informing them of the wishes of the privy council; at the same time he reported back the actions and even the opinions of local men, made representations to the central government on their behalf, and suggested what policies it would be unwise to push through.

As the duties of the lords lieutenant were growing, those of the sheriff were declining. Even before the opening of the Tudor period the shire court, over which the sheriff presided, and the sheriff's tourn had lost most of their importance. Nevertheless, the sheriff had a part to play in local government.[21] He was still responsible for seeing that justice was done by executing the king's writs in the shire, and for the secure keeping of prisoners, but he had lost most of his financial duties and was no longer the leading man in the shire. The position of 'high

[19] Scott Thomson, *op. cit.*, p. 68.   [20] *Ibid.*, p. 137.
[21] Holdsworth, *op. cit.*, IV, p. 122.

sheriff', as he was sometimes popularly called, although this was not an official term, must still have carried some prestige and the members of well-known Lincolnshire families occupied it during the Tudor period. Members of the Tyrwhit family filled the 'high' sheriffdom in 1494, 1500, 1517, 1519, 1523, 1536, 1540, 1559, 1583, 1595, and 1599. Ayscoughs were 'high' sheriffs on seven occasions and Skipwiths on four, while the Dymoke family held the office no less than eight times. The families of St Paul, Copledike, Willoughby, Carr, Tailboys, Hussey, Heneage, Disney, Thorold, Monson, and Thimbleby provided the sheriff on two or three occasions.[22] Thus, fifteen families filled fifty out of the 118 years between 1485 and 1603.

The coroners whose chief duty had long been to enquire into sudden deaths had their position in this regard strengthened in 1554.[23] The constables also played an important role as executive agents. There were two types of constable—the high constable who acted in the hundreds, and the petty constables who acted in the townships which included all but the smallest villages.[24] Their importance increased in the sixteenth century, and the justices were beginning to act on the present-ment of the constables rather than on that of the hundred jury. In turn the constables became increasingly dependent upon the justices, the high constables being appointed and removed by the quarter sessions and the petty constables by the petty sessions. The duties imposed on the (petty) constables by the poor law legislation also increased their personal importance,[25] and from being the appointees of the old com-munities they became the officials of the new civil parish and were subordinated to the justices of the peace. It is true that some of the older courts survived, especially the private court that had a franchise confer-ring upon it leet jurisdiction, and in the boroughs the form of dispens-ing justice that had evolved during the Middle Ages continued with little alteration. But the older communal courts had been dying long before 1485 and the justices of the peace in Lincolnshire, as in the country generally, became the men who enforced criminal justice, except for the most serious crimes, and administered the shire in the king's name.

This is not the place to catalogue the many duties that the justices had thrust upon them by parliamentary statutes.[26] It was principally the work placed upon them to see that many statutes were enforced that made them vastly more important in local government in 1600 than they had been in 1500. We can only ascertain what the duties of

[22] PRO Lists & Indexes, Sheriffs, sub Lincolnshire.
[23] Holdsworth, op. cit., I, p. 85.
[24] Ibid., IV, pp. 122 et seq.   [25] Ibid., IV, p. 125.
[26] Ibid., IV, pp. 138 et seq.

Fig. 2 Monumental brass to Sir Robert Dymmock, 1545

Lincolnshire justices were from parliamentary statutes: it is impossible
to form a picture of them in the performance of their duties during the
Tudor period since all the sessions records before the 1680s appear to
have been lost, with the exception of Quarter Sessions files for Lindsey
which exist from 1625. But the powers of the justices throughout the
country were the same, and so in Lincolnshire single justices must have
had the power to order rioters to disperse and to act against gypsies,

rogues, and vagabonds and, if parishioners, churchwardens, or constables defaulted, they could assess and levy rates made at the Easter sessions. Two or more justices could punish rioters and make orders concerning bastard children, and their administrative powers enabled them to appoint overseers and licence ale-houses.[27] But it was only in Quarter Sessions that justices could enquire by a jury into all cases within their commission. These general sessions of the peace became increasingly important in Elizabeth I's reign as an appeal court against rates made by the churchwardens and others.

Gradually the justices acquired their own officials. The *custos rotulorum* and the clerk of the peace emerged, and in 1605, at the order of the privy council, divisions were made so that none should have to travel more than seven or eight miles. The *custos rotulorum* acquired a precedence over all other justices as he kept the rolls and records of the sessions and appointed the clerk who was responsible for drawing them up. As the work grew the clerk of the peace appointed a deputy and individual justices began to have clerks.

The justices were the tools of a strong central government. The greatly strengthened executive power that replaced the weak legal and political control exercised by the central government of pre-Tudor times, or at least of the period pre–1460, was exercised, except in outlying parts, by the privy council. Most of the tasks that the justices had to perform were laid upon them by statute, but the way in which they performed them was supervised by the Council. Control came most obviously of course through the selection of justices. The Crown would only grant the commission of the peace to men who were loyal and trustworthy and thus we find that, generation after generation, members of gentry families received the commission. So, in the years 1540–41, to use that period as an example, commissions of the peace were granted to, among others, members of the families of Dymoke, Tyrwhit, Skipwith, Heneage, Mussenden, St Paul, Wingfield, Monson, Grantham, Dalison, Littlebury, Ayscough, Dighton, Hussey, Irby, Ogle, Thimbleby, and Sutton.[28] Although new names such as Hatcher[29] and Saunderson[30] appeared among the justices at the end of the century, the old names continued: they came from families that provided the back-bone of local government through which the privy council could make its influence felt. Such influence was exercised not only through the choice of J.P.s but also by intervention from the council. Sometimes it gave general charges to the justices or even sent them all a circular instructing them how to act; at all times it was ready to rebuke them

[27] *Ibid.*, IV, p. 141.
[28] LP xv (1540), g. 282 (19) and g. 942 (12); xvi (1540–41), g. 305 (69).
[29] CSPD 1591–4, p. 191.   [30] CSPD 1595–7, p. 70.

individually or collectively for wrong actions on their part or to praise them for zeal in the performance of their duties.[31] At times the judges of assize were instructed to oversee the work of the justices or to hear reports from them but, by whatever method, control of the justices by the central government was close and effective.

Perhaps the most sensitive area of government policy was that dealing with the treatment of the poor. The government's correct mix of stern measures against the undeserving poor, and the prevention of the ultimate consequences of dire poverty for the deserving, had to be carried out at the local level by officials working under the justices. It was essential that the mix should be correct for over-harshness might engender rebellion which the Tudors with their inadequate armed forces always feared, while softness in some areas towards rogues and vagabonds would create problems by concentrating them in those areas. The unit for the relief of the poor was the parish, and it was the task of having to deal with the poor which turned the parish into an important unit of secular government. In 1563 the justices had thrust upon them the duty of seeing that the new poor rate was collected.[32] Powers in connection with the apprenticeship of children had been given in 1549–50, and over the maintenance of houses of correction and stocks of materials to provide work in 1575–6. By the great codifying statute of 1597,[33] the churchwardens and four overseers of the poor in each parish were saddled with the obligation to maintain and set children on work, to purchase stocks of material on which the poor might work, and to maintain the impotent poor. The justices were empowered to levy a rate for the maintenance of the poor and of hospitals and almshouses; they also had the powers to rate a richer parish in aid of a poorer one. Essentially the state espoused a paternalistic policy the object of which was, in the interests of the preservation of order, the maintenance of the prosperity of all classes in the community, and that policy could only be effectively carried out by local men firmly controlled and constantly checked by the privy council. The justices knew the local economic situation and the churchwardens and overseers knew the merits and demerits of the persons who applied for relief.

Of the detailed working of the poor law in Lincolnshire during the Tudor period we know relatively little and nothing of the part played in it by the justices. We can, however, trace the implementation of the government's policy of poor law relief at the fundamental level in the parish of Leverton, some 6½ miles east of Boston. 'The book for the collection for the poor' begins by listing under the date of 20 June 1563

[31] Holdsworth, op. cit., IV, pp. 77 et seq.
[32] By 5 Eliz. c. 3, see Holdsworth op. cit., IV, pp. 373 et seq.
[33] 40 Eliz. c. 3.

'the names of all the inhabitants which are able to help and relieve the poor and impotent people.' The principle of compulsory contribution had been established in 1552,[34] and in 1563[35] the sessions were empowered to assess the contribution of those who had refused to meet their obligations. The names of thirty-six villagers appear who were able to contribute varying sums towards the upkeep of the impotent poor: it is not easy to be certain as to the figure at which they were assessed or how much they in fact contributed individually, but sums ranging from 5s. a year to 4d. are recorded. In 1565 appears an item of 5s. 8d. that was given by several of the parishioners—unnamed—whom the archdeacon had commanded to contribute, thus, ecclesiastical pressure clearly had to be employed.[36] The total collection in 1563 was £2 8s. 2d. and the total sum spent on relief was 11s. 2d.[37]

Some of this money was given to four needy people who could not support themselves, Janet Pynder, Agnes Marynge, Thomas Casse, and John Roberdson, but sums were also given to proctors or collectors from hospitals and poor houses throughout the country. These men came with licences to beg which are referred to as 'testimonials', as did certain individuals who collected alms for themselves. In 1563 proctors or gatherers came from Enfield in Middlesex, from Surrey and from Malton in Yorkshire and received sums of 6d. for their houses, while in subsequent years during the 1560s and 1570s such men came from Cambridge, Grimsby, Stamford, York, and Knightsbridge in west London, and were given 6d. or 8d.: Patrick Madawle may even have been a professional collector for he represented Enfield in 1563 and York in 1565. This begging round the country on behalf of almshouses and poor houses is an interesting phenomenon. Being near the sea, Leverton had its fair share of distressed mariners many of whom had been robbed at sea and they were given sums of money in 1565[38] and 1571.[39] Also maimed men and soldiers received some charity.[40] The 'maymed sawdyor that came from Ireland beyng servyd ij tymes',[41] and who obtained 1s. 4d. in 1572 reminds us of the similarities that have survived in Anglo-Irish relations over 400 years and of the differences that have developed in welfare policies. Also at the receiving end of Leverton's charity were poor scholars of both universities: John Broke and Richard Richardson of Oxford obtained 12d. on the Sunday after Easter in 1565,[42] while, in 1572, Thomas Banyard of Cambridge secured 3s. 4d. towards an exhibition.[43] Contributions were made towards the construction of Sprott Bridge and to the new hospital at Louth,[44] and also payments to

[34] By 5, 6 Ed. VI c. 2.   [35] By 5 Eliz. c. 3.
[36] Leverton, Overseers' accounts, 1563–98, f. 6v.   [37] Ibid., ff. 2v, 4v.
[38] Ibid., f. 8.   [39] Ibid., ff. 15, 17.   [40] Ibid., ff. 7v, 8.   [41] Ibid., f. 19.
[42] Ibid., f. 7v.   [43] Ibid., f. 19.   [44] Ibid., ff. 7, 7v.

certain players in 1575[45] and 1577,[46] and to the waits of Boston in 1578.[47] These three payments of 12d. could hardly be justified as payments in aid of the poor unless it was necessary to maintain their morale along with that of the other villagers.

The main concern of the overseers was, however, the impotent poor who had to be supported by them. Old Thomas Badyard as he is called received 2s. in 1563,[48] and he appears annually until 1567, getting 2s. in the former year. In 1565–66 he was being paid 4d. or 8d. at irregular intervals, usually each month, and the following year he had 6s. 8d. Others also were maintained for lengthy periods. Another form of help was given by making payments to villagers to look after those who fell sick. When Mrs Bennytt nursed William Scalfleet for a week, it was her husband Richard who received the fee of 8d., but John Staves and his wife appear to have taken on the task jointly for forty-nine weeks for which they were paid 32s. up to 4 April 1586.[49] The overseers also made payments to parishioners who agreed to bring up children— William Browne received 14s. for maintaining Edward Elcocke for half a year—[50] and others were helped by the purchase for them of shoes at 12d. to 1s. 4d. a pair, shirts, and cloth. Coal and barley were purchased in small quantities for distribution to poor individuals in 1596–8.[51] In these ways the problem of the poor was tackled.

So far we have looked mostly at the ways in which central government attempted to control the government of the shire, although it has been pointed out that lords lieutenant had a two-way function. But the principal influence that could be exercised by the shire on central government was through members of parliament.[52] A county history is not the place to discuss the influence which the house of commons had on the sovereign or on the government, but if any group of men could influence central government, it was the elected members for the shire and for the incorporated boroughs. It would be generally agreed that their influence grew in the period during which the Tudor dynasty ruled England, but it would be unwise to assume that governmental policy was frequently altered as a result of parliamentary pressure: the techniques of governmental persuasion could sometimes be brutal. Moreover, during the Tudor period parliament never attained the freedom to initiate: it might amend or reject the sovereign's proposals, but the initiative remained with the monarch.[53] The Crown also

[45] Ibid., f. 24.   [46] Ibid., f. 27v.   [47] Ibid., f. 29v.   [48] Ibid., f. 4v.
[49] Ibid., f. 39.   [50] Ibid., f. 43.   [51] Ibid., ff. 48, 50v.
[52] The author wishes to express his profound gratitude to the History of Parliament Trust for making available to him information, without the use of which the rest of this chapter could not have been written.
[53] Holdsworth, op. cit., IV, p. 89.

exercised considerable control over the election of members. The policy of the payment of members did not die out completely in the sixteenth century and constituencies might be promised that if they elected the right men their representation would cost them nothing.[54] When, later in the century, payment was less frequent the Crown, until 1586, created boroughs, often at the instance of patrons, where Court nominees might be elected or the council might write to the sheriffs recommending them to elect certain persons or certain types of person. Grimsby on more than one occasion was ordered to choose an inhabitant of the town.[55] On occasion also, orders were sent to elect the same members as had sat in the previous parliament.

At the opening of the Tudor period, in addition to the two knights of the shire, four boroughs in Lincolnshire returned two members each to parliament: these were Lincoln city and the boroughs of Grimsby, Stamford, and Grantham, to which Boston was added from 1547. As might be expected, the same families that supplied J.P.s and 'high' sheriffs provided many M.P.s. The city of Lincoln usually chose at least as one of its members someone who either was, or had been, closely connected with the government of the city; frequently the recorder or an ex-mayor held one of the seats.

The shire knights were considered somewhat more prestigious than the borough representatives and, as is to be expected, Lincolnshire was represented by members of leading families in the county. During the Tudor period, from Henry VII's first parliament of 1485–6 to Elizabeth I's last parliament of 1601, we know the names of twenty-seven men who represented the county in twenty-four out of the thirty-three parliaments held in those years: the names of the shire members in the parliaments of 1487, 1497, 1504, 1510, 1512, 1515, 1536, 1542, and 1572 have not as yet come to light. The Hussey family provided two members to three parliaments, the Tyrwhits three members to six parliaments; Sir William Skipwith attended two parliaments, while Sir Edward Dymoke (1509–66) and his grandson, also Sir Edward (1558–1624), were M.P.s on two and four occasions respectively. In addition, two members of the Heneage family, John in 1539 and Thomas in 1571, represented the shire in parliament, and George St Paul sat for the shire in 1555, while his grandson Sir George was member in 1589 and 1592. Thus, these six families provided twelve M.P.s to twenty-two out of the twenty-four parliaments of which we have some, though not always a complete, record of the names of the members.[56] Moreover, the six well-known Lincolnshire families of Tailboys, Willoughby, Dalison,

[54] *Ibid.*, IV, p. 94.   [55] HMC *14th Rep., App.*, pt. VIII, pp. 254–5.
[56] Only the names of one of the two members are known for the parliaments of 1489, 1495, 1523, April 1554, 1559, 1584, 1586, and 1601.

Copledike, Thimbleby, and Monson provided one of their members to be an M.P. for the shire on one occasion. If we accept Sir Edward Burgh, Sir William Cecil, and Richard Bertie, who were also M.P.s on one or two occasions, as Lincolnshire men, despite their interests outside the county, it will be seen that virtually no M.P.s for the county during the Tudor period came from outside the shire, and that representation was confined to about fifteen families. Some of the knights of the shire had, however, previously sat for other constituencies,[57] so some men were beginning to acquire considerable knowledge of parliamentary affairs.

For the city of Lincoln the names of thirty-one men who represented it in twenty-seven parliaments have been established. The names of the members in only six parliaments, those of 1485–6, 1487, 1489, 1497, 1504, and 1510, are unknown. Here again, as in the county, certain families, notably the Alansons and the Granthams, provided more than one local M.P., but the reasons for members of the same family serving the office, as for continuity of representation, lies in office-holding rather than in family ties. Of the ninety-two mayors in the 117 years of Tudor rule, eleven served the city in parliament.[58] William Bell served in the parliaments of 1491–2 and 1495, Robert Alanson, four times mayor of Lincoln, sat as M.P. in 1512, one of the years of his mayoralty, and again in 1515. Robert's son William, who was mayor in 1542–3, was also a burgess for the city in the parliament of 1542. Vincent Grantham, twice mayor, was twice M.P., sitting in the parliaments of 1529 and 1536, and his son Thomas sat in 1547, ten years before he became mayor. William Long, mayor in 1487–8, was an M.P. in the parliament of 1495; John Halton, mayor 1522–3, was an M.P. in the parliament which met during his term of office. William Sammes, mayor 1515–16, had his disagreements with the city fathers, but he became sufficiently reconciled to become M.P. in the 'Reformation Parliament' of 1529. William Yates, twice mayor, first in 1539–40 and again in 1549–50, sat as member in 1545; William Rotheram, mayor 1554–5, sat in the parliament of April 1554, and John Welcome who held the principal civic office in 1568–9, went to Westminster in 1572.

Other officers of the city also served in parliament. The recorder, a judicial official who existed in Lincoln from the later Middle Ages, was frequently chosen as one of the burgesses to represent the city.[59]

[57] See *post* pp. 102–10.

[58] J. B. King, (Comp.), A list of mayors, bailiffs etc. in the city of Lincoln, (part typescript, part MS.) 1945; corrected and supplemented by the History of Parliament Trust.

[59] King, *op. cit.*

Anthony Mussenden, recorder of Lincoln from 14 December 1536[60] until his death in 1542, sat as member for the city in 1539 and 1542 as his predecessor, the attainted Thomas Moigne (recorder 1532–6), had done in 1536. When Mussenden died in 1542, he was replaced as recorder by George St Paul who also went to parliament to take the dead man's place as burgess for the city. Thereafter, he represented Lincoln in the parliaments of 1545, 1547, October 1553, November 1554, and 1558. Apparently he did not sit in the parliament of April 1554, but he represented the shire in 1555; thus, George St Paul sat, between 1542 and his death early in 1559, in at least seven parliaments.[61] George St Paul's mother was a Thimbleby,[62] and he married an Ayscough;[63] he provides one of the outstanding examples of the way in which a member of the landed establishment in Lincolnshire was gaining a knowledge of parliamentary ways by repeated service at Westminster. Opportunities to gain such experience were occurring in other counties. His successor, as recorder, Anthony Thorold served in that office until July 1570, but he sat as M.P. only in the parliament of 1559. He had had previous experience as he had represented the borough of Grantham in 1558, but he did not act as M.P. for Lincoln in the parliament of 1563 as might have been expected. In that year one of the members was Robert Monson who again represented the city in the parliament of 1571. He sat as M.P. therefore before being elected to the recordership, which office he held briefly between 1570 and 1572.[64] Stephen Thimbleby was recorder for almost fifteen years from November 1572 but he sat only in the parliament of 1584. Son of Sir Matthew Thimbleby, his mother was Ann, a daughter of Sir Robert Hussey, a younger brother of lord Hussey. It is not known why he did not sit in the parliament of 1586 since he remained recorder until his death on 21 August 1587, but he had had previous experience in the house of commons in 1572.[65] The last recorder of the Tudor period was George Anton who held office from 22 August 1587 until 1613: he was M.P. for Lincoln city in 1589, 1593, 1597, and 1601.

In all, seven recorders and eleven mayors represented the city. Eighteen out of the thirty-one M.P.s had held one of these two offices, and doubtless others who sat in parliament held inferior offices since

[60] *Ibid.*

[61] The representation in the parliament of March 1553 is not known but St Paul may have been one of the M.P.s.

[62] Helen, dr. of Richard Thimbleby of Poolham—A. R. Maddison (ed.), *Lincs. Pedigrees*, III, Harl. Soc., vol. 52, 1904.

[63] Jane, dr. of Sir William Ayscough of South Kelsey—*Ibid.*

[64] J. B. King says he resigned in 1570 but no new recorder was appointed until 3 November 1572.

[65] See *post* p. 110.

many of them were local men such as Robert Clerk[66] of Lincoln, Washingborough, and London, and Robert Dighton[67] of Lincoln and Little Sturton, whose father had been mayor. Thomas Wilson, later secretary of state, M.P. in 1571 and 1572, came from Washingborough; John Savile[68] (M.P. 1586) was established at Great Humby-in-Somerby; and Thomas Fairfax who sat with Savile may well belong to the Swarby family of that name. Peter Eure (M.P. 1589)[69] was of the family with lands in Belton in the isle of Axholme and also in Washingborough, while Charles Dymoke (1592) was of the Scrivelsby family though domiciled at Coates near Stow. Thomas Grantham (1597) was the great grandson of the M.P. in 1529, and the grandson of the Thomas who had represented the city in 1547, and Francis Bullingham (1601) was the son of the former bishop. Very few M.P.s for the city of Lincoln were men from outside the county. Francis Kemp, M.P., in 1558, is said to have been of Wye in Kent and London,[70] and there are two other members who do not appear to have been of local families. One of them, Robert Farrar, represented the city on four occasions, in October 1553, April and November 1554, and in 1555, while the other, John Joye was M.P. in 1584 but although influence may have been brought to bear in elections it seems to have been exercised in favour of local men. The principal patrons were the earls of Rutland and the duke of Suffolk. There are reasons for thinking that Anthony Mussenden was a nominee of Thomas Manners, the first earl of Rutland, and that the second earl supported Robert Farrar. Francis Kemp was certainly a nominee of the second earl while Edward, the third earl, probably pressed the claims of John Joye. George St Paul is said to have been a nominee of the duke of Suffolk[71] and Anthony Thorold may also have been a Suffolk protégé.

The borough of Great Grimsby returned forty-three men to twenty-nine parliaments for we have a record of M.P.s for all the assemblies except those of 1504, 1536, 1539, and March 1553. Unlike Lincoln, local men—those who had served as mayor and in other offices—did not predominate as representatives and even some of the gentry families such as Heneages, Tyrwhits, Suttons, and Skipwiths came from a little distance and, in that sense, could hardly be described as local. The Heneage seat at Hainton was fifteen miles from Great Grimsby, the Tyrwhits at Scotter and Cammeringham were above twenty-five miles distant, Ambrose Sutton was probably one of the family

[66] M.P. in 1512, 1515, and 1523.　　[67] M.P. 1539.
[68] Maddison, Lincs. Pedigrees, III, p. 860.
[69] In Maddison, op. cit., said to be M.P. in 1571, but in the History of Parliament Trust in 1589.
[70] The History of Parliament Trust.
[71] Ex inf. Sir Francis Hill.

settled in Burton-by-Lincoln and Washingborough, and Edward Skipwith may have belonged either to the Metheringham or the Ketsby branch of that far-flung family. These places were about thirty-three miles and twenty miles from the constituency. However, many gentry are said[72] to have owned property in Grimsby among whom Richard Thimbleby of Irnham, Sir Robert Tyrwhit, George and William Heneage, Lionel Skipwith, Francis Mussenden, and William Bard are to be found. Three ex-mayors, Stephen de la See, Thomas Pormad, and Thomas Broughton sat in the parliaments of 1485–6 and of 1495, and an ex-coroner, alderman Hugh Eden, was also M.P. in the latter year. Other local men who served as members were George Banardiston and Robert Vicars in 1512, Philip Hamby in 1515, and Robert Lord in 1523.[73]

But the electors of Grimsby tended to choose as their M.P.s either Lincolnshire gentry or even men from outside the county. John Heneage represented the borough in 1497, and almost certainly his son John was member in 1523 and 1529, and it was this John who sat for the county in 1539.[74] William Tyrwhit, possibly the grandfather of Sir Robert Tyrwhit the knight of the shire in 1553, 1554, and 1558,[75] sat as member for Grimsby in the parliament of 1510, and his great grandsons Marmaduke and Tristram represented the borough in 1558 and in 1586 and 1589 respectively. The member who sat with John Heneage in the Reformation Parliament was William Ayscough, the father of the martyr Anne, and a man of considerable influence in the locality as he held a large estate in Stallingborough. In 1545, Thomas Hussey, a grandson of Sir William who was lord Hussey's brother, was M.P. The Thimblebies of Irnham provided one of the members in 1571: he was John who was connected with Stephen the recorder of Lincoln. Thomas Grantham (1572) although he does not appear in the Grantham pedigree may have belonged to the family established in Lincoln, and Goltho or, more probably, to a humbler branch in Barrow, Claxby, and Stallingborough. Thomas St Paul was the son of the recorder of Lincoln, and the father of George, the knight of the shire in 1589 and 1593: he sat only once as member for Great Grimsby in 1571. His daughter-in-law was the sister of William Wray, son of the lord chief justice, who represented the borough in 1584 as his father had done in 1563. If parliamentary experience was to be obtained by attendance at

[72] E. Gillett, *A History of Grimsby*, London, 1970, p. 93. Mr Gillett informs me that members of the Cracroft, Kirton, Monson, Thimbleby, and Hatcliffe families were resident in the town.

[73] The History of Parliament Trust. Also for the elections of 1485 and 1487, see A. Rogers, 'Parliamentary Elections in Grimsby in the Fifteenth Century', *Bull*. IHR, XI, 1969, II, pp. 216, 219–20.

[74] See *ante* p. 100.   [75] See *ante* p. 100.

many assemblies, it was also to be acquired by accounts passed down from father to son as must have happened in the St Paul family. If Thomas Morrison who sat for the borough in the parliaments of 1572, 1584, 1586, and 1589 is the Thomas Moryson of Cadeby,[76] then he is both of the landed gentry and also an office-holder for he was mayor of Great Grimsby in 1576.[77] He had married Elizabeth, the daughter of Thomas Moigne, who sat briefly for Lincoln before his execution in 1537. If he came from Wyham-cum-Cadeby he was only about eight miles from the borough and about the same distance from his wife's interests in North Willingham. Thomas Hatcliffe may have been resident in Grimsby or he may have been from the eponymous village some five miles inland. In 1593 the borough was represented by one of the gentry who was on his way up to higher things. Nicholas Saunderson, heir of Robert Saunderson of Saxby and Fillingham, whose mother was Katherine, youngest daughter of Vincent Grantham, sat as M.P. in 1593 and was eventually created viscount Castleton.[78] In the last Tudor parliament a nobleman, Thomas lord Clinton and Saye, son and heir of Henry second earl of Lincoln, who had himself sat as knight of the shire in 1571, was elected member for Grimsby from which constituency he went on to represent the county between 1604 and 1610. Edward Skipwith who sat with Thomas lord Clinton was of the South Ormsby family although he eventually bought Ketsby.

One of the most remarkable Grimsby M.P.s of the sixteenth century was the land 'speculator' John Bellow who represented the borough in 1547, October 1553, April and November 1554, 1555, 1558, and 1559. He was, along with John Broxholme, one of the *nouveaux riches* of the district who made a fortune out of monastic property. Probably the son of a Stallingborough husbandman, he became mayor of Great Grimsby four times and an M.P.[79] Here was a man of humble origins whose rise may be attributed to his legal practice and his governmental service under Cromwell. But the borough, largely on account of its poverty, was willing to ask any to serve it who would do so without charge, and so outsiders such as Sir Edward Warner[80] and Edward Fitzgerald appear as members. Richard Goodrich, probably of the Bolingbroke family of that name, assured the mayor and his brethren in 1545 that he would serve as M.P. without any charge as did Thomas Hussey the same year.[81] Thomas Hatcliffe and Thomas Ellis in 1597, and Thomas, lord Clinton in 1601 indemnified the borough against any expense: free representation was important for the town.[82]

[76] Maddison, *op. cit.*, p. 693.   [77] *Ibid.*
[78] GEC *Complete Peerage, sub* Castleton.   [79] E. Gillett, *op. cit.*, p. 91.
[80] See *post* p. 108.   [81] HMC *14th Rep., App.*, pt. VIII, p. 254.
[82] *Ibid.*, p. 279.

Grimsby provides an outstanding example of interference in the election of members both by the Crown and by local gentry and magnates. Francis Mussenden, writing from Healing to Michael Empringham, said that his father-in-law, Sir Francis Ayscough, desired Empringham to choose Francis's uncle, George Skipwith, and William Marbury as M.P.s.[83] Sir Francis again intervened in 1557 when, in writing to the mayor and burgesses, he required them 'to choose for one of your burgesses (M.P.s) Christopher Winch.' He said that this would also please the earl of Westmorland who had influence in the town, as Winch was one of his council, and he guaranteed that Winch would take no fee from the town. In 1559, Sir Robert Tyrwhit of Kettleby informed the mayor and his brethren by letter that 'lord Clinton required them to commit the nomination of one of the burgesses for parliament to his lordship' and, once again, the assurance was given that, in so doing, the town would be put to no charges.[84] Lord Clinton made a direct approach in 1562 desiring that Edward Tarrat should be elected and assuring the town that no expense would result if he were chosen.[85] The fact that, on these occasions, the nominees were unsuccessful does not cancel out the interference.

The record of members for the borough of Stamford is unusually full. We have the names of its M.P.s for all thirty-three parliaments of the Tudor period: in all, only thirty-nine members sat between 1485 and 1601. The Cecil family, as might be expected, dominated the borough, and five members of the family, commencing with David in 1504 and ending with William in 1589, represented it in twelve parliaments to say nothing of cousins and nephews who bore other names. David Cecil, designated a merchant of Stamford and already in Henry VII's favour, was elected to the parliament of 1504 when he was thirty-three years of age,[86] and continued to sit in 1510, 1512, 1515, and 1523 and his son Richard, lord Burghley's father, represented the borough in 1539. The great statesman himself was M.P. for Stamford in 1547 before going on to be knight of the shire in 1555 and 1559. In due course his eldest son Thomas claimed the seat and was returned to the parliaments of 1563, 1571, and 1572. In 1586 and 1589 another son William sat, while Francis Harrington, a cousin[87] of lord Burghley, was returned in 1572. Robert Wingfield,[88] lord Burghley's nephew, was member for Stamford in every parliament from 1584 to 1601. In the earlier years of the Tudor period local men in the persons of Christopher Browne, merchant of the Staple and an ex-alderman (M.P. 1485-6,

---

[83] *Ibid.*   [84] *Ibid.*, p. 255.   [85] *Ibid.*, p. 256.

[86] J. C. Wedgwood, (ed.), *History of Parliament: Register 1439–1509*, London, 1938, *sub nomine*.

[87] The History of Parliament Trust.   [88] *Ibid.*

1489, and 1495), William Radclyffe, an ex-alderman (1497), and another Stapler, alderman Richard Cauvell (1497 and 1504) were elected but even then an outsider like Thomas Lacy of Granchester appeared in 1487 and Christopher Browne's interests often took him away from the town. Although William Hussey sat once in 1512 many of the members appear to have been outsiders, probably nominees of the growing Cecil interest. George Kirkeham (1515), Maurice Johnson (1523, 1529, and 1536), John Hardgrave (1529) may or may not have been local men, but Henry Lacy (1536, 1542, and 1545) appears to have been established there as was his father Thomas.[89] Kenelm Digby, member in 1539 probably came from Stoke Dry[90] in Rutlandshire, and was well connected with many important families. John Allen, mercer of Grantham and Stoke Rochford, was probably the same as the member in the parliaments of 1542, 1547, October 1553, and April 1554, and Thomas Heneage (October 1553) was undoubtedly of the well-known Lincolnshire family. Leonard Irby of Gosberton, later M.P. for Boston, may have started his parliamentary career in Stamford in 1545[91] and Francis Yaxley (1555) may have belonged to a family of that name in Boston.[92] Thomas Balgey or Balguy was the son of a London merchant, and he became recorder of Stamford in 1594 and sat in the parliament elected in 1597.

But there are still many M.P.s with no apparent local connection. Rowland Durant, member in April 1554, and John Fenton and Henry Lee who sat in November of that year fall into this category. Francis Thorneff, member in 1555 and 1563, and the two Cookes, Richard in March 1553 and William in 1559, do not appear to have belonged to the local gentry. John Houghton (1558 and 1559), Michael Lewis (1571), George Lynne (1584), Richard Shute (1593), and Edward Watson (1601) do not seem to have been local men, but further research may show that they were nominees of the Cecils whose influence certainly from the middle of the sixteenth century was paramount.

In sharp contrast to the position in Stamford, the names of many Grantham M.P.s are missing. No names are known for the parliaments of 1485-6, 1487, 1489, 1497, 1504, 1510, 1512, 1523, 1536, 1539, and 1542, so that the names of members of only twenty parliaments are available. In these parliaments, extending from 1491-2 to 1601, twenty men were elected by the borough. But Grantham had similarities with Stamford for it was under the influence of the Manners family as Stamford was dominated by the Cecils, and few of the members would appear to have been office-holders. In the only earlier parliament of which we have a record, that of 1491-2, the members were Sir William

[89] Maddison, op. cit., p. 576.   [90] DNB sub Digby, Everard.
[91] See post p. 109.   [92] Although he does not appear in Lincs. Pedigrees.

Knevytt and John Mordaunte, neither of whom appears to have been a local man.

Local gentry, however, frequently represented the borough at West-minster. In the 'Reformation Parliament' Francis Hall of Grantham was one of the members. It is difficult to say whether this was the man who was surveyor of the works of Calais[93] and who died in 1553, or his father who had married the daughter of Sir John Wingfield. The family, still remained active in politics since Arthur Hall, son or grand-son of the 1529 member, sat as M.P. for the borough in 1571, 1572, and 1584, and Arthur's sister Jane married Francis Neale, whose son Francis was probably M.P. in the parliaments of 1593 and 1597. The Hussey family also had an interest in the seat for William, M.P. in 1529, may be the same William who represented Stamford in 1512. Later in the century Thomas Hussey, probably a younger son of lord Hussey, was member in the parliaments of March 1553 and April 1554, having been one of the knights of the shire in the intervening assembly. Two near-by families, the Disneys of Norton Disney, some sixteen miles away, and the Thorolds of Marston, only five miles distant, provided members. Richard Disney was M.P. in April 1554 and Anthony Thorold in 1558. To the parliament of 1584 was sent William Thorold who may have been Anthony's brother or his son or his nephew. George Williams[94] M.P. for 1555 may have belonged to the family established at near-by Denton, while his colleague William Porter certainly came from the adjacent Belton or from Grantham itself. Henry Savile of Barrowby and Somerby was descended from an ancient Yorkshire family and represented the borough only once in the house of commons in 1558.

One of the members for 1589 was William Armyn of Osgodby, a place over thirty-five miles from Grantham, whose mother Mary was the eldest daughter of Henry Sutton of Burton-by-Lincoln. But, in addition to electing local gentry, the burgesses of Grantham chose members of the aristocracy. The Manners family lived only a few miles from the town, and in 1563 Roger Manners the third son of Thomas the first earl of Rutland sat in the Commons for the borough, while in the last Elizabethan parliament Oliver, the fourth son of John, the fourth earl, was one of the members.

Sir Edward Warner who sat for Grimsby in 1559 apparently began his parliamentary career in Grantham for which borough he was member in 1545, 1547, and March and October 1553. He was a government placeman who was appointed lieutenant of the Tower in October 1552, although he was removed in July of the following year and fell foul of the government in January 1554 on account of his religious

[93] *Lincs. Pedigrees*, p. 441.   [94] Although he does not appear in *Lincs. Pedigrees*.

sympathies.[95] On Elizabeth's accession he was re-instated as lieutenant, and sat for Grimsby until he was returned as a knight of the shire for Norfolk in 1563.

Whether William More the M.P. for 1559 was the father of Richard who sat in 1589 is not certain but, if this were so, he was in all probability new to the district. There is reason to believe that this family served the town as office-holders since Richard's son Alexander held the position of alderman, the equivalent in other boroughs of mayor. But there were members who cannot be traced as local gentry and who, because of the lack of municipal records in the sixteenth century, cannot be traced as office-holders. James Walles (October 1553), Richard Sharpe and Roger Johnson (both November 1554) have the surnames of local gentry families, but cannot be traced in the pedigrees of those families which are readily available. Of Thomas Randolph (1559), William Killigrew (1571), and John Vaughan (1572) we can say little beyond the fact that the Vaughans may, like the Williams family, be Welshmen who settled in the district as a result of Henry Tudor's success in 1485. William Ashby and Robert Markham, who were the two M.P.s in 1586, and Thomas Horsman (1593 and 1601) remain shadowy characters, but they may, like some of the other members at present barely identified or identifiable, be nominees of the earls of Rutland.

Boston falls into a special category because it did not return any members to parliament before 1547 following its incorporation two years previously. It has a most unusual record for the continuity of service of its members since, in the seventeen parliaments that were called between 1547 and 1601, only fifteen men represented the borough. One of the seats was almost permanently in the hands of the Irby family. Leonard Irby who had sat for Stamford in 1545,[96] was M.P. for Boston in every parliament with the exception of the first assembly of Mary's reign between March 1553 and 1571. He was lord Clinton's surveyor and the second son of Anthony Irby, a family originally from Irby-on-Humber, but which had settled in Gosberton some ten miles from Boston during Henry VIII's reign. Leonard was succeeded in the house of commons by his nephew Anthony who sat in the parliaments of 1589, 1593, 1597, and 1601. He was a distinguished lawyer and founder of the line of Boston M.P.s, one of whom was eventually raised to the peerage as lord Boston. Another long-staying member was George Forster, a local lawyer who sat in all five parliaments between March 1553 and 1558.[97]

[95] DNB sub nomine.   [96] See ante p. 107.
[97] The History of Parliament Trust, quoting Boston Corp. Min. Bk., 1545–1607, ff. 13–13b.

The custom here then was to send local men to Westminster, but from time to time local gentry acted as members. Robert Carr of Sleaford, the former associate of lord Hussey, represented the borough in 1559, and Stephen Thimbleby[98] sat in 1572 and later was member for Lincoln of which city he was recorder. John Tamworth, son of Thomas Tamworth of Leake, some seven miles out of Boston, was not only a member of a gentry family but also a placeman. He sat for Boston in 1563 and was, according to A. R. Maddison, a privy councillor.[99] Vincent Skinner, finally established at Thornton Curtis but the son of John Skinner of Thorpe near Wainfleet, was thrice member, in 1584, 1586, and 1589. Francis Allen M.P. in October 1553 was the bishop of Winchester's secretary[100] who replaced for one parliament Leonard Irby, probably a Protestant who had favoured Queen Jane. Of the remaining members, William Naunton and John Wendon, who were the borough's first M.P.s, Thomas Lyfield (1571), William Doddington (1572), Richard Stevenson (1586, 1593, and 1597), and Henry Capell (1601) little at present is known but some of them may well have been local men who had served the municipality. Whether Nicholas Gorges M.P. in 1584 was a member of the Somerset family which produced so many brilliant statesmen and *littérateurs* has not been established.

What influence did these members of the house of commons have upon central government? How far could they make the voice of the shire known? It must be admitted that, at the best, what they could represent was only the opinion of a small section of the community. The knights of the shire were elected by all those who held freehold land to the value of 40s. *per annum*,[101] but it would be a well-nigh impossible task to enumerate the qualified voters, and a completely impossible one to say how many of those qualified actually voted. However, absolutely, the county electorate was much larger than that in the boroughs and may in fact have represented a larger proportion of the population, especially in some areas where freeholders predominated. Parts of Holland may have produced many county voters. We know that in 1510 riots broke out at the election of knights of the shire but no reasons for them have been vouchsafed. In the boroughs the percentage of the inhabitants enjoying the franchise varied from one to another. In the city of Lincoln the freemen apparently chose the two members and, although it is not possible to say how large a percentage of the total population they formed, they were a larger electing body than in some places. In Grimsby also the freemen voted and marriage to a freeman's

[98] See *ante* p. 102.   [99] *Lincs. Pedigrees*, III, p. 948 but not according to APC 1558–70.
[100] The History of Parliament Trust.
[101] SR II, p. 243.

daughter gave her husband the right to vote.[102] In Boston it would appear that the franchise was extremely limited until 1628 when those who paid scot and lot were allowed to vote.[103] In Grantham apparently the free burgesses had the vote,[104] but the numbers of electors in the sixteenth century were perhaps not high for the borough was controlled by the Manners family,[105] although the view has been expressed that the inhabitants as well had the right to vote.[106] Stamford on the other hand, although so much under Cecil control during the Tudor period, had a somewhat larger electorate, and even in the sixteenth century those paying scot and lot may have been eligible to vote.[107]

It is not only the smallness of the electorate that casts doubt upon the truly representative nature of the members who sat in the house of commons, but also the fact that the electors were manipulated in the interests of control by leading magnates. Reference has already been made to the influence exercised by lord Burghley in Stamford and the earl of Rutland in Grantham: Sir H. Bagnell writing in 1586 asked to be nominated by Edward, third Earl of Rutland to 'his borough of Grantham.' But the Manners family also managed matters to some extent in Lincoln where they contended with the city council in the earlier part of the century.[108] In so far as the recorder was invariably one of the members, anyone who controlled the appointment to that office had a friend in the lower house. After the suppression of the Lincolnshire rebellion the duke of Suffolk was allowed by the corporation to nominate the recorder. Boston gives clear proof of the influence of lord Clinton, later the earl of Lincoln, in that city as he was able to secure the election of his official Leonard Irby many times, even on one occasion against the influence of William Cecil. Cecil in March 1553 was recorder of Boston as well as secretary of state, but he could not secure the election of his nominee. Great Grimsby during part of the Tudor epoch was dominated by the earls of Westmorland. In return for a reduction of £30 in the fee farm rent of £50 that the town had to pay to him, he was granted the nomination of one of the members. During the minority of the fourth earl from 1499, this arrangement seems to have fallen into abeyance, but attempts were made to revive his influence from the late 1520s or from the 1540s. Richard Goodrich M.P. in 1542 was a nominee of the earl.[109]

The control of aristocratic families was made easy by the decayed

[102] E. Porritt, *The Unreformed House of Commons*, I, London, 1903, p. 78.
[103] Porritt, *op. cit.*, I, p. 47 quoting *H. of C. Journals*, 1628.
[104] Browne, Willis, *Notitia Parliamentaria*, I, edn. 1750, p. 33.
[105] Porritt, *op. cit.*, I, p. 378.
[106] The History of Parliament Trust.
[107] Browne Willis, *op. cit.*, I, p. 32.   [108] See *post* pp. 123-4.
[109] The History of Parliament Trust, and HMC *14th Rep., App., pt. VIII*, p. 252.

state of some of the boroughs, many of which professed that they were no longer able to pay their members. No doubt the wages and expenses of members were a considerable drain upon municipal resources for, by a statute of 1323, citizens and burgesses were entitled to a wage of 2s. a day and knights of the shire to 4s.[110] In addition, travel expenses to and from parliament were allowed, twenty miles in winter and thirty miles in summer being regarded as a full day's journey.[111] With the multi-session parliaments of the Tudor period, especially with the one of 1529–36, these charges mounted up, and Vincent Grantham in 1535 'out of his zeal and love for the city' remitted part of his parliamentary wages.[112] He took only £4 3s. 4d. while his colleague William Sammes received £41 0s. 8d. Shortly after this, wages ceased to be paid in Lincoln and reports in the Council minute book of addresses from the returning M.P.s cease. This wish to be rid of expense led boroughs to look favourably upon outsiders who would offer to serve in parliament without incurring the electors in any expense, and it was the entry of outsiders that to some degree gave the aristocracy their chance. Members of leading families in the shire were able to put forward a nominee who might promise to serve at reduced charges or even at no cost at all to the constituency, and thus they obtained a loyal member of the lower house who would reflect their views perhaps to the exclusion of the views of the constituents. In this way members became even less representative of the electorate in the sixteenth century.

On the other hand, although perhaps less truly representative than the local office-holders of the past, the outside members, many of them drawn from the gentry families in the vicinity of the constituencies, did not necessarily exercise less influence upon the government. On the contrary, long continuity of service in the Commons increased their potential effectiveness as an opposition to the Crown. Out of the 185 members who represented the shire, the city of Lincoln and the three (later four) boroughs in the Tudor period, relatively few went only once to parliament and these tended to be in the early years. As the sixteenth century progressed it became increasingly usual for a member to sit time and time again. Leonard Irby is an outstanding example of this trend: he sat in nine out of the eleven parliaments that met between 1545 and 1571. George Forster sat in all six parliaments between March 1553 and 1558. Robert Wingfield represented Stamford in every parliament —and there were six of them—between 1584 and 1601; John Bellow was M.P. for Grimsby in seven of the eight parliaments between 1547 and 1559 and may have sat in March 1553 for which we have no returns. Robert Farrar represented Lincoln city on six occasions between October 1553 and 1563, missing only the assembly of 1558,

[110] Porritt, op. cit., p. 155.　　[111] Ibid., p. 157.　　[112] Ibid., p. 257.

while Sir Edward Dymoke was knight of the shire in 1547, October 1553, and 1558, and his grandson sat in all four parliaments between 1584 and 1593.

Continuous re-election however did not necessarily mean exercising greater influence on government for such influence as could be asserted —and the government did its best to minimize it—depended upon the members' calibre, the independence, or otherwise, of their opinions, their devotion to the needs of their constituents and their diligence in attendance at the House. To take the last point, it cannot be assumed that Arthur Hall was an isolated example of an absentee. Arthur Hall represented the borough of Grantham in the house of commons in the parliaments of 1571, 1572, and 1584 and, in 1585, the House made a special order that he should attend.[113] Of course, attendance could never be effectively enforced by the House and often members left parliament early with the approval of the mayor and corporation in order to save wages, but a member could not exercise influence unless he remained in attendance. Arthur Hall caused a considerable stir in the House but it might be doubted whether he advanced in any degree the interests of his constituents in Grantham. On 20 February 1576 the case of Edward Smalley yeoman,[114] Hall's servant, was discussed, and on 7 March he was judged guilty of contempt of the House and it was decided that he was no longer to enjoy the status of a member's servant. Matthew Kirtleton described as 'school master to Mr Hall' was similarly judged and both were committed to the Tower for a month. The cause concerned a debt of £100 owed to the executors of Melchisedech Malory and five years later it had further repercussions. Arthur Hall in the meantime had written a book charging the House with spite towards him and its members with drunkenness. He was examined by the privy council as to whether he had caused the book to be printed, and its findings were reported to the House by Mr Secretary Wilson, M.P. for Lincoln city, on 4 February 1581.[115] Eventually after lengthy discussion in the Commons, in which he was accused of publishing conferences of the House abroad in print and of impeaching the memory of the late Speaker, he was imprisoned in the Tower for six months, fined 500 marks and deprived of his seat. The order was given to issue a writ for a new burgess for Grantham. All this did not however prevent him from being returned in the next parliament of 1584 although whether he ever appeared is uncertain. Hall was a man of considerable literary talents: he translated Homer's

[113] *Ibid.*, p. 238, quoting Sir Simonds D'Ewes' *Journals*, pp. 338–9.
[114] For this affair see DNB *sub* Hall, Arthur, and Sir Simonds D'Ewes, *Journals*, pp. 249, 254, 258.
[115] DNB *sub* Hall and D'Ewes, *Journals*, pp. 291–2, 296.

'Iliad' from French and he was also a *protégé* of lord Burghley: he was a member with a liberal outlook almost verging upon anarchy, but seemingly he was not a very open channel to pass forward Lincolnshire views to Westminster or a means to influence central government.

Perhaps the most influential ordinary member was Sir Edward Dymoke, M.P. for the shire between 1584 and 1593. He spoke in debate and sat assiduously on committees.[116] We find him first on Saturday 5 December 1584 bringing in a bill to secure a good supply of fish—an interest that was no doubt important to the coastal regions of the county—and a week later he was bringing in a petition to secure a good supply of godly preachers to 'places destitute of means of salvation'. He was placed on the committee for the fish bill, and on Friday 11 December he brought it back to the full House unaltered. Quite a busy week for Sir Edward was that of 5 to 11 December. The following week on 16 December he was sitting on a committee to conflate the various petitions on ministers and to draw up a composite petition for presentation to the house of lords. Here he was working with, among others, Sir Thomas Heneage, a Lincolnshire man, but by 1584 sitting for Essex. He was already emerging as a committee man and an active working member of the House. Because Dymoke was also 'high' sheriff he was given permission to depart on 23 February 1585: Mr Stephen Thimbleby, recorder of Lincoln, who received similar leave on 4 March to attend the assizes does not appear to have been so active as a member. Sir Edward spoke and sat on committees many times during his parliamentary career. On 26 February 1589[117] he argued unto a bill concerning captains and soldiers, the next day he was on a committee to discuss the subsidy with members of the upper house, and the following month he introduced a bill for the relief of the city of Lincoln.[118] On 15 March 1593 he brought in an amended bill for Lincoln, and a week later he spoke vigorously against home engrossers who, he said, did more to ruin native retailers than foreign retailers did. Reading carefully such reports of his speeches as we have, it can be seen that Dymoke was a good member who knew his shire, represented its grievances, and attempted to improve the common weal.

On 7 April 1571 Mr Sampoole *i.e.* Thomas St Paul, M.P. for Grimsby, in commending a subsidy complained that collectors sometimes kept the money for more than a year, and urged that the better sort of men should be appointed collectors. Here doubtless he was expressing the grievances of his constituents who may have experienced this misdemeanour. In May 1571 Mr St Paul and Mr Irby, presumably the M.P. for Boston, sat with Mr Thomas Heneage, the knight of the shire, on a committee. But apart from Hall, Dymoke, Thimbleby, St

[116] D'Ewes, *op. cit.*, p. 337.   [117] *Ibid.*, p. 439.   [118] *Ibid.*, p. 448.

Paul, and Irby no other M.P.s appear to have done much to bring the influence of the county to bear upon central government.

There remains, however, a group of three members who did not so much bring influence to bear on central government in the sense of checking or controlling it for they were at one time or another the government or, at least, part of the governmental establishment. These were Robert Monson (?c. 1525–83) M.P. for Lincoln city 1563–66; Dr Thomas Wilson (? 1525–81) M.P. for Lincoln city 1571–81; and Sir Thomas Heneage (1532–95) M.P. for Stamford October 1553 and, returned both for Boston and Lincolnshire in 1562–63, he preferred to sit as knight of the shire,[119] which seat he held until 1583. Robert Monson, one of the family of Burton and South Carlton, was probably the most independent minded of the three, though it is difficult to say how far he pressed specifically Lincoln problems. Sir Thomas Heneage may well have done more for the city, but Monson was a fearless critic in the House: in the autumn of 1566 he was very outspoken in pressing upon the Queen that she should marry, and so earned her majesty's displeasure, but this did not prevent his appointment as a justice of Common Pleas in 1572.

Dr Thomas Wilson was undoubtedly the most learned member who sat for any Lincolnshire constituency in the sixteenth century. He came from a family established in Washingborough. From his appointment to the privy council on 12 November 1577 and as secretary of state he played an active part in the business of the lower house, but even before that date he had been a prominent member. In 1571[120] he had spoken on a bill to control vagabonds, and his speech on usury must have been one of the longest made in the House at this period, for it takes up 2½ columns in Sir Simonds D'Ewes's *Journals*.[121] Wilson was a national rather than a Lincolnshire figure, a man who may well have lost touch to some extent with the county of his birth, but he sat for Lincoln in the last five years of his life when his power was at its zenith.

Sir Thomas Heneage, a privy councillor from 5 September 1587 until his death in 1595, did not sit for a Lincolnshire seat during the time of his great influence as vice-chamberlain of the queen's household. But he had Lincolnshire roots, though his life, like his father's before him, lay in official circles. He was the son of Robert Heneage who had been surveyor of woods and had been returned for Stamford at an early age. By 1571 we find him as a hearer of petitions and on committees of the House,[122] and the following year he was on a committee that discussed the situation of Mary queen of Scots.[123] But after he had become knight of the shire for Essex (in 1585) he continued to have an interest

[119] *Ibid.*, p. 82.   [120] *Ibid.*, p. 165.   [121] *Ibid.*, p. 173.
[122] *Ibid.*, p. 189.   [123] *Ibid.*, p. 206.

in his native county for on 18 March 1589 he introduced a bill for the
relief of Lincoln.[124] Of the Cecil representation little can be said that
refers specifically to the county. Sir Thomas sat on a committee on
24 February 1576 while he was representing Stamford, but the intervention of the various Cecil M.P.s was usually upon matters of national
rather than local significance.

[124] *Ibid.*, p. 448.

CHAPTER VIII

LOCAL GOVERNMENT

THE detailed history of the local government of the shire, as distinct from that of the boroughs, cannot be written in the absence of the justices' sessions records. So vital a part was played in local government by the J.P.s, that the lack of petty and quarter sessions' records inevitably means that nothing beyond the generalizations which have already been made can be written. Of other officials with jurisdictions over the whole county, either in itself, or as part of a group of shires, such as coroners, escheators, tax-collectors, purveyors, lords lieutenant, a little can be said, although the functions of many of their offices affected individuals rather than the community as a whole and, to that extent, they cannot be regarded truly as local government officials. Our lack of evidence of the day-to-day activities of the justices is all the more serious because it means that we cannot pinpoint the changes in local government that were effected during the Tudor period and which were described by the late Sir William Holdsworth in the following words: 'by the latter part of the sixteenth century the conduct of the local government of the country had definitely passed from the old communities of township, hundred, and shire, to the justices of the peace assisted by the sheriffs, coroners, and constables'.[1]

The role played by the lord lieutenant in local government was largely a military one since his was the ultimate responsibility for calling out the muster when ordered. Men might be mustered to meet a local threat or they might be called upon to serve far away from the county. The troubles, especially those in Ireland, that vexed the later years of Elizabeth's reign had their effect upon the shire, for the county was expected to provide men to serve there. In 1602 the shire had to levy 200 men to be sent to Chester. The shortness of the notice made it impossible to get them there by 20 April, but they fulfilled the quota a little later and collected £750, an average of £3 15s. a man.[2] As there was no lord lieutenant at that time, commissioners undertook the levying and mustering of the men: Thomas, lord Clinton, Charles, lord Willoughby

---

[1] Holdsworth, *op. cit.*, London, 4th edn. 1935, III, p. 601.
[2] LAO, microfilm copy of two papers relating to the mustering of 200 men.

of Parham, John Savile, John Bolle himself a commander in Ireland,[3] William Wray, and Nicholas Saunderson, also implicated in Ireland,[3] were in charge.

Not only, however, did the lord lieutenant have to find men to serve, he had also to obtain monetary contributions towards the defence of the county, usually by way of loans which were frequently disguised gifts to the Crown. In March 1588, in the face of the gathering storm, privy seals were sent into Lincolnshire to 115 people demanding in effect that they should lend to the Crown certain sums of money.[4] These sums ranged from a maximum of £100 to a minimum of £25. Only two men were asked to subscribe £100, Robert Carr of Sleaford and Thomas Cony of Bassingthorpe, although they should not therefore be dubbed the two wealthiest inhabitants. A dozen, George St Paul, William Hamby of Tathwell, John Smith of Kelby, Nicholas Thornedike of Greenfield, Francis Copledyke of Harrington, Robert Grantham of Dunham, Thomas Taylor of Lincoln (later of Doddington), Sir George Heneage, Sir John Monson, John Savile, Charles Hussey of Linwood, a nephew of the attainted peer, and Richard Bowles of Boston paid £50. The remaining 101, among whom appear Skipwiths, Heneages, Tyrwhits, and Dymokes, contributed £25 to the loan. Captains brought soldiers to the musters, and gentlemen had to muster with their household servants. On 13 June 1580[5] the lord treasurer, the earls of Lincoln and Rutland, lord Willoughby, the lord chief justice, the mayor of Lincoln, four esquires, Robert Monson, Richard Bertie, Philip Tyrwhit, and Anthony Thorold, the recorder Stephen Thimbleby, and six aldermen—George Porter, Richard Carter, William Goodknapp, Martin Mason, Thomas Dawson and Thomas Hanson—received orders to take musters in the city of Lincoln. In June 1587,[6] 300 recruits for the Low Countries were raised from the shire, and the next year in August, 700 foot and 30 horse had to reinforce the troops in the North under the earl of Huntingdon.[7] Such were the duties of the lords lieutenant and their deputies assisted by special commissioners and by the justices.

The working of local government in the city of Lincoln and in some of the boroughs in the county can be more closely followed because records exist that make this possible. For Lincoln the minutes of the meetings of the Common Council which are collected together in one book for the thirty-year period from 1511 to 1541,[8] continue in a second

[3] Lincs. Pedigrees, p. 151.
[4] BM Lansdowne MS. 81 (55); T. C. Noble (ed.), The Names of those Persons who subscribed towards the Defence of this Country . . . 1588, London, 1886, pp. 37-40.
[5] APC XII, pp. 55-6.   [6] Ibid., XV, p. 119.   [7] Ibid., XVI, p. 231.
[8] LAO L1/1/1/1.

volume covering the years 1542 to 1564[9] and a third book almost completes the Tudor period as it contains items of business down to Michaelmas 1599.[10,11] The so-called White Book,[12] which begins at 1421, although it contains some items of business, is rather a register relating to properties between that year and 1729. It is, however, primarily important for its 'custemare' or code of customs which determined the government of the city. This was drawn up, although certainly following earlier tradition, in 1480 and these were the rules that were in force during the Tudor era. Certain changes in government had sprung from Henry IV's conferring upon the city in 1409 the status of a county, which had resulted in the conversion of the two bailiffs into sheriffs, and by 1421 specific rules as to business had emerged.[13] When a motion was advanced by the mayor he had to call twelve of his compeers (*i.e.* alderman), twenty-four of the more approved citizens and forty men (ten from each ward) and these groups of the twelve, the twenty-four, and the forty had powers to argue and object to articles submitted to them. When the decision of the twenty-four and the forty had been arrived at, they submitted it to the mayor and the twelve aldermen. In the sixteenth century the 'Secret Council', composed of the mayor, aldermen, and sheriffs, frequently met in the Inner Hall for the conduct of business.[14]

Three records enable us to obtain a clearer picture of the government of Tudor Lincoln. Reference has already been made to the customs[15] that were 'compiled and drawn out of French into English by Thomas Grantham' in the time of Robert Huddleston's mayoralty and William Long's and Henry Higden's shrievalty. Among the customs that Grantham preserved was the form of the freeman's oath and the form of the mayor's election. The mayor was to be chosen on the day of the Exaltation of the Holy Cross (14 September) and all the franchise men were to assemble. Those who had passed the mayoral chair were to sit on the bench and the sheriffs within the Chequer, while the mayor sitting with those who had been mayors was to make a calendar (short list) of four men's names of which none had been mayor within the last seven years. The freemen then named two out of the four, and the mayor and sheriffs together were to choose one to be mayor out of the two so named. If the man chosen refused to be mayor he was to be imprisoned for a whole year and have his goods sequestrated for that

[9] LAO L1/1/1/2.   [10] LAO L1/1/1/.
[11] The major items of all these volumes are calendared in HMC *14th Report, App., pt. VIII,* 1895, pp. 24–75.
[12] LAO L1/3/1.
[13] J. W. F. Hill, 'The Corporation of the City of Lincoln', LAAS 36, 1923–25, pp. 177–232.
[14] *Ibid.*, p. 192.   [15] LAO L1/3/1 ff. 46v–59.

period, at the end of which time he was to be sent out of the city for ever. With the sheriff a short list of six was prepared and two were selected: if they refused to serve, their goods within the liberties were to be seized for the king. The mayor took up his office at noon on Michaelmas day (29 September) for twelve months, and on the following Monday the J.P.s, coroners, members of the Common Council (the twenty-four), and the common clerks took their oaths before him. The duties of the various officers, the sheriffs, aldermen, J.P.s, common councillors, coroners, and chamberlains are all set down in detail. The common clerk kept the register, and other officials included the sheriff's clerk and his bailiff, the common sergeant, the sword-bearer, and the city swineherd. Each ward had a constable and under-constable while the chief constable served in the East ward.

The judicial powers of the city were considerable. No man was to be chosen a J.P. unless he had been mayor and none was to be a coroner unless he had served the office of sheriff, but if he were so chosen without having been a sheriff he had to be worth at least 40s. a year. A court known as the Burghmanmote was to be held before the mayor and sheriffs every Monday, except immediately following Michaelmas and Low Sunday, for the hearing of personal pleas and those concerning property, and the same court sat on Thursdays for the trial of cases with a jury and for special inquiries and inquests. As was common practice, no freeman was allowed to implead another freeman in any court except the Burghmanmote, unless in a cause that was not pleadable there. If he did so he was liable to lose the freedom of the city and, moreover, inhabitants of Lincoln who were not freemen had to use the court or else be subject to a penalty of 20s. Details of the procedures to be followed especially in cases of debt are laid down. A debtor was permitted three essoins, that is to say, he could absent himself on three occasions before he had to answer the charge. Procedure is also laid down for the examination of those accused of trespass, and the penalty for anyone convicted of an affray was 20d. There were at least two prisons for we read that no non-freeman should be put in 'the chamber called "franchist mans prison" unless he be a priest, gentlemen, or a clerk within orders.'[16]

Questions of property and other rights inevitably filled much of the time of the court of Burghmanmote. A woman who engaged in a craft was to be treated as a *femme sole* in law as regards the operation and the tools of her craft. The court also was one in which wills were to be enrolled. Any questions concerning lands and tenements in the city were brought before it. Any man or woman who was disseissed of lands or tenements might have an assize of fresh force which was to be

[16] *Ibid.*, f. 55.

taken within forty days of the actual disseisin, and this provision afforded speedy redress for any allegedly wrong dispossession. At the next court of Burghmanmote, after the sheriff had attached the disseisor, a jury was to be empanelled, and the procedure was that of an assize of novel disseisin. Because Lincoln claimed to have the same privileges as the city of London, the inhabitants were able to give or devise lands in the city contrary to the statute of mortmain, but upon making these gifts or bequests to ecclesiastical corporations they had to pay 20s. to the Common Chamber, otherwise such transactions were void. All land in the city was held of the Crown in burgage tenure. These passages in the White Book contain many by-laws, in particular those which forbade the deposit of 'muck, earth, rammell (rubbish), or other filth' on the streets. From St Thomas's day (21 December) until Twelfth Night the Christmas jollifications extended so far that no one was to be arrested or have his goods attached in the city in any personal action except by the king's writ. The White Book also contains copies of the charter of 1424, and Edward IV's confirmation, upon which the customs and privileges of the city were based, and from which sprang the forms of procedure that tell so much about the local government of Lincoln.

The second record is one that defines the area over which the city corporation had jurisdiction. It was very large. Within less than a year of the opening of the Tudor period, Richard III issued letters patent[17] incorporating within the city the villages of Washingborough, Heighington, Fiskerton, Cherry Willingham, Greetwell, and Burton-by-Lincoln, but this charter was never effective.[18] Bracebridge, Branston, Waddington, and Canwick were, however, already part of the medieval city by a grant of 1466,[19] and these additions meant that the area of the city's jurisdiction was over six miles across at its widest extent. The third record is not a document but a record in stone. The Guildhall placed over the Stonebow is of late fifteenth-century date, and may not have been finished until the first decade of the sixteenth century.[20] If this dating is correct, with the beginning of the continuous record of municipal proceedings in 1511, the election of a new town clerk Richard Hunston about the same year and a new recorder Richard Clarke in 1512, it is possible that municipal government, if it did not take a fresh turn, may have been refurbished at the beginning of the

[17] HMC *14th Rep., App., pt. VIII*, p. 14 says 2 December 1484, but there is no record on the Patent Roll according to *Cal. Pat. Rolls, 1476–85*.

[18] J. W. F. Hill, *Medieval Lincoln*, London, 1948, p. 285.

[19] *Cal. Pat. Rolls, 1461–7*, p. 499.

[20] N. Pevsner and J. Harris, *The Buildings of England: Lincolnshire*, Penguin Books, 1964, p. 148.

sixteenth century. Both the town clerk, known as the common clerk, and the recorder, once elected, held office for life.

We are able then to follow the continuous history of the administration of the city from 1511. At the beginning of each year in late September the names of the mayor and other officials for the ensuing year are recorded. The headings of the register are usually in Latin but the business is written in English. So the first folio commences, to translate, 'the Register of Robert Alanson mayor of the city of Lincoln and of Christopher Burton and Robert Mylner sheriffs from the feast of St Michael Archangel in the third year of the reign of Henry VIII (1511) until the same feast through one whole year.' There follow the names of the aldermen, thirteen including the mayor; the names of the justices for the year, four in number; the names of the chamberlains of the four wards, South, East, West, and North; and a heading, 'the names of the paviors' although none was appointed that year. Neither the coroners nor the head constable were entered in the record, but the names of the common clerk, Richard Hunston, and the sheriffs' clerk, Bartholomew Willesford, the sword-bearer, John Ingylbright, and the bearer of the bell (town crier), Richard Hygdon, were all sworn along with the chamberlains. For some reason no swineheard and no cowherd were appointed that year.

The first Common Council of Alanson's mayoralty was held on 8 October 1511[21] when, in addition to the mayor and the recorder, thirty members were present, and the principal item of business was to hear the new mayor take his oath of office. Then it was agreed that twenty-four discreet and honest persons should be chosen who, along with the twelve aldermen, should have full authority to make ordinances for the 'common profit' of the city. These common councillors had to forfeit a sum of money if they failed to put in an appearance at Council meetings. The common seal of the city was to be in the custody of Robert Dighton, a man who had been thrice mayor (1494, 1506, 1510) and who must have been well known and trusted by the municipal establishment of the early sixteenth century.

The poverty of the city comes clearly through the pages of the minute book: various citizens are continually coming to its aid and paying its debts. During Mr Dighton's period of office as mayor 1510–11, he gave 10 marks (£6 13s. 4d.) towards paying off the debts that the corporation owed to one Robert Wymark, and in return he was allowed between 1511 and 1514 to provide once to the sheriffship.[22] The remainder of the debt to Wymark was paid out of the rents of two closes that Thomas Burton and John Fox held of the city.

One of the problems that Lincoln had to face at this period was pres-

[21] LAO Li/i/i/i, f. iv.   [22] Ibid., f. 2.

sure put upon it by magnates—pressures that were not unconnected with the city's poverty. In 1511, Sir John Hussey (later lord Hussey) sent his brother Robert with a letter about the choice of Christopher Burton of Branston as sheriff to which election he objected. Branston was one of the outlying villages over which the degree of the city's control was in dispute. At the council meeting on 12 October a reply to Sir John was agreed upon which insisted that Christopher Burton should perform the duties of his office, but conceded that, in return for a payment of £20 into the Common Chamber, the householders of Branston should for ever be discharged from the obligation to be sheriff. They had, however, to continue to pay scot and lot which the authorities said was granted to the city by charter. Citizens of Lincoln were not to 'flit or remove their goods to Branston by fraud' for if they did so they were still liable, but otherwise the inhabitants of Branston were exempt from being mayor, sheriff, or chamberlain and were not in fact to be called to serve any office without the consent of Sir John Hussey, his heirs, and assigns.[23]

The challenge from Thomas Manners, who became twelfth lord Ros in 1513, after the death of his father who had become eleventh baron in 1512 following the death of his maternal uncle in 1508 and of his maternal aunt (a co-heiress with him) in 1512, and who inherited a claim to £100 *per annum* to be paid by the city of Lincoln, was much more serious. During the time of the tenth baron's insanity between 1492 and 1508, his affairs had been managed by his sister's husband, Sir Thomas Lovell, and he had demanded nothing from the city for many years and only took 20 marks out of the £100.[24] Presumably between 1508 and 1512 this happy state of affairs had continued, and apparently the eleventh lord Ros had not received any payment, but Thomas Manners, the twelfth baron, a royal favourite whose star was rising fast in the early 1520s and who was created earl of Rutland in 1525, began to demand his rights. This probably followed the death of Sir Thomas Lovell who had been granted control of the Ros lands for his lifetime. The fee farm, originally a payment by the city for the collection of royal dues itself, whereby it excluded royal tax-collectors, had at some time become payable to the Ros family, but Edward IV appreciating the city's poverty had excused it from the £100 a year payment to lord Ros. From that time and throughout Richard III's reign no payments were made,[25] and Henry VII, understanding that the city was 'seven or nine parts' in ruin and that 200 houses were decayed, it is implied, scaled down the payments. On 7 September 1528—the dispute had been going on since 1524—it was stated that scarcely £30[26] could be collected, and the following month it was agreed to pay no

[23] *Ibid.*, f. 6.   [24] *Ibid.*, f. 166v.   [25] *Ibid.*, ff. 207, 208.   [26] *Ibid.*

more than 20 marks to lord Ros, thus continuing the same rate as had been paid to Sir Thomas Lovell.[27] The dispute dragged on and gave an opportunity to lord Ros—he is always so called and never referred to as the earl of Rutland—to intervene in the election of the new recorder after Richard Clarke's death in April 1530; at any rate Thomas Moigne was the only candidate for election in 1532. Eventually, help was given in the payment of the fee farm rent at the expense of the Church for, in 1544, Henry VIII by impropriating to the city certain benefices provided an income from which the levy might be paid.[28] But Rutland influence remained strong, and the second earl had constantly to be placated usually by gifts of fish which he certainly received in 1550,[29] and with the nomination of one of the burgesses in parliament and a tun of claret in 1553.[30] In 1558 a final settlement was arrived at whereby the city's liabilities to the earl were satisfied by granting him the parsonage of Surfleet and a payment of £300.[31] Nevertheless, the question was still being discussed in 1574, when it was finally settled by a payment of £300 to the third earl.[32]

One of the functions of local government in the sixteenth century, as in the twentieth, was to collect rates. Money was essential to run local government and the city fathers of Lincoln had difficulty in obtaining enough of it. As well as the fee farm granted to the earl of Rutland's ancestors, the city had to pay £80 a year to the dean and chapter, and in February 1542 it was averred that only £20 per annum could be levied.[33] The householders of Lincoln were liable for the payment of a due known as buscage. It may have been collected in instalments, for on 5 April 1512 half the last buscage was to be gathered from every parish by Thursday in Whit week (3 June), and at a council meeting on the latter day it was decided that a new buscage should be levied and gathered in with the old buscage and the money received be devoted to the payment for the new charter.[34] In 1532 a new buscage was levied to pay the burgesses' expenses at the last parliament.[35] Of course, the council not only had to levy money to maintain the costs of local government but also to subscribe to national taxation. The city was so impoverished, and every indicator we have confirms this poverty in the early sixteenth century, that it had been exempt from payments of fifteenths and tenths until 1540–41 when it had been charged for four fifteenths and tenths and had to find £400 in four years. This levy compelled the council to petition the king in February 1542 to appropriate revenues to the dean and chapter so that the city might be

[27] Ibid.   [28] HMC 14th Rep., App., pt. VIII, p. 39.   [29] Ibid., p. 43.
[30] Ibid., p. 47.   [31] Ibid., p. 49.
[32] Ibid., p. 66; J. W. F. Hill, Tudor and Stuart Lincoln, p. 73.
[33] LAO L1/1/1/1, f. 289v.   [34] Ibid., f. 5v.   [35] Ibid., f. 220.

relieved of the £80 a year that it had to pay to that body. The corporation did however have other resources besides taxation. It had land and property which presumably brought in considerable rents. At any rate disputes arose over rents, for arbitrators had to be appointed over the payments from lessees of the New Closes in 1511.[36] The following year a lease of a pasture called 'Frereholme' was made to Robert Smyth, a mercer, for sixty-one years, later amended to forty-one years, at a rent of 16s. *per annum*, and throughout the proceedings of the Common Council, records of leases are fairly common. In 1523 the tavern under the Stonebow was let to William Archbold for 8s. a year.[37]

The reasons why the council wanted money were varied. One expense that it had to bear was the renewal of the charter; it was always a wise precaution to obtain an *inspeximus* and confirmation of the city's privileges from each new monarch. In January 1515 an interesting breakdown of the costs of renewal occurs.[38] The four skins cost four nobles each, that is, in total, £5 6s. 8d., the fee for examining the charter £1 6s. 8d., the lace 1s. 4d., the fee for the man who prepared the wax 8d., the seal £1 0s. 4d., the enrolling of the new charter £4, and a payment to the king in the chancery, at the king's pleasure but at least £4. This comes to at least £15 15s. 8d.[39] probably in the region of £6,000 in modern money. Another heavy expense connected with the Crown was the king's visit to Lincoln in 1541. At a meeting of the council held on 9 July 1541 it was decided to present to the king twenty fat oxen and a hundred fat sheep, which gift would set the city back £50; the whole commonalty had to bear the cost. The king's arms were to be set up on Bargate and on the south side of the Guildhall, and the aldermen who had passed the mayoral chair were to wear scarlet gowns although these were to be paid for at their own expense. On 9 August when the king and queen (Katherine Howard) arrived about 4 p.m. they were met at the border of the city franchise area by the mayor and recorder who conducted them to the bishop's palace. They made the gift to the king, and the queen had a present of pike, tench, and bream worth £7. Another charge on the city funds was the maintenance and expenses of its representatives in parliament. The Foss dyke which had fallen into disrepair was a further call on the city's resources: the mayor laid out £17 in 1521[40] to keep men on the work, but most of this expenditure may have been recovered as men were sent to Hull and York to gather money for the work, as we have seen, and a collection had been made in the city as early as June 1518 towards its cleaning and repair.[41]

[36] *Ibid.*, f. 1v.   [37] HMC *14th Rep., App. pt. VIII*, p. 31.
[38] LAO L1/1/1/1, f. 40v.   [39] HMC *14th Rep. op. cit.*, p. 275.
[40] LAO L1/1/1/1, f. 115v.   [41] HMC *14th Rep. op. cit.*, p. 26.

Not many of the functions of local government were the same in the sixteenth century as they are today but one of the tasks was the preservation of law and order. The constables were primarily charged with these duties, and in June 1512 they were ordered to produce lists of all the able-bodied men in their parishes.[42] Five years later every constable was to instruct the under-constables in each parish to make search for vagabonds and certify to the mayor the names of men and women who were idle and would not work,[43] and in 1525 the threat of vagabonds was still a real one. In the Secret Council meeting of 27 November 1515 the councillors decreed organization by wards against vagabonds. Disorder might often arise from too much drinking, and in 1553 the number of tippling houses was limited to thirty.[44] Another facet of the law and order problem was that the mayor was ultimately responsible for levying troops which might have to meet the king's demands for service. In 1512–13 we find that a group of between three and seven parishes was responsible for the supplying of body armour for one soldier. There were six groupings, one of which included the franchise men resident in the Bail and those of the four out-towns. The mayor took the muster of the 'sawdyors' in St Hugh Croft on Monday 2 May 1513.

The promotion of ceremonial was another function of the mayor and his brethren particularly with regard to St Anne's gild. St Anne's was a religious gild to which free men and women could belong, and like all such bodies it mounted pageants. The spontaneous success of these seems to have been somewhat doubtful if we are to take seriously the injunctions that sanctions would be taken against those who did not support them. In 1515 the plague made it difficult for the warden of the gild (the graceman) to hire garments from knights and gentlemen, and every alderman had to provide two gowns, and every sheriff and chamberlain one gown each.[45] Three years later every alderman under pain of paying 6s. 8d. was to provide a servant with a lighted torch for the procession on St Anne's day (26 July) and the constables were to wait on the procession or else forfeit 12d. In 1525 the aldermen were each to supply a gown of silk for the Kings, but continual complaints were made that people were not supporting the pageants as they should. Every trade had to be urged to put on a good show at the pageant or else forfeit the large sum of £10. The lack of support in the 1520s for the gild pageant on St Anne's day was perhaps rather an indicator of the poverty in the city and of the decline in its population than a sign of any anti-religious feeling. The city waits or musicians also had to be maintained at the city's expense, and although they were

[42] LAO L1/1/1/1, f. 3v.   [43] Ibid., f. 70v.   [44] HMC 14th Rep. op. cit., p. 47.
[45] Ibid., p. 25.

IX Louth steeple. Among the late medieval building projects, Louth tower
(late fifteenth century) and spire (1501–15) stand pre-eminent. At 295
feet high, it is the tallest in the county and represents the final flourish of
ecclesiastical architecture in Lincolnshire.

X Boston Grammar School, dated 1567; one of a number of borough schools built in Lincolnshire during the sixteenth century. The roof is restored.

(a) Six-poster alabaster tomb-chest and canopy of Sir Thomas St. Pol, described in 1564 as 'earnest in religion' (died 1582), and his wife in Snarford Church. Colourful and 'jolly' (to use Pevsner's description).

(b) Alabaster tomb of Sir Edward Ayscough (died 1612) and his wife in Stallingborough Church.

XI Tudor effigies

XII Tudor effigies: (a) Tomb of Sir William Cecil, Lord Treasurer of England (died 1598), in St. Martin's Church, Stamford. (b) The pretentious monument to Richard Bertie (died 1582) and his wife, the former Duchess of Suffolk (died 1580): 'a most remarkable monument'. This photograph shows the east-facing side of what amounts to a wall, built within an arched opening. The west side is covered with Biblical texts; on the east side, a monk and two 'wild men' (an emblem used by the Willoughby family) provide the setting for small busts of Bertie and his wife.

XIII Tudor memorials: (a) A humble memorial to Alice Smith (died 1605) in Keelby Church. (b) Monument to Sir William Pelham, soldier and lord justice of Ireland (died 1587), in Brocklesby Church. The alabaster was highly coloured.

XIV Tudor memorials: an alabaster tablet to Sir Francis Velles de Guevara, a Spanish gentleman who settled in Lincolnshire and died in 1592. This is one of two such monuments in Stenigot Church.

XV Tudor plate: typical of much of the new post-Reformation plate provided to Lincolnshire churches in the 1570s, apparently by John Morley of Lincoln, these chalices belong to Roxby Church.

XVI The Sudbury Hutch. This chest in Louth Church, given by Thomas Sudbury some time before 1504, is decorated with portraits which are alleged to be those of Henry VII and his queen Elizabeth of York.

down to two in number at one time, a band of musicians was always available for civic functions.

Tricky disputes over jurisdiction arose from time to time as certain privileged areas existed within the city over which the mayor's writ did not run. The Bail, the Close, a liberty known as Beaumont's Rent or Fee were three such regions.[46] On 10 September 1512, Paul Brandys a citizen had been attached for debt in the Close by John Barnes, porter and officer of the Close, at the suit of one William Willesford of the Bail for the sum of £3 and Brandys was put in gaol in the Close. Thence he escaped and Barnes came to the mayor to ask for his prisoner, but the mayor did not know where he was, and then the officer of the Close along with the mayor's officer went into Beaumont Rent but there they could not touch the escapee. After the archdeacon had been called in and further moves made, Brandys agreed to leave the liberty of his own free will and return to face justice in the Close. The inhabitants of the Bail apparently paid buscage since arrangements were made in 1512 for collecting it at rates varying from 1d. to 6s. 8d. from eighty residents in that area[47] and when they failed to return their precept (writ) ordering them to pay the subsidy they were fined £20.[48]

But one of the main duties of the city government was to maintain the economic prosperity of Lincoln. This was a difficult task since the decline of Lincoln's cloth industry from the late fourteenth century, and its reduced importance as a centre for the purchase of wool, had subjected the city to growing poverty and consequently to a decline in population. Opportunities for gainful employment did not exist, and throughout the fifteenth and most of the sixteenth centuries continual pleas of poverty were advanced in order to seek a reduction in the tax burden that the city had to bear. Exemptions from royal taxation were frequent in the fifteenth century and generally helpful, but they did not solve the question of how to attract more industry or more apprentices to the city. One of the traditional methods of fostering trade was to favour natives as against 'foreigners'. The bakers were specifically protected in 1524 when it was laid down that only freemen of the city could sell bread and that not even apprentices and journeymen could bake until they had their freedom.[49] The previous year the council minute book recorded the signs of all fifteen bakers in the city and presumably this fairly small number had a monopoly.[50] It is easily forgotten how strict municipal control was over the various crafts for, in 1524, detailed instructions were given that allowed the bakers to bake

---

[46] On the Close and the Bail see Hill, *Medieval Lincoln*, pp. 99–102, 123–9, *et al.*
[47] LAO L1/1/1/1, f. 13.   [48] *Ibid.*, f. 17.   [49] *Ibid.*, f. 164.
[50] There are photographs of bakers' marks in Hill, *Tudor and Stuart Lincoln*, London, 1956, plate 2 at p. 30.

white bread in Lent, provided they served the city and suburbs with wastel, cracknel, simnels, and cocket bread. In the victualling trades and especially in the supply of bread and ale the municipality, like all others, exercised statutory control over prices. The assize of bread was given to the bakers in the form of the price of a quarter of wheat, and the size and quality of the 'standard loaf' would vary according to the price of the quarter of wheat or other grain. Between 1513 and 1518, the assize given to bakers varied between 5s. and 8s. 6d. per quarter of wheat, in June 1520 it was 12s. 6d., at Michaelmas 15s. 6d., in 1522 it rose to 24s. a quarter, then in 1523 it fell to 5s. In 1527 the assize was 4s. 6d., on 15 December 1532 it was 13s. 6d. The records do not show a fixing every year but they may well be defective in this regard as at some periods it is obvious that the city fathers exercised close control. The explanation of the violent fluctuations in corn prices belongs rather to economic history than to the history of local government, but the municipality was ever mindful of the unsettling effect that high food prices might have upon the citizens, and strove to control them as far as possible with a view to minimizing the chance of riots. Similarly with ale, the municipality exercised price control. The price of a gallon of ale was fixed at various times at 2d., 2½d. and 3d. The cost of candles for lighting, thatch, turf and wood for fuel, and of building materials was also of great importance, particularly to the poorer citizens, and so attempts were made to control the price of these commodities in the 1550s and 1560s.[51]

Efforts to encourage the growth of crafts in the city consisted of some reorganization of the gilds and some relaxation in apprenticeship regulations. After the confirmation of the charter by Henry VIII in 1515, all the crafts, except the gilds of weavers and cordwainers which claimed royal charters, were reviewed and they drew up new rules that were approved by the Common Council since their powers derived from the city. Some amalgamation took place for the numbers of masters in some crafts were not large enough to support a full scale organization: one such was the gild of smiths, ironmongers, armourers, spurriers, cutlers, and wire-drawers; another, the glovers, girdlers, skinners, pinners, point-makers, scriveners, and parchment-makers. The admission of boys to learn various crafts was strictly controlled. Year by year boys were enrolled before the mayor or his deputy, and from these very full returns a picture can be established of the economic health or sickness of various trades. The rule about enrolment, laid down in 1525, was that all masters should enrol their apprentices within a year, and if they did not do so the apprentice was free to go to another master by the advice and control of the mayor and council. But ten

[51] Hill, *Tudor and Stuart Lincoln*, pp. 83-4.

years later masters could obtain a grace to enrol the boy even though it was out of time. No master appears throughout the years 1511 to 1541 to have been seriously penalized for non-observance of these rules: instances of delays in enrolment of up to three years are not infrequent.

It was in the general interest of the city's economy to encourage apprenticeship, but not to the extent where there would be large numbers of qualified men who could not find work since that would have fostered potential disorder. Very few masters therefore had more than one apprentice since, if they turned out too many qualified men, the risk of redundancy among the skilled labour force would have been considerable. The term of apprenticeship varied from one trade to another, from one master to another, and from one apprentice to another. How else can we explain the apprenticeship of four glovers in 1516, one for fourteen years, one for eight years, and two for seven years? It may be that the boy apprenticed for fourteen years—a uniquely long period—was younger than the other three, but on that we have no information. By far the most frequently found term is seven years: of 259 apprentices enrolled between 1511 and 1541, 126 or 48·6 per cent served for this period, 18·1 per cent served for eight years, and 4·2 per cent for nine years. The duration of apprenticeship is not recorded in some instances, but it can safely be said that over three-quarters of the boys served for a period of seven to nine years. Perhaps it was a form of cheap labour since it is difficult to believe that any but the dullest boy would need so long to learn some of the crafts.

During the years between 1511 and 1541 the masters of thirty-five different crafts took on apprentices. Again our statistics are not complete for, if we exclude the last two years when the records are defective, the craft affiliation of eleven apprentices is omitted although it is not likely that the number of thirty-five different crafts would be greatly increased. An analysis of these apprenticeships indicates that the leather-working crafts took on more boys than any others. The cordwainers apprenticed twenty, the glovers twenty, the tanners, seventeen although strangely, only one saddler's apprentice is recorded. In fact the glovers of Lincoln attracted apprentice boys from considerable distances; eight of them coming from places between 50 and 150 miles from the city. These figures clearly indicate the flourishing state of the leather preparing and manufacturing trades which is to be expected in a town that, because of the livestock farming in parts of the county, would have had a good supply of raw materials. The other branch of trade that was flourishing in early sixteenth-century Lincoln was the metal-working industry. The smiths took on eighteen apprentices in this period, the braziers, twelve, and the pewterers nine. Lincoln, as the county town and as a place of some size, even though its population was declining, had a number of wealthy residents, and attracted into it many of the near-by gentry. Hence mercers and tailors flourished: the former took on eighteen, the latter fifteen apprentices. Food demands meant that the victualling trades flourished moderately: the bakers enrolled seventeen and the butchers eight apprentices. But the lack of apprentices in the building trades (only four tilers, four carpenters, one sawyer) demonstrates clearly that maintenance work was probably all that was required. The complaints of the decline of the clothing trade made by the council are fully borne out by the pitiably small number of apprentices. In thirty years only three weavers, three fullers, and two dyers were enrolled to learn their respective trades. The dyers' fortunes apparently revived in the 1560s,[52] but the cloth trade was still stagnant and negotiations were entered into in 1591 with a Mr Grene of Boston who promised to give employment to 400 poor people in the wool trade. A decade earlier the city council had established a knitting school.

From a reading of the council minutes there emerges clearly the cantankerous nature of many of the city rulers in the Tudor period. Frequently the real causes of the numerous quarrels are not specifically stated for these disputes were usually dealt with in the Inner Chamber and the minute of record is tantalizingly general. The quarrels are obviously sometimes reflections of the power struggles that went on in a small closed body, struggles sometimes fanned by outside influences. In 1511 Thomas Norton had declared that Francis Whytwell had not been lawfully elected chamberlain, whereupon he was committed to ward and had to apologize to the mayor and Common Council for his seditious sayings. Some years later John Hutchinson alleged that Mr Norton had committed perjury and, although sent to prison, he continued to use opprobrious words against the mayor and aldermen: eventually he submitted but we have no clue as to what the discord was about. The authorities complained of opprobrious words against the mayor and council by Thomas Hart in 1524: it seems as if the city fathers were rather thin-skinned for this complaint was frequently recorded. Earlier, on 19 November 1521 Ralph Smyth, a fisherman, had used seditious words and we know what they were. He alleged that any victualler coming into the city could sell at his pleasure provided he gave the mayor any part or dish of fish, otherwise he would be plundered and cheated.[53] This allegation was more than the establishment could or would stand as it cast grave doubts on its probity. Smyth submitted, was fined, and had to provide sureties to be of good behaviour. Justice may or may not have been done but it was certainly not seen to be done for the whole matter was handled in the Secret

[52] HMC *14th Rep.*, *op. cit.*, p. 55.   [53] LAO Li/1/1/1, f. 125.

Council: the mayor and aldermen were assuredly judge and jury in their own cause.

Why the recorder wanted to resign because of the 'misdemeanours of the best of the city as well as the commonalty' in 1521 is not clear nor do we know what the dean said to him to induce him to continue in office. It may be that he had been disturbed by the energetic mayoralty of Peter Effard between 14 April and Michaelmas 1520 and his continuance in office for the year 1520–21[54] In 1554 David Brian was committed to ward for fourteen days for calling the mayor a false man and a butcherly harlot and the aldermen all false harlots, but he submitted and was fined 40s.[55] On 25 February 1559 William Rotheram, an alderman, justice of the peace and a former mayor, rebuked the mayor and was committed to prison from which he broke out. He was deprived of all his privileges and disfranchised, but the justice of assize quashed his disfranchisement although he was never again to hold office. On 16 March 1573 John Welcome, a former mayor and the current M.P., was deprived of his aldermanship and perpetually barred from office for opprobrious language and factious proceedings and for disclosing to Dr Wilson, his fellow burgess, a secret letter from the mayor and aldermen to Justice Monson, said to be the recorder, although probably by that time he had resigned the office.[56] The mayor's charge was that by revealing the contents of the letter he did his best to turn Dr Wilson against the city and this apparently the corporation did not desire. What the letter contained is not known but it may have been somewhat critical of the learned man who was to become secretary of state. These petty local quarrels had, on occasion, wider significance.

Signs emerge that from the 1560s Lincoln was becoming more prosperous. The decline in its fortunes that had been apparent for nearly 200 years gave way to a period of modest prosperity. Some of the encumbrances were shed, the fee farm business was settled, and relief secured from taxation, and, at the same time, trade took a slight upturn although the clothing industry never recovered its earlier prosperity. In 1562 the city felt itself able to buy a house for the mayor, and expenditure on education, charitable outlays, entertainment, and ceremonial increased. Above all, the continual complaints about poverty that had occurred before Elizabeth's reign seem to diminish and finally to disappear.

It can be assumed that during the Tudor period the problems that the Lincolnshire boroughs had to face were similar to those facing the county town. Of Grantham we have no record and very little information from Stamford. The local government of Great Grimsby cannot be as fully studied as that of Lincoln because the documentation is less

[54] HMC *14th Rep., op. cit.,* p. 48.   [55] *Ibid.,* p. 50.   [56] *Ibid.,* p. 66.

ample.[57] A number of royal charters and letters exist, some court rolls of the mayor's court, and the Court Books that contain copies of letters, receipts, enrolments of deeds, wills, and other documents, but there is nothing like the books of council minutes available for Lincoln.

In the early Tudor period considerable friction arose between the town and the Austin canons at Wellow. Like Lincoln, Grimsby had trouble with the fee farm rent. It had been reduced in 1256 from £111 to £50,[58] and Edward II, had granted it to the ancestors of the earl of Westmorland. Although it is difficult to ascertain precisely how the claim had come down from Edmund of Woodstock, earl of Kent, to the Nevilles, earls of Westmorland, Henry VII undoubtedly recognized its validity when he announced to the earl that the town could not afford to pay. The king proposed to make a survey of the town's value,[59] as the corporation was threatening to surrender all its liabilities and in that event no fee farm rent would have been payable to the earl.[60] On 4 March 1500 the fee farm was granted for life to Edith the widow of Ralph Neville as part of a gift that her father-in-law Ralph, the third earl, had given to her late husband,[61] but the threat to surrender the privileges had been made some ten years previously.[62] On that occasion the mayor and twenty-one burgesses had threatened to surrender to the king if the earl demanded more than £30 out of the £50, the lower figure being presumably the maximum that could be raised. The extent is referred to and thus it would appear that £30 was the agreed payment to the earl who was pressing for the original figure. In fact in 1487, the town had threatened to surrender its charter if the earl demanded more than £26 13s. 4d.[63] The burgesses were prepared to pay more if more money could be raised but that would have meant doing something to increase the town's prosperity.

Just as Lincoln was suffering a reversal in its fortunes by the diminution of the cloth trade, so Grimsby suffered by the shrinkage in the volume of shipping using the port. The silting up of the harbour was a serious problem, but a gradual one, for up to the middle of the century trade in coal and corn played a significant part in the life of the town and in that of the villages for fifteen to twenty miles around.[64] But despite improvements in the harbour, referred to elsewhere,[65] Grimsby's share of the fish trade was less than in the fifteenth century. The mayor played a vital part in the corn and coal trades since he licensed the export of

[57] *Ibid.*, pp. 237–91.   [58] *Ibid.*, p. 238.
[59] Probably this was done by the commissioners appointed 3 December 1490—*Ibid.*, p. 262.
[60] *Ibid.*, p. 247.   [61] *Cal. Cl. Rolls Hy. VII*, I, p. 355.
[62] HMC *14th Rep.*, *op. cit.*, p. 268.   [63] *Ibid.*, p. 270.
[64] Gillett, *op. cit.*, p. 98.   [65] See *ante* p. 82.

corn and fixed the price of coal. But the second half of the sixteenth century saw a diminishing use of the haven and by 1571–72 only two keels, possibly loaded with turf, another loaded with lime, a crayer with salt, four hoys with coal, a Scottish ship with fish, and three other ships used Grimsby. As the port declined the mainstay of Grimsby's prosperity was its market which met on Wednesdays and Saturdays. As at Lincoln efforts were made to help the victualling trades by prohibiting 'foreigners' to trade: for example only on market days and during St Bartholomew's fair could 'foreigners' sell bread or baked meats in the town.

During the Tudor period the town was governed by a mayor and comburgesses. They held a court which enjoyed leet jurisdiction, and not infrequently it came into conflict with the Admiralty court that had jurisdictional competence in seaports. In fact the lord admiral's authority seriously limited the borough court, and it led to a clash in 1579 when the mayor and burgesses disfranchised Richard Holmes who had been acting for the Admiralty: this in turn led to the intervention of the lord high admiral, lord Clinton. Also, besides the mayor, the town had a bailiff and a treasurer.[66] The fullest evidence for Grimsby is on the judicial side with court books of 1539–48 and 1562–75 that contain the records of many cases of which a large number concerned affrays and bloodshed.[67] The usual quarrels and disputes arose but they seem to have been less frequent than at the county town.

The corporation exercised all the usual controls, regulating the corn supply and controlling the stint of pasture. Pasture was becoming scarce in the late sixteenth century and then an ordinary inhabitant was allowed five sheep and one beast, a burgess twenty sheep and two beasts, one of the 'Twelve' thirty sheep and three beasts, an alderman forty sheep and four cattle, and the mayor, during his year of office, sixty sheep, four beasts, and a horse on the little field. The policy of the council seemed to be to keep the poor away from the town by laying down that no house should be let to more than one tenant. The usual cases of the playing of unlawful games are to be found with a strict prohibition on football, although in 1589 the Reverend Robert Hundleby was alleged to have played it in the streets.[68] Travelling players on the other hand received the blessing of the town fathers: the queen's players performed on 11 June and the earl of Leicester's on 6 August 1572.

Admittance to the freedom of the town, or to burgess status, could apparently be conferred upon men who married women who had that status in virtue of an earlier marriage,[69] but the fee for the purchase of the

[66] HMC *14th Rep.*, *op. cit.*, p. 273.   [67] *Ibid.*, p. 280.
[68] Gillett, *op. cit.*, p. 113.   [69] HMC *14th Rep.*, *op. cit.*, pp. 272–3.

freedom was fixed at 20s.[70] In 1582, all artificers who came to work in the town could do so only if they were admitted by the mayor and his brethren and had to pay 2s. for the privilege. Every shoemaker, tailor, glover, cobbler, smith, weaver, and tinker had to pay 3s. 4d. for admittance if married, and 5s. if single, every pedlar, mercer, and draper 10s. and every merchant venturer 20s. They were not excessive sums and it is apparent that Grimsby wanted to attract workers into the town while giving some advantages to those who were already free.

Boston was an ancient and important port that had reached the height of its prosperity in the thirteenth and early fourteenth centuries but it, like Lincoln and Grimsby, was suffering economic decline at this period. Leland describes vividly the desolation and decay that he found in the late 1530s or early 1540s.[71] It was the result of the abandonment of the port by the Hanseatic merchants possibly in Edward IV's reign,[72] the removal of the Staple, and of the silting up of the port. It is rather remarkable that Boston was not an incorporated borough in its heyday, but it did not receive a charter until 1545 when it was hoped to restore the town to prosperity. It was a forlorn hope for the port, and in the 1570s it was described as 'destitute of ships and trade of shipping.'[73] In the period before 1540 Boston had been dominated by the friars, all four main orders being represented, and by the gilds. The gild of St Mary was predominant and much is known of its working from the accounts of its officials for the year 1525-6 which have survived, and from an inventory made in 1534 of its goods and properties. Other gilds were those of St Peter and St Paul, of Holy Trinity, and of St George. That the granting of the charter was part of a policy of restoration is to be seen from the fact that the new corporation was to annex all Boston's rich gild properties and to spend the proceeds on municipal repairs.[74] Monastic lands and lands of Henry duke of Somerset and Richmond were acquired for £1,646 15s. 4d., and some of the chantry lands that passed to William Parr later marquess of Northampton were given so that he might establish a hospital or almshouse there. But on his attainder the lands reverted to the Crown and they were re-granted to the mayor and burgesses for the establishment and maintenance of a free grammar school.

By the 1545 charter Boston was given a governing body of a mayor, twelve aldermen, and eighteen common councillors. The Assembly Books or minutes of the corporation give us some indication of the problems that the town fathers had to face. Poverty was the main con-

[70] Ibid., p. 273.
[71] L. Toulmin Smith (ed.), Leland's Itinerary, Centaur Press, 1964, IV, pp. 114-15.
[72] Ibid., IV, p. 181.   [73] Pevsner and Harris, op. cit., p. 463.
[74] LP xx, i, g. 846 (87).

cern of the council. Relief from taxation was obtained, as in 1592 when the town was exempt from fifteenths and tenths, and attempts were made to attract new inhabitants, to which reference has already been made.[75] The first mayor and aldermen chose the common council, and the same officers were to choose by majority vote a recorder and town clerk. The aldermen and the men of the common council thereafter elected a new mayor every Lady Day (25 March) and he was to take his oath in the Guildhall before the outgoing mayor, aldermen, councillors, and the recorder on 1 May. The aldermen and councillors held office for life and vacancies were filled as they occurred by the Assembly—a method of election that continued until 1835. The mayor and four aldermen were always to be the justices of the peace for the borough, and the mayor and the recorder together with the two eldest and most discreet of the four aldermen were to form the quorum. They had all the powers of justices in the county, holding quarter sessions, but all records of those sessions between 1545 and 1728 have been lost.

Lord Burghley did his best for the borough. A royal licence to hold two fairs or marts every year, one on St George's day (23rd April) and the two following days, the other on St James's day (25th July) and the two subsequent days. The details of these fairs are unknown to us as there are no Piepowder Court books extant before 1723 although the mayor was clerk of the markets. Another attempt to fight decline was for the corporation to acquire more land and jurisdiction. The manors of Hallgarth, Hussey Hall, and Roos Hall were sold to the mayor and burgesses and, in 1594, the citizens were permitted to enjoy all the rights granted by their charters in areas that extended into the territory of the duchy of Lancaster. But it was an uphill fight. In 1565 there were probably about 470 households in the borough which would indicate a total population of about 2,500, and in the 1570s the approaches to the harbour were difficult because the course of the river Welland through the Deeps had changed.[76] The company of Merchant Venturers of London admitted ten inhabitants of Boston to be members in 1576, and refugees from the Low Countries were arriving in the 1570s, but the problems that local government in Boston had to solve were not alleviated before the eighteenth century.

Of Stamford and Bourne little is known in detail. Stamford, it would appear, was, like Lincoln, Grimsby, and Boston, in decline during the sixteenth century. The town council at Stamford had some similarities to that of Grimsby for local government was in the hands of thirteen comburgesses and a mayor who was known in the south Lincolnshire

[75] See *ante* p. 90.
[76] Pishey Thompson, *The History and Antiquities of Boston*, 1856, p. 71.

borough as an alderman. But in Stamford the alderman and the 'First Twelve' were assisted by a 'second Twelve'; there were, in fact, two councils here despite the charter of 1462 which made no clear provision for such an arrangement.[77] The 'First Twelve' consisted mostly of those who had been aldermen, and they were the justices of the peace for the borough, but apart from this the two parts appear to have been treated as a whole. A confirmation of the 1462 charter secured in 1504 made no alteration to the terms of the grant but, in fact, the system of government by an alderman and a council of twenty-four continued. Also like Grimsby, Stamford was dominated by great men from outside. In the latter town, the *seigneur*, Cecily duchess of York, probably insisted upon the alderman being sworn in before her steward, but her successor Lady Margaret Beaufort's influence is difficult to determine.[78] From 1481 the borough nominated its legal adviser and, from 1490, two men, John Walcote and William Elmes, jointly served what was in effect the office of recorder, although, when the recordership was formally established in 1502, the latter was appointed to the office. The other officers were the coroner who was chosen from the 'First Twelve', two chamberlains, usually members of the 'Second Twelve' but after 1485 not necessarily so, three constables and two serjeants who held their paid offices for many years but who were reappointed every year.

From time to time a 'third twelve' emerged as representative of the community of the burgesses resident in the town, but they clearly had no official standing since in the stinting of sheep on the common, the 'First Twelve' were allowed sixty, the 'Second Twelve' forty, and every commoner twenty. In fact, at Stamford, councillors appear to have enjoyed few rewards for their service other than a little patronage which came to the alderman. They served because of the prestige of the office and because of their desire to help the town.

The decline that resulted from the virtual cessation of cloth manufacture in the town and from the discontinuance of its wool market was not arrested and clearly reversed until the second half of the seventeenth century. Tudor Stamford was a depressed town: the amalgamation of parishes bears witness to that fact.[79] In 1548 the parishes were reduced from eleven to six, and in 1574 the town council was concerned at the extent of unemployment and poverty in the town. Ten years later the town council could only obtain the money to pay the fifteenth by leasing the common tenter meadows where cloth was dried and stretched. The population of Stamford rose very little during the Tudor period: including St Martin's, 242 households in 1524 had only increased to some

---

[77] A. Everitt (ed.), *Perspectives in English Urban History*, London, 1971, pp. 17 *et seq.*
[78] A. Rogers, 'Late Medieval Stamford etc.' in A. Everitt (ed.), *op. cit.*, pp. 22–3.
[79] A. Rogers, *The Making of Stamford*, Leicester U.P., 1965, p. 59.

263 in 1583, and perhaps to 300 families in 1603. Other Midland townships and many Lincolnshire villages had, by contrast, increased their
populations by between 50 per cent and 100 per cent.[80] Although on the
major north–south route and despite having a number of crafts, of
which leather-working was prominent, in addition to marketing facilities, Stamford in the Tudor period did not emerge from the decline
which had overtaken it in the fifteenth century.

The reasons for this failure have been well described and analysed by
Dr Joan Thirsk. An attempted revival of the weaving industry, not of
broadcloth manufacture but of canvas weaving and the making of the
New Draperies, never got off the ground in the sixteenth century. In
the 1560s the town council decided to buy hemp to set the poor on work
weaving canvas and in the same decade a project was put forward to
invite Dutch immigrants to settle in the town. What success the Dutch
had is not as yet clearly known but it is certain that they did not re-
establish a woollen cloth industry.

Moreover, Stamford did not establish itself as a marketing centre
probably because it failed to specialize in one commodity which would
have attracted merchants from a distance. Another cause of its failure in
this respect was that in a large area surrounding it lay the fens and the
forest where large numbers of middling peasants lived who were too
poor to travel to market and who therefore acquired such goods as they
needed in their large villages. In the heathland, where gentry and rich
yeomen dwelt, clients might be found, but these farmers were able to
travel farther afield to the best markets, and so they went to Newark,
Grantham, Nottingham, Spilsby, Market Harborough, Melton Mow-
bray, and elsewhere and in this way the scope for marketing at Stamford was limited. The fact that the river Welland was not navigable as
far as Stamford, the inhabitants thought was responsible for the continuance of the town's commercial decline, and it may well be that the
reversal of its ill fortune was due to the clearing of a passage to the sea
in the 1660s.

And yet during the long period of decline which lasted throughout
the Tudor period, Stamford had wealthy citizens. William Ratclif
supported the grammar school,[81] and William Browne, like Ratclif
a merchant of the Staple, at one time alderman, founded Browne's
Hospital and endowed it from grants of land in Swayfield and elsewhere. Another alderman, John Haughton, who held office in 1558,
built a new town hall on the bridge, and lord Burghley founded a
hospital in Stamford Baron in 1597. The Cecil family did much for
the borough. David Cecil, alderman in 1504, 1515, and 1526, was the
first of the family to settle in the area and to support the borough of his

[80] *Ibid.*, pp. 60–1.   [81] See p. 143.

adoption. His son Richard did perhaps less for the town, but his distinguished son William, later lord Burghley, amid all the cares of public office did much for Stamford although not enough to make it prosperous.

Bourne, it would seem, went against the trend towards decline that hit the larger Lincolnshire towns in the sixteenth century. It was a market town specializing in corn, dominated by its Augustinian abbey until 1536, and as there had been little industrial activity apart from leather-working, limitation or cessation of manufacture, as happened at Lincoln, Stamford, Grimsby, or Boston, did not affect it to the same degree. Population seems to have grown between 1563 and 1603; probably an increase of about 400 souls from around 700 to 1,100 took place, if we add a fifth for those under age to the 900 communicants registered in 1603. In the light of later figures, 1,100 may be too high an estimate of Bourne's population.[82] But apart from the population figures and the manifest prosperity of some Bourne families, such as the Trollopes and the Fishers, little firm evidence exists on which to base the prosperity of Tudor Bourne. Inventories of various families such as the Mores, Clarks, and Harringtons demonstrate the increasing wealth of individuals but are hardly sufficient to provide a certain picture of prosperity for the town as a whole.

Local government in the boroughs, then, had many facets. Partly it was keeping in touch with central government and carrying out the orders of the privy council, but it was also putting pressure upon ministers—and Lincolnshire was perhaps fortunate in having Justice Monson, Dr Wilson, Sir Thomas Heneage and, above all, lord Burghley so close to the centre of royal power—to do something in favour of the locality. Another aspect of local government were the courts that administered the law of the land and the local by-laws but, primarily, economic well-being was as much a function of local government in the sixteenth as in the twentieth century. Minor matters such as the supervision of ceremonial functions and entertainments formed part of the duties of the councils and, as we shall see later, the encouragement of educational facilities.

[82] J. D. Birkbeck, *A History of Bourne*, printed Warners Ltd., Bourne & London, n.d., p. 29.

CHAPTER IX

LINCOLNSHIRE EDUCATION

THE opportunities open to Lincolnshire boys and girls in the Tudor period to obtain a good education were somewhat limited but they were better than in many shires. A few children doubtless had private tutors but there were a number of schools in the principal towns. Reasonably good as the overall provision of school education was, it significantly improved during the sixteenth century since during that period many new schools were founded and many old ones resuscitated. Especially between 1585 and 1604 an increase in the number of schoolmasters occurred. The increased interest in classical Latin and, above all, in Greek provided the impetus to found new schools or to revive old ones. Two forms of the Latin language co-existed in Tudor England. The one was the old form of Latin, used in legal documents, in manorial accounts and court rolls, virtually unaltered from the thirteenth century, and although some of these documents were drawn up in the vernacular from the last quarter of the sixteenth century, at least the headings, of account rolls for example, remained in medieval Latin. This medieval Latin was the sort that all lawyers had to know and use. The other form was the Latin as it had been written by the great writers of antiquity, which had been introduced into England only shortly before 1485, and which did not really influence the country before Henry VIII's reign. To this widening knowledge of classical Latin was added at the turn of the century a knowledge of Greek, but it was doubtless several decades before the latter spread into Lincolnshire. Erasmus, Colet, Linacre, and Grocyn may not have had any direct influence on the county, but their writings which encouraged the study of humane letters stimulated education there in the long term.

Little can be written about the curriculum and daily routine of Tudor schools in the county, rather more about their financing and their headmasters.[1] Despite the presence in sixteenth-century Engand of a number of blue-stockings—and Lincolnshire had at least Katherine

[1] A. F. Leach, 'Schools', VCH *Lincs.*, II, pp. 421–92 on which this chapter is largely based, supplemented by Joan Simon, *Education and society in Tudor England*, London, 1966, and N. Orme, *English Schools in the Middle Ages*, London, 1973.

Willoughby and Anne Askew (Ayscough)—the opportunities for boys far outnumbered those for girls since most of the foundations of which records exist specify that the educational provision is for boys and youths. It would be safe to say that what instruction girls received was normally from tutors, although the school at Alford which apparently provided both elementary and secondary education may have admitted them.[2] The curriculum of the grammar school, basically Latin grammar, was not thought suitable for girls, while the means by which reading and writing English, and arithmetic, and accounts were taught, and the people who taught them appear to have left no traces.

As might be expected, the county town had an ancient grammar school which was part of the foundation of the cathedral church, and by the early fourteenth century eleven other grammar schools were in existence in the county. The intricate relationships between the grammar school in the Close and the ancient grammar school of the city, complicated by the emergence of a choristers' Song School by the beginning of the fifteenth century and by the teaching of six boys on the Burghersh chantry foundation, have been amply dealt with by the late A. F. Leach.[3] He also exposed the myth of the many so-called foundations of Edward VI, demonstrating quite clearly that the parts of chantry and gild endowments devoted to educational purposes were not exempt from expropriation and that, in some instances, considerable struggles had to be mounted to retain the existing facilities. But in his necessary revaluation of Edward VI's educational work his reaction was too strong: nevertheless, the dissolution of the chantries did lead to the suppression of elementary schools. In Lincoln, consequent upon the dissolution of the chantries, Edward VI ordered on 25 April 1548 that, out of the cathedral revenues, 20 marks ($£13$ 6s. 8d.) and a rent-free house should be given to a schoolmaster and $£6$ 13s. 4d. and a free room to an usher. The usher was an assistant master competent to teach, not a man merely responsible for keeping order. From 1548 the school was to be completely free whereas previously tuition fees had been charged to all pupils except the choristers. Those choristers who had served in the cathedral choir for five years or more were, when their voices broke, to be given $£3$ 6s. 8d. per annum for another five years provided they studied at a grammar school. For a variety of reasons amalgamation took place between the Close grammar school and the city grammar school. The agreement reached between the dean and chapter and the mayor and aldermen in 1584 brought this about. From the 1560s the city had taken an active interest in improving its school, and in 1567 Robert Monson, M.P., future

[2] Leach, loc. cit., p. 483.   [3] Ibid., loc. cit.

recorder and justice of Common Pleas, agreed to pay the cost of establishing a new free school in the building of the former Grey Friars in Free School Lane. He was to have the glass out of the old school building to use in his repair of the conventual edifice. When, in 1575, sufficient gifts for the sustenance of the schoolmaster were not forthcoming, a compulsory levy was raised. This was the beginning of an 'education rate' in Lincoln.

Meanwhile, after 1548 the grammar school in the Close had had its difficulties. From 1559 the schoolmaster was well paid at £20 a year and the usher from the same date had £10, but the school's position may have been to some degree undermined by the teaching of the choristers who must have spent some considerable time in the Song School. From 1563 to 1570 or 1572 John Maydwell, the pedagogue in the Close, had as his rival the song master, William Byrd, one of the leading, if not the foremost musician of his day. The headmaster after Maydwell, Christopher Digles, was academically well qualified but negligent in his duties to such a degree that, after less than five years, he had to be found a living, and this vacancy in 1582 probably helped the negotiations which had been going on since 1580 between the chapter and the mayor. The final agreement of 18 January 1584 stipulated that the schoolmaster of the city school should be a Master of Arts competent to teach Greek and Latin: it is noticeable that Greek is a requirement not only for the schoolmaster but also for the usher. The dean and chapter, in view of their liability to provide a free school under the 1548 provisions, contracted to pay the schoolmaster £20 *per annum* to which the city added £6 13s. 4d. While the dean and chapter chose the master, the usher was chosen by a committee composed of the mayor, recorder, and aldermen who had been mayors, and paid £13 6s. 8d. by the city. The bishop promised not to promote any other school in the city or within three miles of it. Tuition fees were waived only for the children of freemen, and poor clerks had to pay 6d. to study under the usher and 1s. to be taught by the schoolmaster. It was the opening of a new era for grammar school education in Lincoln for without other competition the authorities were able to provide salaries that attracted well qualified teachers. The school had its ups and downs but it continued to flourish for over 300 years.

A. F. Leach thought that many schools in Lincolnshire, the origin of which tradition had ascribed to sixteenth-century benefactors, were indeed much older. Grammar schools, he showed, existed at Barton-upon-Humber, Partney, Grimsby, Horncastle, Boston, Grantham, Bourne, Louth, and Strubby—or at least these places had schoolmasters in the fourteenth century. Moreover, he thought that schools at Alford and Gainsborough had precursors before the sixteenth century: in the latter town a schoolmaster is mentioned in 1578–9.[4] Schoolmasters were teaching in Boston from the fourteenth century, and in 1514 it is known that St Mary's gild paid the master, George Watson, the sum of £9. Most of our information, however, is not about the school but about the land deals made by the corporation to endow it. In 1555 the corporation acquired certain lands of the attainted marquess of Northampton to maintain a school, and new building took place in 1567–8. Boston appears to have been mean in the financial provision it made for the schoolmaster and the usher: at one time in the 1570s and 1580s the mayor's chaplain acted as usher but got no extra fee. In 1596, although the usher James Harry was a bachelor of arts, he received only £3 a year. Moreover, Greek as well as Latin was being studied, since in 1601 both Greek and Latin dictionaries were bought for school use. In Market Rasen a Mr Hawke was schoolmaster in 1585[5] and Sir Thomas St Paul had left an exhibition of £17 a year to the school in 1583.[6]

The town of Louth had a schoolmaster as early as 1276 and by the early sixteenth century the gilds were helping to maintain him. The gild of St Mary contributed 10s. and the gilds of Corpus Christi and St Peter 5s. each, and from all gild sources the schoolmaster was receiving 40s. a year in 1533 and doubtless had some other income. He was a man named John Goodall who dominated education in the town for an unusually lengthy period. One of the notable features of sixteenth-century schools is the rapidity of turnover of masters and ushers, but Goodall taught from 1533 to 1538 before going to Thornton whence he returned about 1548 and stayed until his death in 1576. Here again some reorganization took place for, in 1551, John Bradley persuaded his half brother Richard Goodriche, attorney of the court of Augmentations, to petition Edward VI to convert into a school what had been a chamber of priests.[7] Lands worth £40 per annum were set aside from the property of dissolved gilds and of John Louthe's chantry towards the maintenance of twelve poor folk and of a schoolmaster and usher. From that time onwards a schoolmaster (John Goodall) was paid £20 and an usher £10, and the governing body of a Warden and six Assistants presented its first accounts in 1553. Education at Louth was not limited, however, to the free grammar school newly built in 1557–58. There was also a Song school, of which there is mention as late as 1556–57, and an elementary school. The latter was known as the 'petie'

[4] *Ex inf.* Mr Ian Beckwith who has kindly made the results of some of his researches available to me.

[5] *Ex inf.* Ian Beckwith.   [6] A. R. Maddison (ed.), *Lincs.Wills*, I, 272, p. 98.

[7] *The Charters of the Corporation of the Town of Louth and the Free Grammar School*, Louth, 1831, pp. 1–16.

school and John Laycoke was paid at the rate of £6 *per annum* in 1553-54 for teaching the young children. We do not know what he taught but it would be reasonable to suppose that he instructed the young in reading, writing, and arithmetic, essential preparatory subjects, before some of them went on to learn Latin grammar. This elementary school had a life of about 200 years continuing until the mid-eighteenth century. The grammar school went from strength to strength under Goodall's direction, the head being responsible for the Corpus Christi play under Mary while later the pupils' histrionic talents were exercised in the performance of interludes. Education in Louth flourished under the Tudors.

Stamford also had a schoolmaster as early as 1309, but the endowment of the present school dates from 1 June 1532 when alderman William Ratclif, a merchant of the staple at Calais, directed by his last will that a secular chaplain should be found to pray for his soul and teach the art of grammar.[8] A remarkable teacher, one Libeus Bayard, remained schoolmaster for at least fifteen years and taught William Cecil, later lord Burghley, and Ralph Robinson, the first translator of More's *Utopia*. They left, the former in 1535 to go to St John's college Cambridge, the latter the following year to become an undergraduate at Corpus Christi college, Oxford. William Cecil's position of authority enabled him in 1548 to get a private act passed through parliament re-founding the school and thus avoiding any loss to the school that might have resulted as a consequence of the dissolution of gilds and chantries. The alderman, as the mayor of Stamford was called, was to choose the master with the approval of the Master of St John's college Cambridge, who was also to draw up the rules. This link with St John's was further strengthened in 1581 when lord Burghley, as part of his further endowment of the Lady Margaret scholars there, was granted the privilege of founding a tied scholarship for the school. The patronage of the Cecils and of St John's college together with the interest shown by the corporation of Stamford secured the prosperity of the school. A reference in 1535 to a school in Stamford without a master may indicate that there was another school in the town.[9]

Some twenty miles to the north, Grantham also had a master in the early fourteenth century, which indicates that there was some educational provision there before bishop Fox's interest, an interest that A. F. Leach has shown to be minimal. Henry Curteys, an alderman of Grantham who died in 1479, and his son Richard, were the real refounders of the school who gave the bulk of the endowment since the Curteys chantry in 1487 provided for one of its two chaplains to keep a

---

[8] B. L. Deed, *A History of Stamford School*, 1954, p. 10.   [9] LP IX, 1107, p. 381.

school and to instruct boys 'as well in good manners as in the art of grammar'.[10] But Richard Fox(e), bishop of Winchester built the school-house and the master's house and gave an additional endowment of £6 13s. 4d. *per annum* through his foundation of Corpus Christi college, Oxford. He was a native of Ropsley, five miles east of Grantham, and his distinction together with his other foundations, Corpus Christi Oxford, and the school at Taunton, perhaps made it inevitable that he should be given over-large merit for his work in Grantham. The endow-ment of the school was enlarged in 1551 when lands of the late chantries of Holy Trinity and of St Mary and obit lands in Manthorpe came to the school. The alderman (mayor) and comburgesses were the governors of the school known from that date onwards as the Free Grammar School of king Edward VI or as the King's School.

Another town which is known to have had a master in the early fourteenth century is Great Grimsby. The school was connected with a chantry known as Rayner's chantry, because the endowment made in the 1340s was to provide for prayers for the souls of Sir John and William Rayner and for the mayor and all burgesses of Grimsby. The burgesses converted this chantry to educational purposes by royal licence.[11] At the petition of Sir Edward North, chancellor of the court of Augmentations, letters patent allowed the endowment to be used to teach grammar to boys and youths, and John Bellow, then mayor, and the burgesses of Grimsby were to acquire land to the value of forty marks a year for the upkeep of the school. Thomas Thomlynson, chaplain of Rayner's chantry, sold its lands to the mayor and burgesses for £80 so that the 1548 act did not involve the confiscation of the chantry lands. The schoolmasters of Grimsby were more poorly paid than elsewhere, and Harry Fotherbye in 1557–58 was having to collect the rents himself from the lands which provided his salary.

Two Wolds towns, Horncastle and Spilsby, and the not distant town of Alford, just in the marsh, had schools in Tudor times. A master was appointed at Horncastle in the fourteenth century and Mr Andreweson the schoolmaster in 1536 was among the ringleaders of the Rising,[12] but it was in 1571 at the petition of Edward Fiennes K. G., later first earl of Lincoln, that queen Elizabeth granted the foundation of the Free Grammar School of queen Elizabeth in Horncastle.[13] A master, an usher, and ten governors were to be appointed: the first ten, two clerics, three gentlemen, and five yeomen, being named in the letters to those to whom the powers of appointment and drawing up statutes were assigned. They could hold lands to the value of £40 a year for the

[10] D. M. Owen, *Church and Society in Medieval Lincolnshire*, Lincoln, 1971, p. 101.
[11] *Cal. Pat. Rolls* Ed. VI, 1547–8, pp. 176–7.   [12] LP XI, 568, p. 225.
[13] *Cal. Pat. Rolls* Eliz. 1569–72, no. 1824.

maintenance of the school. Whether lord Clinton gave any endowment is uncertain but, in 1574, John Neale a tanner gave lands in Sutton, Huttoft, and Thornton, and fourteen years later John Spenluffe of Farlesthorpe left £20 to the school.[14] Alford school was an unusual creation in that it seems to have been for elementary and secondary education. By a deed of 18 March 1566, Francis Spanning a merchant gave £50 to six governors and four auditors. Some £40 of this was to be used to maintain a schoolmaster and a free school for teaching young children the alphabet and also to read both English and Latin. Three years later William Gubbe gave an additional £30. On 2 July 1576, at the instance of lord Burghley, the queen issued letters patent establishing a free grammar school in the town of Alford of the petitioner's foundation and of his son, Sir Thomas Cecil. Ten governors were given licences in mortmain to hold lands up to the value of £40 a year. It is clear that Burghley gave nothing but his name, but the incorporated governors took over control of the Spanning and Gubbe bequests, and Richard and John Spendley (Spenlove) gave lands in Strubby, Woodthorpe, Withern, and Cumberworth in 1585, but in 1598, the elementary aspect of the teaching disappeared when new statutes made Alford a grammar school alone. Spilsby had a free school founded by letters patent of Edward VI in December 1550,[15] although there had been an instructor of scholars there named John Fenne in 1479.[16] The school was to teach Latin grammar and polite letters, but no mention is made of Greek. The first schoolmaster was Robert Lathum, but his successors were to be appointed by Katherine, duchess of Suffolk, her son lord Brandon (sic), and their heirs. The interest of the Willoughby family was strong and, in 1611, an additional endowment was given by Robert Bertie, thirteenth baron Willoughby d'Eresby later created first earl of Lindsey.

Wainfleet school was already in existence at the opening of the Tudor period. It had been founded by William of Waynflete in 1484 to match the school at Magdalen itself, and to act as a 'feeder' to Magdalen college just as Winchester acted for New college, Oxford, and Eton for King's college, Cambridge. We know that it cost £27 to build the hall, 70ft by 20ft, and that Henry Alsbroke of Tattershall was the architect.[17] The President of Magdalen appointed the headmaster, but we do not know why the school failed to develop along the somewhat grandiose lines that its founder had envisaged. Moulton, between Spalding and Holbeach, acquired a free grammar school under the will,

---

[14] A. R. Maddison (ed.), *Lincs. Wills*, I, 312, p. 115.
[15] *Cal. Pat. Rolls* Ed. VI, 1549–51, p. 264. [16] LAO, 2 Anc. 1/24/47.
[17] R. Chandler, *Life of Waynflete*, London, 1811, p. 171 gives the dimensions as 76 ft. by 26 ft.

dated 19 September 1560, of a yeoman John Horrocks. It is known to have had boarders as well as day scholars from its inception but of its early days, disputes over its landed endowment form the chief part of the record. In 1599 the school estate was transferred to the master while six overseers resident in Elloe wapentake were to appoint the master who was to be proficient in Latin and Greek and who was not to hold a benefice. Great stress was laid upon training in manners and reverent behaviour, and two monitors were to be chosen on a weekly basis to enforce these virtues: by 1608 the school had forty-five boys in it. Near-by Spalding obtained a grammar school by the will, 27 May 1568, of John Blank, and further endowments from John Gamlyn who died 10 December 1588. In the same district Wrangle and Bolingbroke received schools in the Tudor period. The former by the will of the vicar Thomas Alenson dated 1 August 1555 benefited from a bequest for the teaching of Latin and English, while the latter acquired a school sometime between 1548 and 1562. In the latter year Richard Goodriche out of the lands of John Goodriche deceased gave a rent charge of £5 a year for the support of the school.

Kirton-in-Lindsey free grammar school was founded by a decree of the Exchequer of 15 June 1577 with an endowment provided by certain copyhold lands. These lands provided £12 a year for the wages of a schoolmaster and it is clear that there was a strong communal interest in having a town school. Laughton free school resulted from the will of Roger Dalison, precentor of Lincoln cathedral who, on 31 May 1566, left lands to William Dalison on condition that a grammar school was set up in the family village of Laughton. In the same region, Gainsborough free grammar school was established by letters patent of 21 November 1589 on the petition of Robert Somerscales but it may be that some teaching had taken place previously in a town of such importance. The parish register mentions a schoolmaster in May 1578.[18] Carre's free grammar school at Sleaford was founded by Robert Carr's deed of 1 September 1604 whereby he gave 129 acres in Gedney to support the school in New Sleaford, where it then was, or in some other convenient place in the town. This wording of the deed would support the view that some form of teaching was already going on. It cannot be known whether the school had been recently established or whether it was of long duration, but it was the last school to be envisaged, if not quite founded, within the Tudor period. From this brief survey of Lincolnshire education, it can be seen that boys, at least, were fairly well provided for and that girls were not left completely destitute of educational opportunity although the opportunities for them were slender.

[18] See *ante* p. 141.

Undoubtedly a tremendous growth in educational provision took place in Lincolnshire in the last twenty years of the Tudor period.[19] The *Libri Cleri* show that, in 1580 and 1585, twenty townships had schoolmasters and other sources show another eleven places to have had at least one teacher. By 1594 these thirty-one places had risen to thirty-three, while a decade later seventy-seven parishes are known from the *Libri Cleri* to have had schoolmasters. If we add those known from other sources, eighty-five townships in all had instructors of some sort in 1604. If eighty-five places offered some form of education, it might be thought that few boys would have been too far distant from a source of instruction where they could have obtained some schooling, but these schoolmasters were not evenly spread throughout the county. It appears that superior educational provision was available in the parishes in the southern and eastern parts of the county, and it cannot be by chance that the richer areas of Lincolnshire—the marshland and fen and part of the wolds—had more instructors than the poor clay lands. Mr Beckwith's researches into wills and inventories have revealed schoolmasters before 1590 in Pinchbeck (Henry Smith) and Rippingale (Ralph Haye), and these documents also demonstrate an increase in the possession of books.

Already from the Lincolnshire wills that were calendared in 1888 and 1891,[20] and from a further series published between 1914 and 1927,[21] we can obtain some information as to the books owned by Lincolnshire men and women at the time of their death, and continuing research will, in due course, add to our knowledge. In the early Tudor period it appears that, for the most part, it was the clergy who owned books although a few laymen had a volume or two. Books in the possession of Lincolnshire men were mostly either religious or legal, but a few men, as is reflected in their holdings, had linguistic and literary interests. William Gaunt, whose will is dated 1531, left *The Golden Legend*, *Chronicles*, *Canterbury Tales* and Lyttelton's *Treatise on Tenures*,[22] but, in the early years of the sixteenth century, a man might leave just one book as did John Cocke in 1534.[23] Clerics usually had a greater number of books than laymen: William Johnson, vicar of Alford, had, in 1541, Lyndwood's *Provinciale*, Radulphus, *Super Evangelia per totum annum*, otherwise called *Vita Jesu Christi*, a Holy Bible and a portable breviary[24]

[19] *Ex inf.* Ian Beckwith.
[20] A. R. Maddison (ed.), *Lincolnshire Wills 1500–1600 & 1600–1617*, Lincoln, 1888 & 1891.
[21] C. W. Foster (ed.), *Lincoln Wills, 1271–1526*, LRS 5, 1914; *1505–30*, LRS 10, 1918; *1530–32*, LRS 24, 1927.
[22] A. R. Maddison (ed.), *Lincs. Wills*, I, 17, p. 8.   [23] *Ibid.*, I, 35, p. 16.
[24] *Ibid.*, I, 83, p. 32.

while Thomas Flower, the sub-chanter of the cathedral possessed, in 1555, *De Vita Christi, Ortus Vocabulorum*, several grammar books, and an English-Latin dictionary.[25] By the early seventeenth century, however, some clerics were in the habit of acquiring many volumes. Francis Beresford of Rowston had lent a Greco-Latin Thesaurus, a Livy, Demosthenes in Greek and Latin, and a volume of Seneca's *Philosophy*, and he doubtless had other books.[26] Moses Wilton of Fleet, who died in 1609, probably collected much of his library during Elizabeth's reign, for, among "all my Hebrew, Greek, and Latin books with maps and shelves and glass in my study" which he left to the next incumbent and to all his successors, he cited twenty-three folios, seventeen quartos, thirty-nine octavo volumes, and six smaller books.[27] Many of Wilton's books were works of biblical criticism, commentaries on the Gospels and the Psalms, patristic texts, works by Erasmus, Calvin, and Bellarmine, dictionaries, and Plutarch's 'Lives'. They are priced at between 50s. for a dictionary down to 6d. for a book by Dr Perkins on 'Predestination'.

Wills provide evidence not only of the existence of well-read men but also of legatees' willingness to bequeath money or lands for educational purposes. These bequests fall into two categories: those in which provision is made for a relative, and those that endow educational facilities more generally. William Foster of Gosberton, in 1512, expressed the wish that his wife should do all in her power to send his son Thomas to school,[28] and forty-five years later William Cracroft made a similar request to his wife.[29] Elizabeth Hustwaite, a gentlewoman of Waltham near Grimsby, left 40s. to support her brother Edward at school.[30] Edward Disney of Carlton-le-Moorland, in 1595, willed that his son Thomas should remain a student at Cambridge till he was 18, and have £20 a year for his 'exhibition' there, and then he was to go on to the Inns of Court where he was to stay until he reached 21 years of age, enjoying an income of £26 13s. 4d. His son William was to do the same.[31] Charles Bolles of Haugh, in 1590, left £5 a year to his nephew, Richard Cracroft, for his education up to the age of 22 years.[32]

Richard Clarke of Horncastle, a tanner, left money to scholars in 1520. John Spenluffe or Spenley, who had helped with the endowment of Horncastle and Alford schools, founded a fellowship for five years at Magdalene college, Cambridge,[33] and the bibliophile Moses Wilton left twenty acres to Emmanuel college towards the support of two scholars chosen from Moulton school until they became M.A.s. It

---

[25] *Ibid.*, I, 133, p. 46.   [26] *Ibid.*, II, 6, p. 4.   [27] *Ibid.*, II, 36, p. 33.
[28] *Lincoln Wills*, I, 1271–1526, p. 47.
[29] A. R. Maddison (ed.), *Lincs. Wills*, I, 209, p. 74.   [30] *Ibid.*, I, 216, p. 77.
[31] *Ibid.*, I, 326, p. 121.   [32] *Ibid.*, II, 331, p. 123–4.   [33] *Ibid.*, I, 312, p. 116 fn.

would appear, as we might expect because of geographical proximity, that the county had more links with Cambridge than with Oxford. Nevertheless, in 1523 Robert Jolif of Trusthorpe told his executors to help support a priest studying at Oxford by giving him 8 marks annually for three years.[34] The bishop had close connections with Lincoln college and with the university which had been in his diocese until 1541.

In conclusion, Lincolnshire men and women in the Tudor period showed considerable interest in education. In the early years money was left to make boys priests with provision for their maintenance until 24 years of age[35] but also care was taken for simple elementary education, for, in 1525, John Lawes the elder of Wigtoft left 33s. 4d. to his grandson "to keep him at school as he may profitably have the exercise of writing and reading so thereby be more meet to put at a craft."[36] Indeed, as has recently been shown, in regard to numbers of schools, Lincolnshire excelled most counties in its educational provisions,[37] and the number of schoolmasters in places where no endowed schools existed spread those provisions even more widely.

[34] *Lincoln Wills*, I, p. 122.   [35] *Ibid.*, II, pp. 176, 201.   [36] *Ibid.*, I, p. 148.
[37] N. Orme, *op. cit.*, p. 324.

CHAPTER X

GREAT AND SMALL HOUSES AND HOUSEHOLDS

LINCOLNSHIRE cannot today exhibit as large or as fine a selection of Tudor domestic buildings as can some counties, but in the sixteenth century a number of leading men built great houses within the shire. The Renaissance came late to Lincolnshire,[1] and fashions that were introduced into London between 1510 and 1520 did not appear in the county until the 1570s. Gainsborough Old Hall, the home of lord Burgh, was built in the 1470s though much of the present building dates from *c.* 1600 when it was owned by William Hickman, a London merchant.[2] Also to the early Tudor period belong Ayscoughfee Hall in Spalding said to have been built originally in 1429 and the present Great Ponton rectory built for a merchant of the Staple. Irnham Hall, built by Sir Richard Thimbleby between 1510 and 1531,[3] and Halstead Hall, one mile N.N.E. of Stixwould, are two early Tudor houses. But the houses of most of the leading families, of the Heneages at Hainton, the Thorolds at Marston, the Ayscoughs at Stallingborough and South Kelsey, the Skipwiths of South Ormsby and Ketsby, and the St Paul's at Snarford, were either built after 1603 or have disappeared or both, although a few Tudor fragments remain at South Kelsey and Marston. We know that the St Paul family had a great house at Snarford[4] for it was surveyed by John Thorpe in the early seventeenth century. Of Elizabethan houses few remain in the county. Sir Christopher Wray built a large courtyard house at Glentworth soon after 1566 when he purchased the estate from the Brocklesby family, but it was re-built by James Paine in 1753.[5] Sir Robert Jermyn's Torksey Castle was built in the 1560s; an Elizabethan mansion built by a man whose main interests lay outside the county. Of Elizabethan houses that remain in good condition, Barrowby rectory bears a date—1588, and Thomas Cony's manor house at Bassingthorpe built in 1568 is also dated. The latter is an early example of the Elizabethan style in manor houses which did not spread until later to other parts of the county. Thomas Cony, a success-

---

[1] Pevsner and Harris, *op. cit.*, pp. 52, 65.   [2] *Ibid.*, p. 243.
[3] *Ibid.*, p. 583 but *Lincs. Pedigrees* has a Richard but no Sir Richard at these dates.
[4] *Ibid.*, p. 66.   [5] *Ibid.*, p. 249.

ful business man married to the daughter of a lord mayor of London, had ideas about the new styles and the money to implement his tastes. Ashby Hall at Ashby-de-la-Launde was originally built in 1595 by Edward King although little now remains of the sixteenth-century house.

Little or nothing remains of Auborn Hall which was altered considerably by Sir John Meres between 1587 and 1628, or of Dowsby Hall which was built by Sir William Rigdon between 1603 and 1610. The plans of the Sheffield mansion at Butterwick or Normanby have survived,[6] and a barn is the only part remaining of the Willoughby d'Eresby manor house at Belleau. Of Sir William Pelham's stately house at Brocklesby Park we know virtually nothing but part remains of the Copledyke's seat at Harrington. Knaith Hall was built in the later sixteenth century, but whether by lord Willoughby of Parham or by Thomas Sutton is not certain. But Doddington Hall, barely five miles west of Lincoln, is an important late Elizabethan house which endures. It is ascribed to Robert Smithson and was built between 1593 and 1600 for Thomas Taylor, recorder to the bishop of Lincoln.

One house, however, stands pre-eminently among Tudor houses— Grimsthorpe Castle, although it is much altered since its original building. Its pre-eminence to some degree results from the fact that the other Lincolnshire magnate's post-Reformation house at Sempringham is merely on record while Grimsthorpe, despite its many alterations, remains. We know that lord Clinton before he died in 1585 built a large mansion, at Sempringham, 200 feet long, but it may never have been finished. Also his family owned, after 1551, Tattershall castle less than twenty miles from Sempringham. Grimsthorpe, then, the home of the baroness Willoughby d'Eresby and her husbands, the duke of Suffolk and Richard Bertie, was the foremost great house in Tudor Lincolnshire. The reversion of Grimsthorpe was granted to William, tenth lord Willoughby and his wife Mary de Salinas on their marriage in 1516,[7] but it was not until 1537, after the death of the countess of Oxford, that their daughter Katherine and her husband the duke of Suffolk obtained possession of it. The property consisted of a late thirteenth-century castle to which the duke hastily added buildings in order to receive his brother-in-law, Henry VIII, in 1541. Suffolk had also obtained the adjacent Vaudey abbey in September 1538 and he doubtless used its stones in the Grimsthorpe additions. Leland mentioned a second court which may in fact be the addition made at this time. After the duke's death in 1545 the duchess, a widow for over seven years, spent part of her time there until she shared the house with her second husband Richard Bertie. Their initial stay there was

[6] *Ibid.*, p. 67.   [7] LP II, 2172.

probably less than two years as they fled to the Continent in February
1555. When they returned in the summer of 1559, after an absence of
nearly five years, Grimsthorpe again became their principal residence
until the duchess's death on 19 September 1580 and her husband's some
eighteen months later.

In 1541, Henry decided to make a royal progress with his fifth wife
Katherine Howard through parts of his kingdom that had been torn by
rebellion a few years previously and, after entering the county at
Stamford, he travelled on to stay with his trusted friend at Grimsthorpe.[8] Here Charles Brandon had added state rooms for their recep-
tion, but the rebuildings of 1685, 1727, and 1811 make it impossible to
form any conclusive judgement of the work so rapidly undertaken in
1540–41. After their stay at Grimsthorpe on 6–8 August,[9] the king and
queen travelled via Sleaford, some fourteen miles away, and reached
Lincoln, a further eleven miles by way of Temple Bruer, on Tuesday
9 August and stayed there till Friday 12 August when they left for
Gainsborough.[10] This journey of seventeen miles or so brought them to
Gainsborough later that day,[11] and the Court stayed there until Tuesday
16 August when it left for Scrooby in Nottinghamshire. The week-end
must have cost the duke and duchess a considerable sum not only in
entertainment but in rebuilding charges, but they had previously
received great benefits from their sovereign's hands. On the Court's
return from York, Henry and his queen spent the night of 14 October
at Grimsthorpe.[12] They had crossed to Barrow-on-Humber on
5 October,[13] and thence journeyed to Thornton College[14] where they
had remained until 9 October. On 9, 10, and 11 October they were at
Kettleby with the Tyrwhits, and on the 11th, later in the day, at Bishop
Norton,[15] the following day with the Monsons at South Carlton, and
on 13 October at Nocton Park.[16] Whether they spent the night there or
at Sleaford is not clear, but on 14 October the council met at Sleaford
before the Court continued its journey to Grimsthorpe. The following
night it was beyond the county at Colly Weston, a few miles south-
west of Stamford.

Parts of Katherine Willoughby's inheritance had been fought for in
earlier years. Although she had a clear title to her father's barony when
he died in 1526, what part of his lands should descend to heirs general
and what to heirs male was anything but certain. Lord Willoughby's
brother, Sir Christopher, was an awkward and determined man bent on
getting all he could from lord Willoughby's widow and young daugh-

[8] Lady Cecilia Goff, *A Woman of the Tudor Age*, London, 1930, pp. 125–6.
[9] LP XVI, 1074, 1077.   [10] *Ibid.*, 1077, 1079, 1084, 1088.   [11] *Ibid.*, 1092, 1094.
[12] Goff, *op. cit.*, p. 136.   [13] LP XVI, 1234, 1236, 1237.   [14] *Ibid.*, 1245.
[15] *Ibid.*, 1249.   [16] *Ibid.*, 1255.

ter who was only 7 years of age at her father's death. But the dowager Willoughby had friends at Court for she had been in queen Katherine's household and, moreover, her husband had foreseen the difficulties that his brother might make. A settlement of the family estates between Sir Christopher and lord Willoughby had been made in 1512,[17] when Sir Christopher had married Elizabeth, a daughter of Sir George Tailboys: this granted to the married couple lands to the clear value of 300 marks a year. If lord Willoughby d'Eresby died without a male heir, then other lands were to go to Sir Christopher or so the latter asserted but lady Mary Willoughby denied this on the grounds that her brother-in-law had drawn up the indenture by crafty means.[18] Dispute raged over the manors of Eresby, Spilsby, Toynton Willoughby, and Steeping which lord Willoughby's widow said were only to go to Sir Christopher if lord Willoughby had no heirs and, as he had a daughter Katherine, they were not lawfully Sir Christopher's.[19] These quarrels did not of course affect Grimsthorpe which was granted to the duke of Suffolk and his wife jointly. The position of Brandon's lands is made clear by reference to his will made in 1544 and proved in 1547.[20] Some of the lands were to hold to the Crown during the nonage of the duke's heirs but that legal provision did not apply to Grimsthorpe. The dispute continued for many years and in 1534 Sir Christopher entered into the manor of Eresby and complained to the king that the dowager lady Willoughby was preventing him from obtaining his inheritance.[21] By this time, however, she was strengthened by the support of her new son-in-law, and an agreement was finally arrived at between the duke of Suffolk and Sir Christopher which was given added force by act of parliament (27 Henry VIII,c.40). [22] Echoes of this conflict still occurred between Katherine and her second husband, Richard Bertie, and Sir Christopher's son, the first lord Willoughby of Parham,[23] but the interest of that branch of the family in Lincolnshire gradually diminished.

Katherine Willoughby was one of the outstanding women of the Tudor age. From the mid-thirties until her death in 1580 she played a prominent part in national affairs which do not fall within the scope of this volume.[24] She became a very firm Protestant despite the fact that her mother, who died c. 1540, was Spanish and devoted to queen Katherine and therefore, presumably, a devout Catholic. But, after 1529 she probably saw little of her mother as, being a ward of the duke and duchess of Suffolk, she went to live in their household which

---

[17] LAO Anc. 5/B/4d.   [18] LAO Anc. 5/B/1c.   [19] LAO Anc. 5/B/1j.
[20] *Wills in Doctors Commons*, Camden Soc., 83, 1863.   [21] LP vii, i, 223, 224.
[22] SR iii, pp. 596–8.   [23] LAO Anc. 5/B/2 and 5/B/4.
[24] The life by Lady Cecilia Goff may be supplemented by Evelyn Read, *Catherine Duchess of Suffolk*, London, 1962.

was principally resident at Westhorpe near Bury St Edmunds.[25] Presumably the duke, first her guardian and then her husband, was so loyal to his royal benefactor that he accepted whatever religious views his sovereign propounded and so, to that extent, was not a devout follower of the old religion, and Katherine therefore may have learnt through him to accept the new ways in religion. It is more probable, however, that she became a strong Protestant during her widowhood which coincided very largely with Edward VI's reign and that these Protestant views were strengthened by her marriage to Richard Bertie. But even before 1545 she had apparently opposed the views of bishop Gardiner,[26] and in 1546 Ann Askew was asked about her religious beliefs.[27] Sometime in 1551 or 1552 bishop Latimer stayed at Grimsthorpe and probably performed the marriage ceremony early in 1553 between Katherine and Richard Bertie. Her attitude towards her first husband's granddaughter, lady Jane Grey, was probably one of sympathy, and at the time of Mary's advent she must have been a determined Protestant. At any rate she was a source of strength and support to those with Protestant opinions, and from the household accounts of 1560[28] we note that a Mr Coverdale was one of the guests: he is described as a preacher but was more probably a pedagogue[29] and a relation of Miles Coverdale whose translation of the Bible into English had first appeared in 1535. Katherine was a woman who had many personal sorrows— above all, the death of her two sons Henry and Charles Brandon within half an hour of each other on 14 July 1551 and her long exile from 1555 to 1559—although during that period she did not live in poverty. Perhaps her temperament, perhaps her ancient lineage, perhaps the dangers and sorrows of her life gave her 'the sharp wit and sure hand to thrust it home and make it pierce when she pleased' that Fuller remarked.[30] Grimsthorpe was also the home of her two children by her second husband: Peregrine, the 'brave' or the 'stout' lord Willoughby of later years, and her daughter Susan, born early in 1554.[31]

When the great house was opened up again upon the return of its owners from exile on the Continent a picture of its running can be obtained from the household accounts.[32] The accounts begin with a list of the household of 'Mr Richard Bertie and the right honorable lady Katherine duchess of Suffolk his wife'.[33] Some of those listed were perhaps 'guests', others are members of the household staff whose

[25] Goff, op. cit., p. 19.   [26] DNB sub Bertie, Richard.

[27] The Acts and Monuments of John Foxe, 4th edn., London, 1867, v, p. 547.

[28] LAO Anc. 7/A/2.   [29] Goff, op. cit., p. 262.   [30] DNB sub Bertie, Catherine.

[31] Goff, op. cit., p. 219.

[32] LAO Anc. 7/A/2. These household accounts are partly calendared in HMC Rep. MSS of the Earl of Ancaster, HMSO, Dublin, 1907, pp. 459–73.

[33] Ibid., ff. 1–2v.

names have a note of their quarterly wages attached. The list begins with 'my master, my lady's grace, my lady Elinor, Mr Peregrine, and Miss Susan.' Mrs Knowles and Mrs 'Coverdall' appear next, then follow eight married women, each earning wages of 13s. 4d. a quarter and a Miss Beatrice, my lady's woman, presumably lady Willoughby's personal maid. No wages are mentioned for the lady's maid nor for five other women servants one of whom is called little Frances. Mrs Pretie and Mrs 'Coverdall' have no wages because their husbands were respectively cofferer at 25s. a quarter and 'precher' at £5 a quarter. These household officials along with the steward Mr Barnerd, the gentleman usher Mr Jeney, the master of the horse Mr Nauton, Mr Burton, and the comptroller, Mr Whitton, have their own servants. There were eight gentlemen waiters mostly earning 13s. 4d. a quarter and two yeomen ushers. William Benrick the groom had 10s. a quarter as did two other grooms, the yeoman of the cellar, the butler, and the pantler. There was a clerk of the kitchen and a clerk of the provisions, an usher of the hall, a footman, a porter, a brewer, two cooks, Thomas and Rowlande Cooke, who each had 25s. a quarter in wages assisted by two 'children of the kitchen.' Of the outdoor staff, there were four grooms of the stable, three gardeners, although in 1560 two appear to have left, a yeoman of the woodyard, and, to supply fresh meat to the household, a slaughterman was employed at 18s. 3d. a quarter. Three hinds were on the staff and three milkmaids in the dairy. A plough boy named Matthew, a cowherd, and a swineherd were also on the pay roll together with nine others simply called retainers. The list concludes with a carpenter and ten other names. The total household numbered just over 100 excluding the family: the first earl of Rutland had had a staff of ninety-four.

Instructions for the pantry, drawn up in October 1560, follow.[34] The meals served seem to have been breakfast, dinner, supper, 'threaclock', and 'alnight', and a list was kept of the numbers partaking of various repasts. Instructions for the baker told him how much flour was necessary to make a given number of loaves of different sorts.

The next section is headed 'Jewel house and debts' and it is followed by one on the wardrobe.[35] A winter gown for lady Willoughby cost £5 14s. and frieze was purchased at 2s. a yard and 26 yds of black frieze at 1s. 9d. a yard and 9¾ yds at 1s. 10d. for the gentlemen's liveries. Three dozen buttons at 6d. a dozen for the master's Spanish leather jerkin and two dozen for his satin doublet and the same number for his frieze jerkin are noted in the accounts. Cloth, linen, and buckram purchases all testify to the fact that most clothes were made in the house but a hat for Mr Bertie came from Lincoln and cost 5s. More

[34] Ibid., ff. 4–5.   [35] Ibid., ff. 6–51.

exotic clothes, such as velvet shoes for the master had to be purchased for 13s. 4d., and Mr Blande the skinner was paid £14 for sable and squirrel skins for Richard Bertie's gown. £9 8s. 10d. was the cost of the making of the master's taffeta gown, a satin gown, and a doublet, and Katherine bought two waistcoats for her husband for 16s.: she herself spent £3 for 2 oz. of musk purchased from a Portuguese. The master was obviously extremely well dressed for 7s. was paid for Holland linen for ruffs and borders for three shirts, and these same shirts were embroidered with silk thread that cost 12s. 4d. for half an ounce. He arrived back at Grimsthorpe in a silk hat trimmed with a gold band which had cost 18s. Others also were generously attired. Gold and silver lace for Mr Peregrine and Miss Susan cost £12, and Browne, a London capper, charged £6 for hats and caps for the master, her grace, and the children. A poor man who found Miss Susan's brooch had a 5s. reward, players received 10s. while George the trumpeter had 3s. 4d. The beds required the purchase of 5 stone of feathers at 6s. a stone, and a quilt for her grace's bed cost 50s. as compared with 10s. for a covering for a child's bed. Two tin chamber pots cost 2s. 8d., whereas two earthenware ones were only 4d.

The next section of the accounts deals with the victualling departments of this vast household.[36] Richard Browne the baker was paid 2s. 4d. for seven weeks' lodging in London up to 18 February 1562. For the bakehouse and pantry it would appear that standing corn was bought since Mr John Harrington of near-by Witham-on-the-Hill received £29 12s. for 73 acres of wheat, barley, peas, and oats. In January 1561, 10 qrs. of wheat were purchased for £8 10s. and 3 qrs. for £2 16s. and in April, 7 qrs. at 20s. a quarter: most months saw substantial purchases of wheat, and it would seem that the household ate wheaten bread. In October 1560, 21s. had been paid for the freight of 2 tuns of wine from London to Boston, 6d. for part of the charge of the cocket, and 12d. to the porters of Boston for landing the wine. How long this consignment of over 4,000 pints lasted the household is not known. Three quarts of new Rhenish wine and a pottle of Muscatel and one of Malmsey were also purchased, and six months later in April 1561, the cellar bought 3 tuns of Gascon wine at £11 a tun, the carriage of which from Boston to Bourne, a distance of about 24 miles, cost 5s. Wormwood wine at 20d. a gallon may have been drunk as apéritifs and, in addition, sack, claret (not invariably red wine before c. 1600), and Hippocras, a spiced wine, were purchased. Other victualling departments such as the spicery along with the chandlery and the laundry made large purchases. In October 1560, 2 lb. of currants cost 8d., 2 lb. rice 12d., 1 lb. dates 5d., half a ream of paper 4s., ink 20d. and quills 1½d.

[36] Ibid., ff. 112–47.

From Stamford, 1 lb. of aniseed was purchased for 14*d.*, 1 lb. of cumin seed 8*d.*, 2 oz. of cinnamon at 9*d.* an ounce, 2oz. ginger at 3*d.*, half a pound of pepper cost 20*d.*, 1 oz of cloves 6*d.* Also from there were acquired 2 lb. sugar at 1*s.* 4*d.* a pound, almonds at 5*d.* a pound, 1 lb. mace 14*d.*, 14 lb. of prunes at 1½*d.* a pound, 1 lb. of isinglass costing 2*s.* 6*d.*, 4 lb. of gray soap 12*d.*, 1 lb. of 'bisketts' 16*d.*, a quarter of olives 8*d.* and 2 lb. of capers for 2*s.* 11*d.*

Outdoors upkeep was a considerable expense.[37] Payments were made for hedging and for mowing: hedging cost 5*d.* a day for ten days and cutting 16 acres of oats at 1*s.* 3*d.* an acre cost £1. For a winnowing cloth the husbandry department bought 27½yds of 'corse Hardon' at 6*d.* a yard and two pairs of cart wheels for a wain at 15*s.* A man received 5*s.* for winding 300 fleeces at Vaudey. 5,000 nails bought at Fotheringay fair at 20*d.* a thousand cost 8*s.* 4*d.*, while Griffith spent 2*d.* on whipcord on his way from Grimsthorpe to London.

As we might expect, a scholarly family bought books. In January 1561, Mr Coverdale was reimbursed for 12*s.* that he had paid for 'Eliotes dictionarie', no doubt the fourth edition of 1559. Four copies of 'Lillies Gramer' cost 4*s.*, four copies of the 'Dialogues' 2*s.* 8*d.*, and four of Aesop's *Fables* 2*s.*: this purchase indicated that Coverdale was in fact a tutor to the Bertie children. Other household expenses were incurred in the reimbursement of officials who had lost money on the exchange of foreign currency when the English currency had been re-valued. Payments of 2*s.* were also made on several occasions to Richard Bertie, 'to my master at cards for 18th day', *i.e.* on 18 February 1561: rarely did these payments exceed 2*s.* and it may be that he stopped playing when his losses reached 2*s.* One year's household accounts are insufficient on which to base firm conclusions, but from this set of accounts it appears that Mr Bertie was given to rather more expenditure on clothes and entertainment than his lady, or it may simply be that after the years of exile his wardrobe was in greater need of renewal.

Among the Ancaster accounts are preserved some for the year 1522 which must be those of the household of the tenth lord Willoughby and his wife Mary de Salinas.[38] They are mostly receipts and payments from April to September of that year and show for May 1522 total payments of £78 8*s.* 4½*d.* Beef, mutton, and veal cost £7 8*s.* 9½*d.*, wax and tallow candles £1 15*s.* 9⅛*d.*, board wages to servants £1 14*s.* 3*d.*, wood and coal £3 12*s.* 7*d.*, and wheat, malt, and oats £11 17*s.* 11*d.* Most of these items recurred month after month with a purchase of bay salt in June for 7*s.* 11*d.* and in the same month a quarter's wages to servants totalling £51 3*s.* 4*d.* Over the six-month period £400 10*s.* 6½*d.* was spent on maintaining the household indoors.

[37] *Ibid.*, ff. 68–88.   [38] LAO Anc. 7/A/1.

We cannot unfortunately gain so accurate a picture of any small household in the county. If, for example, we knew more about the household in which another outstanding Lincolnshire female, Ann Askew, was brought up we might come to some judgement as to why she embraced the ideas she did. She was the daughter of Sir William Ayscough of Stallingborough and Elizabeth Wrottesley and probably was born there or at South Kelsey. Born in 1521, she is said to have had a good education and was a diligent reader of the Bible. She married Thomas Kyme of Kelsey[39] in 1536[40] and bore him two children, but he put her out of the house as she spent so much time preaching. In 1545 she was summoned to answer for alleged heresy and although she was released that year, the following May and June she was re-arrested. Even under torture she did not reveal the names of any who shared her views and she was particularly asked about the duchess of Suffolk's beliefs. On 16 July 1546 she was burnt at Smithfield, one of the Protestant martyrs whose fate only served to strengthen the cause of those whose radical opinions of church reformation went far beyond the ideas of their sovereign.

Little information can be gathered about the houses and households of the leading gentry beyond the fact that many of them built spacious mansions on the monastic properties that they had acquired.[41] Little documentation has come to light that will permit a description on the same scale as for the life at Grimsthorpe of life in, for example, Anthony Ellys's house at Great Ponton built *c.* 1516[42] or Thomas Cony's manor house at Bassingthorpe built in 1568. The smaller households as well as the larger ones took part in hunting, and on Saxton's map of 1576 a dozen parks are shown and rules for coursing were drawn up by Nottinghamshire and Lincolnshire gentlemen in Elizabeth I's reign.[43]

There exists for the years 1564–96 the Cony Estate Book which belonged to Thomas Cony of Bassingthorpe (1529–1611).[44] His father had been a merchant of the Staple at Calais who had died in 1545, and thus the estate is an example of landed wealth being based on trade. By the 1560s Bassingthorpe was prospering and inventories of the livestock were made during a period of over thirty years. In 1564 Thomas Cony possessed 83 cattle, 847 sheep, an additional 53 cattle and 17 horses. At another time the names of the horses were noted: Bailye, Berril, Chaworth, Farington, Foster, Grantham, Hanson, Harman, Holines,

---

[39] *Sic* in DNB but not in *Lincs. Pedigrees.*   [40] Goff, *op. cit.,* p. 167.

[41] A little information is available in *Notices and Remains of the Family of Tyrwhitt,* reprinted 1872.

[42] M. W. Barley, *Lincolnshire and the Fens,* London, 1952, p. 25.

[43] *Ibid.,* p. 97.

[44] Lincs. NQ, I, 1888–9, pp. 113–16, 132–3, 164–6, 198–9, 230–33.

Holmes, Kinlonge's Mare, Norman, Okeley, Oxeman, Reve, Rookbie, Savile, Stanhop, Stokes, and Warren. In 1577 an inventory was taken of the household goods. The list includes the furniture in the hall, the dining parlour, which had a carpet *i.e.* a tablecloth, the low parlour, and Mr Welby's parlour with his bedroom adjoining. There were five other principal bedrooms, one for the mistress of the house, one called 'my lord Wraies', a boarded chamber, and a painted chamber. The contents of the press in the great chamber were also recorded. Two garrets existed, the high garret and the maids' garret, and it is clear from this reference and from similar ones to the hinds' chamber and the shepherds' chamber that dormitory accommodation was normal for the servants. As well as another sitting-room 'in the court' and a nursery, there were the usual domestic offices of a large household. Mention is made of a kitchen and a far kitchen, a dry larder, the west larder house, a brewhouse, a buttery, a cellar, and a milk-house, and there were ample stables.[45]

Such a well-furnished house had a plentiful supply of chairs and tables. The dining-room had, in addition to the essential tables and stools, two pictures, one of Henry VIII and the other of Edward VI, two Bibles, Grafton's *Chronicle* and an *Abridgement of the Statues.*[46] The furniture is frequently of wainscot, that is oak, and the mistress's chamber had a trundle (truckle) bed as well as a standing bed and a low bed. She also had her husband's portrait and her own on two boards. Curtains, feather beds, coverlets made in a variety of materials, chests, and foot stools appear in abundance, and Mrs Cony even had a sheaf of arrows, two bills, and a halberd in her bedroom. 'Lord Wraies chamber' had portraits of queen Mary and queen Elizabeth and five tapestry hangings. The kitchen was well equipped with spits great and small, three dripping pans, a meat chopper, a brass mortar and iron pestle, two frying-pans, a stone mortar, and a wooden pestle, a grater, and a pair of bellows. In the dairy three pans, thirteen pancheons, eight earthen pots, a butter tub, ten cheese vats, three churns, and a cheese press all testify to the quantity of provisions that was supplied to the household. The brewhouse with mashing vats and cooler supplied ale and beer to the household but, if Mr and Mrs Cony drank wine, no record of it appears in the accounts that are in print.

When we turn to the houses of the poorer farmers it is difficult to estimate just how much accommodation they enjoyed; with farm labourers any assessment is still more difficult. Those who had sufficient worldly possessions to think it worthwhile to make a will or who, dying intestate, had relations who took out letters of administration, usually

[45] See also M. W. Barley, *The English Farmhouse and Cottage*, London, 1961, p. 47.
[46] Lincs. NQ, I, p. 133.

had inventories taken of their moveables, and this return would give some indication of the size and complexity of the house. Certainly the last three decades of Elizabeth's reign saw the beginning of what has been termed 'the first phase of the housing revolution which lasted from 1575 to 1615.'[47] Significant changes were made if we compare the houses of 1600 with those of the early Tudor period. Peasant houses of the late Middle Ages very rarely cooked meat or baked bread in an oven.[48] and only in the last decade of Elizabeth's reign did the kitchen begin to be an integral part of the house.[49] The kitchen, if one had existed, had been a distinct building often free standing and separate, and most cooking was done in the hall where the family lived and where the food was eaten. Only in the limestone belt, especially on the Lincolnshire Edge were cottages built in stone, and there they often had walls of two skins of stone with earth between. Lincolnshire did not have an over-abundant supply of timber, and the shortage became more marked in the second half of the sixteenth century, so, many poor cottagers who could neither obtain timber nor afford the services of a carpenter, developed the art of building mud or clay walls with the minimum of wood. Clay mixed with straw, hay, or cow dung to bind it was the principal building material for poor cottagers' walls. In the isle of Axholme, turf walls continued well into the Tudor era. And yet, changes were taking place even before the housing boom post-1575: the open hall was on its way out by 1500, and the building of chambers over the hall necessitated a brick chimney for the hall fire and a staircase, or at least a ladder, to gain access to the upper floor. By 1500 also in the south-east of the country, the one-roomed house had virtually disappeared, and another room at the end of the hall became the principal sleeping-room.

These refinements, however, spread only slowly from the south-east. The Lincolnshire marshland farmer was as rich as his counterpart in Kent between the 1530s and the 1560s but his household goods were fewer than those of the Kentish farmer.[50] It is significant that the hall was called the house and this definition, found in the inventories, demonstrates quite clearly that one-roomed houses were still quite common in mid-Tudor times. But such humble houses were diminishing since, whereas two-thirds of the inventories for Lincolnshire in the 1530s fail to mention distinct rooms in the house, only one third of those for 1572 omit to mention different rooms. The very fertility of the soil attracted a greater number of small and medium farmers than did poorer soils, and the custom of partible inheritance reinforced that trend. Where common land was unstinted even landless labourers might obtain a

---

[47] M. W. Barley, *The English Farmhouse and Cottage*, pp. 57 et seq.
[48] *Ibid.*, p. 5.   [49] *Ibid.*, p. 94.   [50] *Ibid.*, p. 46.

living. This meant, then, that in these areas—the fens are an outstanding example—wealth was more widely dispersed, and therefore the standard of housing was of greater simplicity. The isle of Axholme, another area where wealth was widely dispersed and where rural industry provided a supplement to agricultural incomes, provides twenty inventories in the year 1557–8 of the goods of deceased persons, and only two of them mention details of different rooms in the house. They were not all poor people for evidence abounds of the hemp industry, but few had ovens and they obviously took food to the bakers to be cooked. Lincolnshire peasants possessed the popular painted cloths, the poor man's tapestry, which were pieces of canvas stretched on wooden frames and painted by a painter-stainer. This was apparently a cheaper form of wall decoration than painting the plaster itself although occasionally richer farmers had the walls painted. The two-roomed houses in Lincolnshire usually had their entrance at the middle of one side, facing a chimney stack, which divided the two rooms, and which might have either one flue for the hall, since the absence of a fire in the sleeping room was common, or two flues, one for the hall and one for the parlour.

Between 1540 and 1570 more land probably changed hands than at any time between the Norman Conquest and the sixteenth century and the yeoman farmer secured a share of it. With more land and with increased prices of corn[51] and other farm products, the yeoman farmer and even the larger husbandman were able to add to their houses or even to build new ones. Moreover, the rise in population necessitated the building of more accommodation, and records show that cottage building especially reached its peak between 1580 and 1630.[52] William Harrison in his *Description of England* written in 1577 noted that building in timber was giving way to stone, that chimneys were everywhere being constructed, and windows glazed. Lincolnshire was, relatively to other counties, poorly supplied with timber as is shown by the burning of cow dung for fuel, but the growing affluence of some farmers permitted them to make some improvements to their houses using even scarce materials. It is interesting to note that some of these improvements such as window glass and floor boards were regarded as tenants' fittings which might be removed on the termination of a tenancy. By the end of Elizabeth's reign even those who, according to their inventories, had goods worth only £10 lived in two-roomed houses,[53] and

[51] The average price for wheat 1540–82 was 13s. 10½d. a qr. as against 6s. 10d. a qr. 1500–40—Thorold Rogers, *A History of Agriculture and Prices in England*, IV, London, 1882, p. 292. In 1583–92 wheat per qr. was 23s. 8¼d., and in 1593–1602 34s. 10¼d.— *Ibid.*, V, p. 276.

[52] M. W. Barley, *The English Farmhouse and Cottage*, p. 59; Barley, *The House and Home*, London 1963, p. 31 *et seq.*

[53] M. W. Barley, *The English Farmhouse*, op. cit., p. 78.

by this period three-roomed houses were as common as two-roomed ones. This third room might be on the ground floor, a service room, or it might be a chamber over the hall or parlour, or it might be merely a loft in the roof at the level of the eaves. In the villages around the Wash a greater homogeneity of housing existed than elsewhere in the county for nearly all the peasants with goods worth from £15 to £50 have a four-roomed house with a hall and parlour and a chamber over one or the other and one service room. All this new building from the 1570s was done mostly in timber with clay walls, except in the limestone uplands where stone was plentiful. In the fens, in the Humberside villages, and those on Trent side, some construction in brick had been used in the Middle Ages. The roofing was usually of thatch. In the fenlands and parts of the marshland there was a little reed thatching but this required skilled labour; elsewhere, wheat, rye, and even barley straw served to roof a house as well as to thatch a hayrick.

Inside these new houses the ground floors were usually of earth. Earth or clay mixed with ox-blood and ashes formed a surface that could even be polished. In the south-west of the county, limestone slabs could be used for there they were fairly cheap, but nowhere do bricks appear to have been common in the Tudor period. Boards, frequently not nailed down, formed the upper floors. By leaving them loose they were regarded as removable by the tenant, and also it was often easier to bring bulky goods to an upper storey by hauling them through a hole than by dragging them up narrow winding stairs. However, some upper floors were made of plaster of which the highest quality, used at Doddington, was gypsum. The shortage of timber and hence its high cost may well have been one factor that persuaded tenants to have plaster floors, and another one was that it was possible to have a more level floor in that material than in wood. Rush matting, probably made in the household or imported from the fenlands, covered these floors.

That houses of yeomen, husbandmen, and even cottagers were becoming larger and more complex is known from a couple of surveys made shortly after Elizabeth I's death. In 1608, the officials of the duchy of Lancaster ordered Ralph Treswell to survey the Duchy properties in Lincolnshire,[54] and six years later Henry Valentine surveyed the Willoughby d'Eresby manor of Toynton on the southern edge of the Wolds. The relevant thing is that they made records of the houses as well as of the lands for they realized that in the event of a rise in rents, the houses were a good indicator of a tenant's prosperity. The size of the houses varied on the Duchy's estates from region to region. The Duchy had estates in the upland area at Waddington near Lincoln for example

<hr>

[54] *Ibid.*, pp. 87–9 quoting PRO DL 42/119.

and at Greetham near Horncastle; in the marsh at Steeping, Ingoldmells, Thoresby, and Saltfleetby; in the fens at Sutton, Wainfleet,
Wrangle, and in the East, West, and North Fen, and also the important
honour of Bolingbroke which covered wolds and fenland. It is possible
therefore to see the difference in the size of houses in the upland villages
and those on the marshland and in the fenland.[55] While the simplest
form of house and parlour forms only 9·3 per cent of the houses surveyed on the uplands, it comprises 41·2 per cent of those on the marshland, and 41·7 per cent of those in the fenland villages. The house and
parlour plus service room was, in 1608, 11·2 per cent of those on the
uplands, 41·2 per cent on the marsh, and 28·4 per cent of those surveyed
in the fen villages. The house and parlour plus chamber over one or the
other of the former was 14 per cent, 5·9 per cent and 3·7 per cent; the
house, parlour, and two chambers, 8·4 per cent, none, and 1·8 per cent;
the house, parlour, service room, and chamber, 17·8 per cent, 11·7 per
cent, and 15·1 per cent. Houses with a hall, parlour, service room, and
two chambers formed 23·4 per cent in upland villages and 1·8 per cent
in the fen, while houses with more than five rooms were 15·9 per cent of
those surveyed on the upland and only 7·5 per cent of those in the fenland villages, with none in the marsh.

Cottages were also measured by the Duchy surveyor and the numbers in the three areas of the one-roomed type were 1, 1, and 3 respectively. The numbers of those with a house and parlour were 17, 8, and
7. Of more elaborate types none is recorded in the fen villages, but in the
upland villages there were 5 with a house, parlour, and service room
and 12 in the marshland villages. The house, parlour, and chamber, and
even larger cottages, *i.e.* above three rooms, appeared only in the
upland, and there were 3 and 7 respectively of these types. Taking these
two surveys of 1608 and 1614 and comparing the houses at the time of
the survey with their state at the time of the tenants' deaths, as recorded
in their inventories, it can be seen that tenants were rebuilding or adding
a room to their properties. Admittedly this is evidence from the post-
Tudor period but there are good general grounds for believing that
this rebuilding and addition had been going on since about 1575. Men
such as Edward Lacon of Tetney and Adam Heneage of Donington-on-
Bain were doing so, but they were gentlemen: nevertheless, even husbandmen with no freehold land were adding to their properties.[56]

Something is also known about the houses of the clergy. Neighbours
made inventories of the goods of deceased clergy but also, from 1571,[57]
rectors and vicars made returns of property belonging to the parish
church, and thus, information about rectories and vicarages is available.
From 1605 the bishops of Lincoln asked very detailed questions 'about

[55] *Ibid.*, p. 88.   [56] *Ibid.*, p. 90.   [57] *Ibid.*, p. 91.

the size of the house, the materials of the walls and roofs, and the number and names of the rooms.'[58] The houses were usually described by the number of bays: the bay sometimes contained more than one room on the ground floor and the returns show quite clearly that at the end of Elizabeth's reign most of the rooms were chambered over. Rarely did parsons have a study at this time and, but for the presence of a few books, the contents of their houses varied little from those of the wealthier yeomen or, in the fens, of the yeomen of middling status. The size of the parsonage houses in Lincolnshire tended to be smaller than in some counties, since in parts of the shire the parishes were small and the incumbents poorly remunerated. In 1605-6, 10·9 per cent of the 166 houses in the returns had only two bays, probably, that is, four rooms, while 36·2 per cent had three. About 21 per cent had four bays; 12 per cent had five; 12·7 per cent had six, and only 7·2 per cent had seven or more bays.

However, parsonages had undoubtedly improved during the century: at Bitchfield and West Rasen in 1540 they contained only a hall and a parlour, and a hall, kitchen, and parlour with a chamber respectively.[59] But considerable differences of wealth existed among parsons. The difference between the housing standard of the parson and his neighbours was, if anything, more marked at the end of Elizabeth's reign than it had been in 1540.[60] The parsonage at Thorpe-on-the-Hill had sixteen rooms but the incumbent did have five children living: he also had a study and a maid's chamber. Most of the parsons appear to have had servants living in, some of whom may have been farm workers if the incumbent had a large glebe that he cultivated attentively. Inventories permit a comparison of the household furnishings at various periods. In the decade 1530-40 they show that few parsons had chairs and they must have sat upon stools which were so common that they were not usually included in an inventory. By 1590 parsons' houses were certainly better furnished for chairs and even desks are frequently mentioned, as are framed tables that had taken the place of trestle tables. Painted cloths, testers, arrases, and stained glass windows which were rare in 1530 were common enough sixty years later. Linen appears in considerable quantities; coverlets, cloths, towels, and a supply of thirty sheets being not uncommon. Generally there were no books in laymen's homes except the Bible, but whereas in the 1530s only one out of seven parsons had any books, by 1590 practically all clergy had books and many had a study. Even the poor parson of

[58] *Ibid.*, p. 92.
[59] F. W. Brooks, 'The Social Position of the Parson in the Sixteenth Century', *Jnl of the Br. Arch. Ass.*, 3rd Ser., X, 1945-7, pp. 23-37.
[60] Brooks, *loc. cit.*, p. 29.

Grainsby, 6½ miles south of Grimsby, who left only £9 2s. had books worth 13s. 4d.

Even earlier in the century parsons also had a reasonable wardrobe for John Bedall, vicar of Bardney, who died in 1541 had four shirts, a surplice, two kerchiefs, a black gown, a worsted gown, two old coats, two old doublets, two pairs of hose, the whole valued at £2 4s., a quarter of his estate.[61] By 1590–1600 the itemizing of clothes had been abandoned and so comparisons cannot be made. The increase in plate probably demonstrates, as accurately as any one item can, the increased wealth of the clergy and laity alike. At Bassingham, a parson left a basin and ewer of pewter, seven basins of 'latyn' (brass), two dishes, a hanging laver, eight saucers, a charger, eleven plates and six pots all of pewter, and the amount of silver plate had much increased by the 1590s. Silver salts, bowls, and spoons turn up in parsons' inventories whereas the average cottager seems to have had little plate—at most one or two pewter dishes. The average countryman of the period ate his food from treen plates, if he did not still use the four-inch trencher of stale bread.

The average parson was, of course, a farmer since their inventories show that they had ploughs, wains, carts, corn in store, oxen, and cattle. In towns parsons usually had no livestock except a pig and some poultry, but even there they kept a few hives of bees, whereas such hives are rarely mentioned in husbandmen's inventories. Flocks of fifty to a hundred sheep are fairly common possessions of country parsons and they also kept more horses than the average yeoman. Nearly all kept poultry, and it has been suggested that increased numbers of poultry in the last decade of the century are due to the attention which parsons' wives lavished on the poultry—three of them were even keeping turkeys.[62] Certain evidence would point to the fact that the Elizabethan clergy were not miserably poor; that they were not only better off in the 1590s than they had been in the 1530s but that they were relatively better off *vis-à-vis* the laity. It all depended on the prosperity of the village and the increased price of corn since both tithes and the profit from the glebe must have risen in the later decades of the sixteenth century. A parson's wife and family were an asset in a peasant economy.

But, it should not be concluded that every house was becoming larger and every household more prosperous in the Elizabethan era. The sources, such as inventories and wills and other returns which are open to us, tell us nothing of the rapidly increasing numbers who did not feature in tax returns or make wills. The era, one of fairly steady wages and rising prices, was a grim one for large sectors of the population. Nor did the poor alone suffer, for some of the gentry, often

[61] *Ibid.*, p. 32.   [62] *Ibid.*, p. 34.

perhaps through their own fault, were forced to sell their lands. Families were rising and falling, as they have done in all historical periods, but perhaps at a slightly accelerated rate between 1540 and 1640. Even noblemen were selling, since Thomas lord Burgh who inherited estates at Lea, Skellingthorpe, and Gainsborough in 1584 had sold them all by the time of his death in 1597. Sir Roger Dalison of Laughton had bought Lea in 1592, only to mortgage it to his cousin Sir Thomas Monson in 1599 who reconveyed it to Dalison. Later, in 1600, Dalison sold it to Sir Edmund Anderson L.C.J.—nevertheless, he died in debt.[63] Anderson, who had been born at Broughton near Brigg, had become Lord Chief Justice of the court of Common Pleas in 1583 and continued in that office until his death in 1605 but he had settled at Eyworth in Bedfordshire, and in 1600 may well have been acquiring the property for one of his sons.

A few Lincolnshire households, some not always in the poorest income bracket, still suffered in the Tudor period from the stigma of servile tenure. Most of these dwelt on royal estates, in particular, on the Lincolnshire estates belonging to the duchy of Lancaster.[64] Fifty-three persons belonging to the manor of Long Bennington (between Grantham and Newark) were bondmen of blood, and their children also shared this unfree status. When, in 1570, the queen considered giving to Sir Henry Lee the privilege of receiving and enforcing the payment of manumission money from these serfs, a jury was appointed to enquire into their numbers and their places of residence. Out of the fifty-three serfs, twenty-nine were resident on the manor or in the adjacent village of Foston, and seven were fairly near but over the county boundary in Nottinghamshire. A further thirteen were living in Lincolnshire only between two and seven miles away from Long Bennington, but two had gone into Norfolk, one to Northamptonshire, and one had settled as far away as Middlesex. The value of the goods of thirty-four out of the fifty-three was assessed at between £199 3s. 6d. and £7 0s. 4d. and attempts were made to reach agreed figures for manumission. The assessment was about one third of their lands and goods and, although there is no proof that these sums were in fact paid, the claim was a heavy one. Bondmen on the duchy of Lancaster's estates were unlucky, for servile tenure elsewhere just died out although some grants of manumission were still being made in the later sixteenth century.

John Copledyke of Harrington, in his will dated 23 June 1582, desired his brother Francis "to manumit and make free Christopher and

[63] LAO 2 Anc. 1/2/1–23.
[64] W. H. Hosford, 'The Elizabethan Serfs of Long Bennington Lincs', *Nottingham Medieval Studies*, IV, 1960, pp. 105–12.

Thomas Guy 'villeynes regardant' belonging to the manor of Frieston."[65] Manumission had also taken place at Frampton in 1562.[66] Bond tenants were recorded at Ingoldmells as late as 1604[67] whereas villeinage was extinct on the wolds and in Kesteven before 1485, while in some of the marsh parishes of Lindsey villeins came by degrees to be copyholders, although a few bondmen remained in the late sixteenth century. These households, though, were an insignificant number of Lincolnshire households but their fate serves to remind us that change in the social structure during the sixteenth century was gradual.

[65] A. R. Maddison (ed.), *Lincs. Wills*, I, 329, p. 122.
[66] Deeds of Magdalen college, Oxford, HMC *4th Rep.*, 1874, p. 458.
[67] C. Brears, *Lincolnshire in the 17th and 18th centuries*, London, 1940, p. 14.

CHAPTER XI

RELIGION IN ELIZABETHAN LINCOLNSHIRE

I N an earlier chapter we reviewed some of the effects of the Henrician legislation upon both clergy and laity, and noted their reactions to the changes in religion during his reign. Although the rebellion was easily suppressed, and although most of the gentry and many of the yeomanry benefited materially from the sale of monastic lands, probably few Lincolnshire men and women were convinced in their hearts of the rightness of the new religious order. As late as 1547 there were probably few Protestants in Lincolnshire, with the notable exception of Katherine Willoughby, and, the previous year, of Ann Askew, while there were many who, although they were not like Henry Litherland and James Mallet (executed in 1538 and 1543 respectively),[1] opposed the reforms in the religious order as much as they dared. It might be presumed that Mary's return to the old ways in religion was popular in the county, for bishop Holbeach (1547–52) had alienated much episcopal property, and his successor John Taylor (1552–53) was a staunch Protestant, and neither of them had been well liked. Neither does any protest appear to have been made against Mary's deprivation of the married clergy. Within the shire at least seventy were deprived of their livings and eleven resigned from them, usually because they had been married, during Edward VI's reign.[2] The conservative religious sentiments of Lincolnshire men and women and the moderation of the two Marian bishops, John White (1554–56) and Thomas Watson (1556–59), brought about a situation where no martyrs' blood stained the county during Mary's reign. Thomas Armstrong of Corby and his wife were convicted of heresy but recanted, and Ambrose Sutton was found guilty of eating meat in Lent, but both suffered light punishment.[3] Anthony Meres of Aubourn, the archdeacon of Stow, John Aylmer, and the archdeacon of Lincoln, Nicholas Bullingham, fled to the Continent,[4] and we know of others who left the county. But it

[1] R. E. G. Cole (ed.), 'Chapter Acts of Lincoln Cathedral', LRS 13, 1917, p. xv.

[2] Lincs. NQ, v, vi, *passim.*

[3] R. E. G. Cole (ed), 'The Chapter Acts of the Cathedral Church of Lincoln', LRS 15, 1920, p. xiv.

[4] *Ibid.,* p. xxi.

would appear that, in general, Lincolnshire men and women were not dissatisfied with a return to Roman obedience.

What then was the attitude in the county to the fourth religious shift in a quarter of a century? After the break with Rome in the 1530s, the ardent Protestantism of 1547-53, and the return to Rome under Mary, a new, a middle way was initiated by Elizabeth I in 1559. To a remarkable degree it appears to have been one of acceptance—at any rate until the 1580s—for the people were accustomed to having their religious life directed for them from above and for twenty-five years the directing power had been the State rather than the Church. Of course in some spheres these changes made little difference to the way in which institutions continued and worked. For example the duties of the bishop, of the dean and chapter of the cathedral church of St Mary, of the archdeacons, and of the probate courts changed remarkably little in many respects throughout the sixteenth century. On the other hand, the new form of divine service, with communion in both kinds, altered church furnishings and the presence of a married clergy made profound differences in the religious life of parishioners. Relics of the old religion could not be banished overnight and lost without a trace. One of the most lasting survivals of the old order was the considerable number of surviving ex-monks, nuns, friars, and chantry priests who were still living in Elizabeth I's reign. In so far as many of them were in receipt of pensions, the government continued to have an interest in them and from time to time asked for returns as to whether they were still living and drawing their pensions.[5]

One such enquiry was initiated in June 1569 when a demand was made to know the date of death of all who had held pensions since 1540 and also what promotions they had obtained before their decease. During the six months following, bishop Bullingham, working through the dean and chapter and the two archdeacons, made diligent enquiries to ascertain which pensioned ex-monks, nuns, friars, and chantry priests had died, and he supplied the Exchequer with as accurate dates of death as he could. Bishop Cooper in response to a similar request, sent returns on 19 June 1574.[6] As late as this, nine laymen and two laywomen were living who were drawing annuities, eleven ex-nuns, at least fourteen ex-monks or ex-canons and probably three more, and four former chantry priests. Of the twenty-one capable of holding a living eight were beneficed. Robert Lindley and William Tofte were vicars of Grimsby and Fotherby respectively, and the parson of Harrington was a former chantry priest there. George Justice at Saleby, Roger Wytters

[5] G. A. J. Hodgett, (ed.) 'The State of the Ex-religious and Chantry Priests, 1547-74', LRS 53, 1959, pp. 126-50.

[6] LRS 53, pp. 146-8.

at Hykeham, Thomas Stevenson, vicar of Langton-by-Wragby, Edward Smyth, vicar of Saxilby, and Edmund Knowles, the parson of Faldingworth, had all been either chantry priests or in religion. Some of them had a long tenure for Edmund Knowles was rector until his death in or shortly before 1582.[7] Smythe was still at Harrington in 1580, John Cooke who had been at Thornton college was at Barrow in 1576, and that same year John Coleman, formerly of St Katherine's Lincoln, was still curate at Waltham. Thomas Powtrell was still vicar of Rauceby in 1574 and Roger Wytters died in or shortly before 1579. So there were many survivors of the old order celebrating in churches in the 1570s and even a few in the 1580s. They were acceptors of the new way in religion either willingly or because they were 'vicars of Bray'.

Apart, however, from these survivors and the lack of change or the minimal change that took place in the administration of the cathedral, with which we shall deal later, what did 1559 really mean? First, it meant, as had happened under Mary to an even larger extent, the deprivation of a number of clergy. They were those who would not accept the abandonment of the old religion, the denial of papal supremacy, and the rejection of the Roman doctrines on transubstantiation. The principal ecclesiastic in the shire, the bishop of Lincoln, Thomas Watson was arrested in London in April 1559; released from the Tower in June, he was given ten days to decide whether to take the new oath and on his refusal to do so he was, on the 26th, deprived of his see of Lincoln. He was to spend the remaining twenty-five years of his life in custody, sometimes in the Tower, sometimes guarded in the households of various bishops, but the county of Lincoln knew him no more. Between Elizabeth's accession and the end of 1562 at least eleven parish clergy were deprived and resigned;[8] probably those who resigned and certainly those who were deprived, suffered because they would not take the oath which in effect compelled them to abandon the old beliefs by accepting the new Prayer Book and acknowledging the queen as supreme over the national church. William Tressam who held the prebendal stall of Asgarby was deprived and Christopher Southouse took his place.[9] Only one bishop, Kitchin of Llandaff, would have anything to do with the new Prayer Book and the supremacy oath, but the solidarity of the bishops in their stand was not reflected among the lower ranks of the clergy: between August and October 1559 most of them fell in with the government's wishes. The surrender of the mass of clergy undoubtedly persuaded the laity to accept the religious changes,

[7] *Ibid.*, p. 80, fn.
[8] Lincs. NQ, v, vi, *passim* and LAAS xxiv, pt. i, 1897, pp. 13–29 and xxv, pt. ii, 1900, pp. 459–519.
[9] LAAS xxv, pt. ii, p. 473.

except in a few parts of the country of which Lincolnshire was not one.

Secondly the religious changes of 1559 meant the abandonment of superstitious objects. The churchwardens made returns of such articles of church furniture, vestments, and vessels as had been used in Mary's reign but which the new régime considered superstitious. An episcopal register called *Inventarium Monumentorum Superstitionis* contains the returns.[10] The lists include such objects as judases (seven-branch candlesticks), cross clothes, altar cloths, 'David psalters', and processioners— either office books or candlesticks used in processions. Vestments became bed-hangings in some places, and bishop Bullingham on a visit to Ashby-by-Horncastle ordered his men to "ryve bowks in peces."[11] At Bilsby the mass books were sold but other papistical books were torn to pieces. Out went the Lenten veil at Bratoft along with the censers, holy water vats, paxes (tablets kissed by the priest and the congregation) and pyxes. At Cadney the clappers, *i.e.* rattles used to summon people to church on the last three days of holy week when bells were not rung, were sold, and at Claxby Pluckacre, and Cumberworth the parishioners disposed of vestments which were made into dresses for players. This, like the use of church bells for cattle, and the report that a man at Usselby put the sacring bell round the neck of one of his sheep, would seem to denote a hard-line Protestant approach. At Walesby someone used the holy water vat to water horses and to wash clothes in, so that it is hardly surprising when we hear that at Skidbrooke Deacon (? near Saltfleet) the cope and the mass books had been stolen probably so that no one might put holy things to profane uses.

Certain changes were made in the fabric of the church itself as a consequence of the new order in religion. Rood screens went out of many churches. In addition to the Holy Rood, many screens had carvings of the Virgin or St John and often a representation of All Hallows for that was the most common dedication in the county. These statues had been objects of veneration and such veneration was frowned upon. Another change apparent to the worshipper was the greater simplicity of the altar or communion table and the presence of new patens as well as new chalices as the communion was given in both kinds.

On this subject interesting evidence has come to light of the way in which many parishes replaced their communion plate, presumably at the instance of the bishop. In 1571, the archbishop of York in a series of questions and articles urged his incumbents, "Ye . . . shall minister the holy communion in no chalice nor a profane cup or glass, but in a communion cup of silver, and with a cover of silver appointed also for

---

[10] Lincs. NQ, XIV, 1916–17, p. 80 *et seq.*
[11] *Ibid.*, p. 85.

the Communion bread."[11a] No such order has been found for the diocese of Lincoln, but the majority of communion cups of the Tudor
period in the county (nearly 70 in all) date from 1569, although some
eleven pieces are before this date. It would thus seem that such an order
was issued in the diocese just before the York provincial visitation of 1571.

Not all parishes could afford newly fashioned chalices from accredited
makers, so many of the poorer churches took advantage of itinerant
silversmiths who sometimes used their own maker's mark, but often no
mark at all. The most prolific of all the marks in Lincolnshire is that of a
silversmith with the symbol I over M. The identification of this crafts-
man is not certain, but that he was based within the county may be seen
from the fact that whereas some sixty or so of his cups survive in Lincolnshire, his mark is only to be seen elsewhere on one chalice in
Nottinghamshire and one in Northamptonshire. He is probably to be
identified as John Morley of Lincoln who is mentioned as paying a fine
of membership in the Goldsmiths' Minute Book in 1573.[11b]

Thus in one sweep many parishes refurbished their plate in or about
1569, often using local craftsmen. How far this represented a re-shaping
of pre-Reformation (and therefore unacceptable to the new Reformed
spirit) chalices, as we know happened in some cases, and how far it
represented new acquisitions, any earlier plate being sold, is not clear.
But throughout the county today it is the Tudor plate which has most
frequently survived.

As preachers became more common in the parish churches, seating
became desirable if not essential. Therefore, pews which had been the
perquisite of the wealthy or the infirm began to multiply and a pulpit
was installed.[12] Thus the parish church began to assume the aspect of the
Anglican church of today rather than that of the typical parish church
of the late Middle Ages.

The whole aim of the government policy, in the years between 1559
and 1562, was to build a Church to which all could conform. Elizabeth's
via media was designed to avoid the excesses of Edward VI's second
Prayer Book, and to give the impression that many of the old forms in
worship remained, and it was thereby hoped that moderate Catholics
would be able to worship within the parish church without too much
offence being given to their consciences. For a number of years many
Catholics managed to do this. On the other hand, the clear breach with
Rome and the denial of the doctrine of transubstantiation was designed

[11a] *Articles of Edmund Grindall* (Parker Society, 1843) p. 124. In this and what follows,
I am particularly grateful to Rev. Mr Peter Hawker of Lincoln, and to Dr. Alan Rogers.
[11b] Charles Oman, *English Church Plate, 597–1830*, 1957; Goldsmiths' Minute Book
(Goldsmiths' Library), i, p. 159.
[12] E. Cardwell, *Documentary Annals*, 1844, I, p. 222.

to attract all but the most ardent Protestants who disliked any ceremonial and who mistrusted episcopal government. Until the Jesuits
stirred up the Catholics, and until Puritan ideas were more boldly
expressed in the 1580s, the government had a measure of success with its
via media, and yet it has often been remarked that the settlement pleased
nobody. One of its sequels was that the privy council was constantly
fearing that opposition to the Church as by law established might
emerge and so it ordered loyalty checks on leading men in the shire to
ascertain where their sympathies lay.

On 20 October 1564 the council sent a letter to bishop Nicholas
Bullingham to which he replied on 7 November.[13] This was his con-
fidential report on the views of various leading men in the shire: those
who approved the new dispensations he described as 'earnest in
religion'; those who did not, as 'hinderers'. Of the Lincoln J.P.s,
Richard Disney, Edmund Hall, Robert Carr, and Anthony Thorold fell
into the first category, while Robert Dymoke, Robert Harrington, and
William Thorold belonged to the second. In Kesteven, Richard Bertie,
Thomas St Paul, John Aylmer (the archdeacon of Lincoln), Thomas
Godwine (canon residentiary), William Porter, Charles Wingfield
gentleman,[14] Richard Meres, and John Harrington gentleman were
earnest in religion and to be trusted there. Of the Kesteven J.P.s,
Adelard Welby, Hunston and John Man were earnest, but Leonard Irby
gentleman, Holland, and Ogle were indifferent. In Holland, Bertie, St
Paul, the archdeacon and the canon with Edmund Lyall, William
Derby, and Laurence Meres were earnest and to be trusted and, of the
justices, Sir Richard Thimbleby, Sir William Skipwith, Thomas St
Paul, Robert Monson, Laurence Meres, and Adelard Welby were
earnest. Sir Edward Dymoke, Richard Bolles, Charles Willoughby,
Christopher Wray, James Smyth, Tristram Tyrwhit, William Manby,
Anthony Tournay, and Richard Cracroft were described as indifferent,
while Sir Robert Tyrwhit, John Copledyke, and Humphrey Littlebury
were hinderers. Turning to the city of Lincoln the bishop thought the
mayor, John Hutchinson, and Nicholas Faulkener, earnest; Thomas
Wright, George Stamp, William Goodknap, William Kent, George
Porter, Leon Ellis, and Thomas[15] Fulbeck, indifferent; Richard Carter,
William Scolfield, and Edward Hallelary, hinderers.[16] Martin
Hollingwourth late alderman was 'veray earnest in religion, honest and
politique.' Then follows a classification of the notables of Grantham

[13] Camden Soc., *Camden Miscellany*, no. 9, 1895, pp. 26–8.
[14] All others in the list are esquires unless stated to the contrary.
[15] The Christian name is supplied from 'A list of Mayors etc.' compiled by J. B. King.
[16] All these men had been or were to become mayors.

into the same three categories; in the first, Roger Johnson, Thomas Tilson and John Taylor; in the indifferent class Simon Hanson, Gabriel Best, John Picke, Thomas Simpson, and Robert Gibbon while the alderman (mayor) Humphrey Duckar with George Atkinson, Robert Wright, John Brotherton and Edward Morton were opposed to the new order. In forming his conclusions the bishop consulted with his archdeacon John Aylmer, his registrar Thomas Tyler (Taylor) and Thomas St Paul. Of course the government wanted to know the extent of conformability among the clergy as well as among the laity, but in the 1560s this was no problem as those who had refused to subscribe the oath had been deprived: it was to become a problem in the 1580s when Puritanism came to the fore. Meanwhile, in 1576 in returns covering 396 clergy in the archdeaconry of Lincoln, only one was 'vehemently suspect' of not conforming.[17] These then were some of the changes which the Elizabethan settlement of 1559–62 entailed.

In some senses the life of the Church continued little changed, and perhaps in no sphere of the Church's activity can this be affirmed with greater certainty than in the activities of the cathedral close. The fabric of the church had suffered damage between 3 a.m. and 4 a.m. on 31 January 1547 when the spire fell in a great storm;[18] its height was said to have been the same as that of the central tower. Other changes doubtless took place from time to time within the great cathedral building with, for example, the movement of the altar or communion table in Edward VI's time but, in essentials, it stood the same from generation to generation. Moreover, the powers and functions of the bishops and of his officials and of the dean and chapter in some ways varied little as a result of the Reformation and the Elizabethan settlement. Admittedly the diocese was smaller than it had been, as the counties of Rutland and Northampton had been cut off from it in 1541 to form the new diocese of Peterborough, and the following year the archdeaconry of Oxford had been formed into a diocese; but it was still immensely large. Admittedly the bishop was much poorer than he had been as a result of the alienation of so many episcopal manors to the nobility and to the Crown during Edward VI's reign since the compensating tithes were potentially less valuable than land. The bishop's income had been reduced from £1,962 17s. 4d. in 1534 to £828 4s. 9d. under Edward VI and rose only to £894 18s. 1d. in 1575: but he was still a prince of the Church even if he were not one of the wealthiest bishops.[19] Moreover,

[17] C. W. Foster (ed.), 'The State of the Church', LRS 23, 1926, p. 462.
[18] Lincs. NQ. III, 1892–3, p. 208 quoting a note on the fly leaf of the Chapter Act Book, 1559–97.
[19] C. W. Foster (ed.), 'Lincoln Episcopal Records temp. Thomas Cooper, 1571–84', LRS 2, 1912, p. ix.

his powers were not vastly different from what they had previously been.

The bishop still controlled his diocese in a way which would not have caused any surprise to his predecessors a couple of hundred years previously. He still visited his diocese, no longer religious houses obviously, as his forbears had done, but the parishes had to be visited, problems solved, and wrongs righted, and vacant benefices had to be filled. The Elizabethan bishops, Nicholas Bullingham 1560–71, Thomas Cooper 1571–84, William Wickham 1584–95 and William Chaderton 1595–1608, though impoverished, continued to fill the office in the same manner as their predecessors. Unfortunately, many of the bishop's Act Books for the period 1545 to 1660 have been lost,[20] but Bishop Cooper's Act Book, although incomplete, is available to us as is his Register, and the returns concerning the clergy known as the *Liber Cleri*. Cooper apparently made a triennial visitation of his diocese and the state of the parson in each parish was carefully noted. In 1576 the younger men, on the whole, appeared more satisfactory in their knowledge than the older incumbents. The bishop had difficulty in filling all the parishes for, in 1576, seventy-eight out of 544 benefices in the county were vacant.[21] This 14·3 per cent of vacancies probably arose for a number of reasons. Many of the livings were very poor, and family responsibilities demanded an adequate income for the clergy but it is also known that at this time fewer university men were entering the Church. The bishop still had powers to grant advowsons and other reversionary rights, and such grants were a source of income which had been much exploited during Mary's reign, and were continued by Bullingham and Cooper. The dean and chapter confirmed many of these grants.

The dean and chapter continued unchanged as a result of the Henririan reform and the Elizabethan settlement since Lincoln had had a secular and not a regular chapter. The main officers, the dean, sub-dean, precentor, and chancellor remained although no treasurer had been appointed after Henry Litherland's execution in August 1538, and the prebendaries, although fewer in numbers, were from time to time in major residence. The names of these officials appear in various records,[22] together with the senior and junior vicars choral, the poor clerks, the choristers, the boys on the Burghersh Foundation, and other officials. These latter ranged from the master of the grammar school through the clerk of the works to the door-keeper, four vergers, and four or five bell-ringers. One of the differences that had occurred as a result of the religious changes was that some of the prebendaries were laymen, and perhaps fewer canons were in residence in the Close than earlier in the

[20] *Ibid.*   [21] LRS 2, p. 333.   [22] LRS 23, pp. 432–9.

century. The dean and chapter still had charge of the fabric of the cathedral, and had the responsibility of filling vacancies that occurred in the peculiars. One important matter which affected most men and women had remained unchanged by the Reformation—the granting of probate of wills. This lucrative professional business had long been in the hands of the ecclesiastical courts, and the religious changes of 1529–59 made virtually no difference to the ordinary man. The bishop, or ordinary, had jurisdiction over legacies and over the administration of intestates' effects,[23] and although the common law courts at the end of the sixteenth century intervened increasingly in testamentary matters, the ecclesiastical courts maintained jurisdiction over probate and administration. The jurisdiction sometimes came before the archdeacon's court and sometimes before the Consistory Court. The Church courts also had wide jurisdiction in matters concerning offences against morals. Adultery and fornication, neglecting to attend church, and tippling in alehouses all continued to bring the ordinary Lincolnshire man and woman before the Courts Christian.

From the administrative labours of the bishop, the dean and chapter, and the archdeacons a clear picture emerges of the state of the Church in Elizabethan Lincolnshire. Reviewing first the state of the clergy, perhaps the most important fact is that they were married—and in increasing numbers. The bishops, all of whom were married, set the example from the top, and the parish clergy were not slow to follow it. In 1560, out of a total of sixty-one cathedral clergy, thirteen were married, thirty-six unmarried, and of twelve no information either way is given.[24] In that same year out of 362 parish clergy in the archdeaconries of Lincoln and Stow, seventy-five were married, 285 unmarried, and two unspecified, while sixteen years later, in 1576, out of 400, 229 were married, 111 unmarried, and sixty unspecified. The late canon Foster broke these returns down into age groups, and only among the higher age groups, 65–70, 71–80, 81–89, and over ninety, and among the small number of 24-year olds were there more unmarried than married clergy.[25] Among the clergy aged 25–64, 216 were married as against sixty-five not married and only two unspecified, so that over 76 per cent of the clergy had taken wives. Figures for the archdeaconry of Stow show that, while thirty out of fifty-seven there were married in 1576, by 1598 sixty out of eighty had wives, with fourteen and seven unstated in the two years respectively. Thus in that part of the county the percentage of those certainly married had risen from 52·6 to seventy-five, and there is no reason to assume that other parts of the diocese showed any difference as regards clerical marriage. That marriage greatly influenced both the parish clergy and parish life is undeniable:

[23] Holdsworth, *op. cit.*, I, pp. 628–9.   [24] LRS 23, p. 455.   [25] *Ibid.*

the influence was perhaps usually for the better, perhaps occasionally for the worse, because sometimes parsons married unsuitable wives. Bishop Cooper had done so.[26] But the royal injunctions of 1559 laid down precautions to guard against undesirable marriages.[27] The bishop of the diocese gave permission for the marriage only after two justices of the peace had issued a certificate and, the parents or near kinsmen of the prospective wife had to give their goodwill. On occasion a clergyman would marry without having secured the necessary consents and then disciplinary action would have to be taken.

What part a wife played in the sixteenth-century parish is not easy to determine but she and her family were undoubtedly an asset in the parsonage and on the glebe land.[28] The wife, as she had had a certificate from two J.P.s would perhaps be a good manager, and she and her daughters in addition to keeping house ran the dairy and looked after the poultry while the sons worked on the land. The typical sixteenth-century parson, although he was perhaps not as impoverished as some historians have thought him to be,[29] was not the hunting parson of the eighteenth and nineteenth centuries: although some of them were scions of the landed gentry, most were of yeoman stock.

In addition to marriage, another clear change was coming over the Elizabethan clergy: they were gradually becoming more learned than their predecessors. Their ecclesiastical superiors expected the clergy to have some knowledge of Latin and of the sacred scriptures, and directed enquiries to ascertain competence in these two branches. Since 1559, of course, the liturgy had no longer been in Latin, and the insistence on a sufficient knowledge of the language may be a cause of surprise. It is partly traditional since the view was still taken, and indeed continued to be taken until the early twentieth century, that no one was properly educated unless he could read Latin, but it was also essential in so far as many scholarly works were written in it. How many of these were read by country parsons is open to doubt. Clergy had to possess the New Testament in Latin and English.[30] Moreover, a few official documents, or at least their rubrics, were in Latin, although their number dwindled towards the end of the century, so that a knowledge of the language was not essential for day-to-day business: but if reference to earlier documents was necessary, a knowledge of Latin was vital. In the arch-deaconries of Lincoln and Stow, returns of 1576 show that out of 396 clergy, 109 had a sufficient knowledge of Latin, forty-five a moderate knowledge, sixty-seven were insufficient, and sixty-eight were quite ignorant, and concerning sixty other non-graduates no specific returns

[26] DNB *sub nomine*.   [27] LRS 23, p. xxi.   [28] F. W. Brooks, art. *cit.*, p. 37.
[29] Notably G. Usher and W. H. Frere, quoted by F. W. Brooks, *loc. cit.*
[30] LRS 2, p. xii.

were made. We can assume that nine clergymen with degrees in theology and thirty-eight M.A.s, B.A.s, or B.C.L.s had good Latin. The position as regards 'knowledge of sacred learning', as it was called, was rather better. Elizabeth I's injunctions of 1559 (number six) had ordered that a Bible should be placed in each parish church and also, between 1560 and 1561, the Paraphrases of Erasmus; the former at the expense of the parish, the cost of the latter to be shared equally between the parson and the parish. With these two volumes and his new Testament in English and in Latin the clergyman was urged to study the scriptures and from time to time the bishop or his deputy examined him. In 1576 in the Lincolnshire archdeaconries out of a total of 396 clergy examined: 123 had sufficient, and seventy-two moderate knowledge and only five were quite ignorant. The nine men with degrees in theology and the twenty-two M.A.s, B.A.s or B.C.L.s presumably had a good knowledge.[31] Thus there were 226 clergy with a reasonable knowledge of the scriptures as against only 201 with similar qualifications in Latin. The standard set to qualify for 'moderate knowledge' or above is not known nor is the method of examination vouchsafed to us, but it would appear to have been a discussion with the bishop or his deputy held during a visitation. When analysed according to the year of their ordination it is obvious that those ordained from the mid-1550s were taking their study of the Bible more seriously than the older clergy who had concentrated on their Mass.

Among those who might be regarded as genuine scholars were the incumbents with university degrees. In 1576 there was one doctor of Sacred Theology, eight bachelors, twenty-four M.A.s and twenty-one B.A.s, one bachelor of canon law, and one doctor of Medicine out of the total of 396 clergy in the two archdeaconries.[32] Nine years later in the same categories the numbers were 5, 9, 63, and 80, and the canon lawyer and medical doctor.[33] Thus 159 out of 573 as against 56 out of a total of 396 had degrees. It is difficult to explain why the total number of clergy in Lincoln and Stow jumped by 177 in nine years but, if we accept these figures, the percentage of graduates leapt from just over 14 per cent to nearly 28 per cent and, in 1585, 266 were said to have been 'bred in the school.' The latter category may well include some clergy who had been at Oxford or Cambridge and who had come down without obtaining a degree.

Probably in the earlier part of Elizabeth I's reign some shortfall in the supply of parish clergy existed. The numbers for the two archdeaconries are, in 1576, 396; 1585, 563; 1594, 589; 1603, 560 and 1607, 560; and we know that several parsons were pluralists. The numbers of these though tended to fall throughout the reign. In many instances it was

31 LRS 23, p. 457. 32 Ibid., p. 453. 33 Ibid., p. 448.

not that suitable clergy were unobtainable, since in 1585 sixty-six parishes had a curate as well as an incumbent (although this figure dropped to fifty-five in 1594 and to two in 1603);[34] it was that patrons would sometimes appoint the same man to two livings. Admittedly some of these benefices had poor stipends and it might have been necessary to hold two of them in order to have an adequate living, but this was not always so. The numbers of pluralities therefore in 1576 were 75; in 1585, 81; 1594, 69; 1602, 65 and in 1603, 47. Most of these were within the same archdeaconry and many of them were held by cathedral dignitaries: very few held three benefices. With pluralists the problem of residence always arose. In 1576, fifty-four out of the seventy-five lived in one of their benefices within the same archdeaconry; in 1602, thirty-nine out of the sixty-five achieved this, while in the latter year seventeen were non-resident within the archdeaconry where they held one of their benefices. Much research would be necessary to ascertain how far was the distance between the two benefices, and whether the incumbents made adequate provisions for their non-residence. Residence involved the question of hospitality: this incumbents were urged to keep although quite what was meant by it is not easy to determine; usually relief of the poor was intended. From the archdeaconry of Stow a return of 1598 produced the following figures that forty-four incumbents were hospitable, ten were not, and about a further twenty-one we do not have any information as to whether they were hospitable or not. Certain other facts about the clergy will be discussed in relation to the problem of nonconformity within *ecclesia Anglicana*.

The Church consists of laity as well as clergy, and much of the ecclesiastical authority that the Church had wielded over the laity continued after the Reformation. The condition of the laity must therefore be noticed as well as the condition of the clergy. The Church's authority was reinforced by the secular power to a greater degree than it had been before the 1530s. Parliament enacted legislation which either limited the ecclesiastical courts or reinforced their authority: some misdemeanours that had been offences against canon law became offences against the law of the land, but the bishops still had standing in finding out or investigating complaints or in giving dispensations. The eating of fish on Wednesdays and Fridays, and the abstention from meat in Lent, were abominable Romish practices but for sound economic, and even for defence needs, the observance was highly desirable if not essential for Elizabeth's government. Archbishop Grindal on 1 February 1577 gave a dispensation to William and lady Anne Ayscough to eat meat in Lent for which they paid 6s. 8d. to the

[34] *Ibid.*, p. 446.

parish poor box.[35] These dispensations were supposedly given on health grounds, but this one was certainly rather suspect on those grounds. Questions involving moral turpitude and matters such as attendance at church and conformity were all matters for the ecclesiastical courts, but until more research has been undertaken into the records of episcopal and archidiaconal courts, judgements on the state of the laity can only be general. What is significant is that the bishop's court of audience and his consistory court, the commissary's court, and the archdeacon's court continued and their powers were substantially unaltered. Questions of non-residence or decay of church fabric sometimes needed great authority, and the chancellor or vicar-general would not have enough power to compel the shortcoming to be rectified. Thus the bishop's personal attendance in his diocese and especially his personal visitation which appears to have become triennial in the Elizabethan period were important. The commissary had probate of wills, jurisdiction over moral offences, and control over non-resident clergy and decayed churches. Cases of disputes between two parties often came to the archdeacon's court where breach of contract, defamation, and tithes cases were heard. He also had probate jurisdiction and the right to judge moral lapses. That the bishop had considerable judicial business is known from his register, and this volume of business is witnessed to by the importance of his registrar.

One problem with two different aspects faced the Elizabethan Church —failure to agree with it. Scarcely anyone in sixteenth-century England believed in religious freedom or in the toleration of different forms of worship within the state. The whole emphasis of the Elizabethan settlement had been laid upon conformity: a *via media* had been constructed so that both extremes of religious belief might find it easier to accept it. Some families in Lincolnshire never abandoned their devotion to the old religion, and Papish recusants who refused the new forms in religion existed from 1559 onwards. But for the first eleven years of the reign they did not create a serious problem for the government nor were they a threat to it. Many recusant families regarded it as satisfactory to attend the parish church and probably to hear Mass in their own private chapel afterwards.[35] But after 1570 Roman Catholics were faced with the choice of abandoning either their loyalty to their faith or to their sovereign. Whereas before 1570 attendance at church had not been strictly enforced, after 1571 the authorities sought out and punished recusancy in the sense of deliberate abstention from the Anglican service. The attitude of the post-Tridentine papacy, and the zeal of the seminarists, made those who did not accept Elizabeth's *via*

[35] Lincs. NQ, VII, 1904–5, pp. 6, 7.
[36] J. B. Black, *The Reign of Queen Elizabeth*, Oxford, 2nd edn., 1959, pp. 22–23, 166.

media a potential threat to the state which took measures to seek out and punish recusants to a degree unknown in the 1560s. Whereas the act of Uniformity inflicted a fine of 1s. for non-attendance at church, an act of 1580 (23 Eliz., c. 1) imposed a payment of £20 a month for such failure, and saying or hearing Mass was punishable by heavy fine and imprisonment.

Officials kept much more careful records of recusants from the 1580s onwards and returns of 1594 show five recusants but they are in the archdeaconry of Leicester.[37] By 1599–1600, visitation books show lists of Papish recusants. Three members of the Yarborough family, Mrs Barbara Heneage, and Mrs Elizabeth Tyrwhit, widow of Marmaduke Tyrwhit of Bigby, appear among those excommunicated at that time for contumacy and a return of 1600 gives the names of sixteen recusants.[38] The next year in two rural deaneries twenty-six names of those refusing to attend church appear in a return, and some of them were mere labourers and their wives. Bishop Chaderton was an ardent warrior against popish recusants, and he chided his commissary Thomas Randes for lack of diligence in furnishing him with the recusants' names.[39] In the returns of 1603 there were twenty men and nineteen women recusants in the archdeaconry of Lincoln, and eight and seven in Stow, a total of fifty-four.[40] The total was not large and the densest concentration was in the rural deaneries of Louthesk and Yarborough, ten in each, and in Manlake where there were thirteen. The following year a probably more accurate survey returned forty men and thirty-six women, in all seventy-six as compared with fifty-four in 1603. To the old families already mentioned, members of the Sapcote, Googe, Thimbleby, Hall, and Dymoke families must be added.

The work of dealing with recusants was carried on at two levels. The bishop, working in close co-operation with the archbishop of Canterbury and through his commissary and the archdeacons, was responsible for trying to get recusants to recant and attend church and, if they would not, for excommunicating them, while laymen were appointed to search out recusants' activities that were against the law of the land. A commission was issued on 9 March 1592 under the great seal to Henry, earl of Lincoln; William Wickham, bishop of Lincoln; Peregrine, lord Willoughby; Edward, lord Sheffield; Charles, lord Willoughby (of Parham); Thomas, lord Clinton; Sir Christopher Wray, chief justice of Common Pleas; Sir Anthony Thorold; Ralph Griffyn, dean of Lincoln; Bartholomew Armine; Edmund Hall and sixteen others to search out seminaries and recusants.[41] Their orders were to enquire into the secret arrival of seminary priests and Jesuits,

[37] LRS 23, p. xli.   [38] *Ibid.*, p. lxxxiii.   [39] *Ibid.*, p. lxxxvi.
[40] *Ibid.*, p. 443.   [41] LAO Anc. XII/A/3.

and power was given to the twenty-seven named or any three of them to search, within the parts of Kesteven, for all those who had come into the realm since Michaelmas 1590. They were to imprison and indict them but not to attempt to convert them, and they were also to proceed against any who had abetted them. An interesting printed sheet is still attached to the commission which tells the commissioners how to execute their duties. The commissioners may divide up the shire between them but they are advised to confer every forty days. Their sole duty is to enquire of people whether they go to church regularly and if not, why not, and then to send a certificate to the bishop and to his chancellor, John Belley, of all such persons with their dwelling place. They also were to ask the *custos rotulorum* or the clerk of the peace for a note of all those who had been presented and indicted as recusants. The leaflet even suggests the type of question the commissioners should ask. 'Have you been moved and by whom to give aid or relief or to adhere to the forces of the pope or the king of Spain?' This question was to be administered on oath but the following one was not—'Have you been at Rome, Rheims, or Spain within these five years?' Another one was, 'Be ye a Jesuit or priest of the Romish order?' Finally the leaflet urged them to find out whether any suspected person had lodged anybody and to send commissioners to other shires if they suspected anyone who should be apprehended had left the shire. Probably there were commissioners for other parts of the shire for these commissioners for recusants were acting all over the county to check any danger to Church and State from these nonconformists.

Although Catholic recusancy in Lincolnshire was not a serious problem for the government, lord Burghley, at one time, is said to have reported that 'part of Lincolnshire is more dangerous than the worst part of Yorkshire.'[42] More certainly we know that Anthony Atkinson, writing to Sir Robert Cecil on 12 July 1597, said that Twigmoor (5½ miles W. of Brigg, 2¼ miles S.W. of Scunthorpe) harboured a number of Jesuit priests and others.[43] He reported that the place was one of the worst in Her Majesty's dominions and that it was used like a popish college, and he sought permission, as the place was only twelve miles by water from Hull, to rout out the recusants with armed ships. Twigmoor belonged to the Tyrwhit family for Robert and William of Twigmoor appear along with John Thimbleby and John Dalison of Irnham on a list of recusants now at Hatfield House.[44] Some of these recusant gentry were imprisoned and some were placed in the guard-

---

[42] C. Brears, *A Short History of Lincolnshire*, London, 1927, p. 138.

[43] HMC *Calendar of MSS of the Marquess of Salisbury (Hatfield)*, pt. VII, HMSO, London, 1899, p. 300.

[44] *Ibid.*, pt. IV, HMSO, London, 1892, p. 264.

ianship of custodians, for William Tyrwhit had permission to leave Kent and go into Lincolnshire in 1586–87 to attend to business matters on his estate.[45] Some of the gentry were arrested and Sir Robert Dymoke, who had married Bridget daughter of Edward Fiennes, the first earl of Lincoln, died in prison on 12 September 1580 as did William Tyrwhit.[46] The homes of the gentry could and did provide resting places for seminary priests who were smuggled into England, but the only priest who was definitely so harboured in the county was William Anlaby who was with Mr Tyrwhit in Lincolnshire in 1586, and who probably stayed there until 1588.[47] Anlaby probably came from Yorkshire, he matriculated at Cambridge (St John's) in 1567, was ordained abroad in 1577, and sent to England the following year. After leaving Lincolnshire, he went to Hampshire and died a martyr's death on 4 July 1597.

Several Catholic priests were Lincolnshire men, but we have no evidence that they undertook their dangerous missions in the county. William Allot is said to have been a Lincolnshire man; he came to England in 1579, was imprisoned at Norwich but he was finally deported and died at Spa in 1597.[48] Roger Dickenson came from the county and Mark Barkworth is said to have come from Searby: both died as martyrs in 1591 and 1601. Thomas Green of Grimsby was a student at Oxford in 1579, and at Grays Inn four years later, before he went to Rheims in 1588. Apparently he never came to England as a priest, and he died, in 1591, at Valladolid. Richard Smith of Welton, born in November 1567, was the son of John and Alice Smith: he came to England in 1603 and, before his death in Paris in 1655, he became bishop of Chalcedon. Two other Lincolnshire priests, Eustace White of Louth, son of William and Anne (née Booth), and Richard Yaxley of Boston, son of William and Rose (née Langton), died a martyr's death, the former at only 31 years of age. A member of one of the well-known county families, Thomas Pormort, a son of Gregory and Anne Pormort of Little Limber, was an undergraduate at Trinity college, Cambridge, who went to Rome in 1581 and who, after ordination six years later, died in 1592.[49] In July 1600, two priests, Thomas Sprott and Thomas Hunt, were found at 'The Saracen's Head' in Lincoln. They were arraigned as priests, which offence was high treason and, being

[45] W. R. Trimble, *The Catholic Laity in Elizabethan England*, Cambridge, Mass., 1964, p. 130.
[46] R. Challoner, *Memoirs of Missionary Priests etc.*, London, 1842 edn., p. xii.
[47] G. Anstruther, *Seminary Priests, 1558–1603*, (collection of source material in ms. in B.M.), *sub nominibus*.
[48] All details about these priests are from Anstruther, *op. cit.*
[49] Thus in Anstruther, *op. cit.*, but Thomas, the son of Gregory Pormort, in Maddison, *Lincs. Pedigrees* is not the same.

condemned, were executed.[50] This constant undercurrent was doubtless troublesome to the government, but it would not appear that the established Church in Lincolnshire was seriously challenged by non-conformists of the Catholic sort.

At the same time as the catholic revival threatened the established church and with it, to some extent, the state, the puritans challenged it also. Nonconformity from this side arose from the feeling that reform had not gone far enough; that too many Romish practices continued. In Lincolnshire this faction was not strong for, as we have seen, men and women within the county were usually conservative in religious matters. But Grimsthorpe Hall must have been a cell of that Protestantism which eventually turned into Puritanism, for its lady, Katherine Willoughby, had long held to that persuasion. She had been on friendly terms with scholars such as Martin Bucer,[51] the martyred bishop Hugh Latimer, and others of advanced Protestant views, and she obviously shared their religious outlook. However, her views were almost certainly not typical of those of the majority of Lincolnshire men and women. Nevertheless, a few in the county held the opinion that public worship should be simpler in form, and that worldliness in the Church, for example in pluralities, should be curbed. Above all, they objected to the vestments prescribed for the use of the clergy, and eventually even to the surplice, and also to the use of the ring in marriage and the sign of the Cross in baptism. Basically, of course, the puritans opposed the episcopal form of church government that the Elizabethan settlement had continued. In order to strengthen themselves, clergy with puritan views met together in 'prophesyings' or *classes* for studying the scriptures to which the laity were sometimes invited, and from 1571 onwards their strength grew. Meanwhile, the government was becoming increasingly alarmed, and in 1576 orders were sent out to test the degree of conformability of the clergy, but in Lincolnshire one only was suspect and he was probably not a puritan. But it was not until the government through archbishop Whitgift (1583–1604) turned the screw on the puritans in the 1580s that the measure of nonconformity in Lincolnshire can first be gauged. Whitgift was a Lincolnshire man, a native of Great Grimsby whose uncle had been abbot of Wellow. He had been away from the county for nearly thirty years when he returned, as dean of Lincoln in 1571. Even then he continued his academic career at Cambridge where he had been based for over twenty years. When, in 1577, he was consecrated bishop of Worcester his links with the county ceased. Shortly after his translation to Canterbury he drew up three articles to which all clergy had to subscribe.

[50] R. Challoner, *op. cit.*, p. 194.   [51] Goff, *op. cit.*, p. 183.

These three articles were that the queen rightfully exercised sover-
eignty over ecclesiastical as well as over lay persons; that the Common
Prayer Book with its order of bishops, priests, and deacons contained
nothing contrary to the word of God and the priest must use it; and
thirdly that the book of Articles of Religion of 1562 was agreeable to the
word of God and must be believed. All clergy had to subscribe to these
three articles. Unfortunately the record of the subscriptions of the clergy
in the two archdeaconries comprising the county of Lincoln are not
fully extant, but Strype says that of the preachers, ninety-four were
conformable and thirteen refused to subscribe.[52] From documents
drawn up by the puritans themselves it would appear that twenty-
three clergymen were suspended from their cures for refusing to subscribe, of whom nine were M.A.s and six B.A.s. They were not
deprived of their livings but suspended from exercising their priestly
functions. Among them were Thomas Fulbeck, parson of Boultham,
John Huddleston, vicar of Saxilby, and James Worship, vicar of Boston:
most of them were young men who had taken their degrees in the
1570s.[53] But, if only twenty-three were suspended, a few others were
restive to the extent of refusing to wear a surplice.[54] The position of the
preachers had a direct bearing upon the championship of the puritan
cause. Preaching had been encouraged by the Elizabethan church, but
the government had a strong desire to keep it under control for many
of the preachers ran towards puritan beliefs. To this end preachers had
to be licensed. The bishop was interested at his visitation to know who
the preachers were, and to check their licences, and in January—
February 1585 the puritans made a survey of the county.[55] The record of
the bishop's visitation of July 1585, the Liber Cleri, and the puritan survey were compared by the late Canon Foster,[56] and the figures of the
former were 109 preachers and 464 non-preachers to 124 and 460 in the
survey. In 1576 the number of licensed preachers within the two archdeaconries was fifty-one with a further twenty who, being variously
described, were probably non-licensed. By 1585 the number had risen
to eighty-eight licensed preachers, plus ten incumbents with theological
degrees who were presumably preachers, and eleven non-licensed
preachers, but by 1603 the county had 145 licensed preachers and
eighty-three presumably non-licensed—a total of 228 preachers.[57] At
the end of Tudor rule the county had far more preachers, and only
forty were designated non-preachers, so that the Lincolnshire church-
goer had a much greater chance of hearing a sermon, good, bad or
indifferent, in 1603 than he would have had twenty years previously.

[52] LRS 23, p. xxiv.   [53] Ibid.   [54] Ibid., p. xxx.
[55] A. Peel (ed.), The Seconde Parte of a Register, Cambridge, 1915, II, pp. 111–29.
[56] LRS 23, pp. xxix, xxxiv–vii.   [57] Ibid., p. 458.

Compared with 1485, the average parishioner of 1603 had immeasurably greater opportunities for hearing sermons and learning more about his religion. In the eyes of some, the break with Rome might not have been complete enough, but in fact the changes were vast. These preachers were supposedly orthodox since the whole point of the licensing system was to ensure that, but, doubtless, some of them were able to get across their reforming views for a number of them refused to wear the surplice.[58] The refusal to wear the surplice, both by incumbents who were preachers and those who were not, had not been completely stamped out by Whitgift nor, in the county, by Chaderton's enthusiasm for orthodoxy.

Another aspect of the Church which had not changed basically, although it was somewhat modified, was lay patronage. To the extent that many religious houses had appropriated livings, their dissolution resulted in more patronage becoming vested in the Crown and other lay patrons.[59] By 1603 the numbers of benefices in the county to which the Crown provided was 130 although to eight of these it presented alternately and the prince of Wales had one benefice. The archbishop of York had one presentation, the bishop of Lincoln, forty, the dean and chapter and the prebendaries fifty-one, and other ecclesiastical persons twenty. Oxford colleges were patrons of nine livings and Cambridge colleges of five, one of which was an alternate presentation. Magdalen college Oxford was the patron of Swaby,[60] Saltfleetby All Saints, and Horsington; Balliol of Bratelby, Fillingham and Riseholme; Trinity college Cambridge had the advowson of Great Coates and Swineshead; Clare Hall of Wrawby; and Christ's of Navenby. Eton college had the presentation to one living, various cities and boroughs to three, and eight patrons were unspecified. But private patrons presented to nearly half of all the benefices in the county: they presented to 333 benefices out of a total of 611. As we should expect, the great nobles were patrons of many livings; the earl of Lincoln presented to nine, lord Burghley to four, and to one of which he had an alternate turn, the earl of Rutland to five, lord Willoughby of Parham to three, and lord Willoughby d'Eresby to eleven, with a further two to which he presented on alternate occasions. Sir William Wray held five advowsons, and other members of the gentry families such as the Skipwiths, Heneages, and Thorolds held between four and six each. The Carrs of Sleaford between Sir Edward and Robert controlled eleven, the Tyrwhits (Sir Philip, Robert, William and Marmaduke) held twelve, and the Dymokes (Sir Edward and Charles) presented to ten livings. If local power is to be equated with the number of advowsons held, the Dymokes appear as a more important family locally than has some-

[58] Ibid., pp. cii–cxvi.   [59] Ibid., p. lvi.   [60] Ibid., p. 305.

times been suggested. As for other gentry families, the Saviles, Armines, Harringtons, Bilsbies, Copledykes, and Booths, mostly owned the advowson of the church of the parish in which their seat was and often one more. This control gave influence to the gentry and also helped to some degree to influence the religious complexion of the parish in so far as the patron might seek to get appointed an incumbent of his own persuasion.

Finally what about the financial status of the clergy in Elizabethan England? The upper clergy, above all the bishop, were poorer than they had been but the incomes of most of the parish clergy were steadily rising; whether the rise was sufficient to keep pace with the increased cost of living is debatable. The order of increase can be demonstrated by ninety benefices in the rural deaneries of Walshcroft, Aslackhoe, Corringham, Lawres, and Manlake.[61] In 1535, the *Valor Ecclesiasticus* had valued them *in toto*, at £1,000 16s. 11d. but a valuation of the benefices taken early in 1604, less than a year after the queen's death, returned a figure of £2,062 4s. 2d. Whereas in 1535 fifteen benefices worth less than £5 had been recorded, in 1604 there were only three. In the range £5 to £10, forty-two were noted in the earlier year as against only twenty-two in the latter; £10–£15, fifteen as against seventeen; £15–£20, six as against eighteen; £20–25, seven as against two and £25–30, five as against thirteen. No benefices worth over £30 existed in these rural deaneries in 1535, but in 1604 there were six between £30 and £40; two between £40 and £50; three between £50 and £60; the same number between £60 and £80 and one at £120.[62] So while 80 per cent of the beneficed clergy were living on under £15 a year in 1535, only 46·3 per cent had had to exist on that income in 1604. Curates' stipends on the other hand were grossly inadequate. In the archdeaconries of Lincoln and Stow in 1604, forty curates had up to £5 a year, twenty-nine between £5 and £10, seven between £10 and £15 and only five had between £15 and £20. The increased price of grain should have given the incumbent both a greater income from tithes and, if he had an extensive glebe, a better price for his own corn on the market. The difficulty about maintaining this argument for a large income is, however, that in many places a composition of tithes had been arrived at, which payment remained stationary at a period of rising grain prices. Moreover, many parsons had paid pensions or granted favourable leases of the glebe to patrons in return for obtaining the living: patrons had simply followed the example set by the queen in her dealings with the higher clergy. In places where the benefice had been impropriated, a lay rector collected the tithes which increased in value while he paid a vicar or curate a pittance. In 1603, 248

[61] *Ibid.*, p. lxi.   [62] *Ibid.*

benefices had been appropriated or impropriated and were served by a vicar and forty-five by a curate, as against 314 in which the rector himself had the tithes. But to some degree the position of the clergy was improved by a judicious amalgamation of benefices. This happened in Grimsby in 1586,[63] and also in Stamford and Lincoln.[64] At Stamford, St Michael's, St Andrews, and St Stephen's were united for seven parish churches were ample for the worshippers, while ten would have been excessive.[65]

In religious matters, then, as in economic and social life the Lincolnshire of 1603 was vastly different in some ways from that of 1485 while in other ways the county saw little change. It was still isolated; its farming methods had not greatly changed although improved drainage was just beginning to add more cultivable land; in trade and commerce its position was probably worse than it had been at the opening of the Tudor era. But in the religious life, after having been an orthodox conservative county, many people of Lincolnshire, under puritan influence and with the greater opportunities for hearing sermons and studying the Bible, were beginning to adopt a radical attitude and a more ready acceptance of nonconformity.

[63] Gillett, *op. cit.*, p. 94.   [64] J. W. F. Hill, *Tudor and Stuart Lincoln*, pp. 56–8.
[65] LRS 23, p. 325.

APPENDIX I

APPENDIX: *Diocesan Return, 1563*
In 1563, the Privy Council required from each diocesan bishop a return
of the parishes and hamlets of each diocese, with the number of families
resident therein. The return for Lincolnshire, made under the authority
of the Archdeacon of Lincoln, Thomas Aylmer, has been preserved in
the British Museum, Harleian MS.618, and is here printed for the first
time. For a discussion of this document, see J. Thirsk, *Sources of Information on Population, 1500–1760*.

DIOCESAN POPULATION RETURN, 1563

Place	House-holds	Place	House-holds
Deanery of Christianity		Eagle	41
i.e. Lincoln		North Hykeham	7
St Peter at Arches	34	North Scarle	35
St Peter at Gowts	58	Norton Disney	30
St Paul's	25	Skellingthorpe	34
St Swithin's	80	South Hykeham	18
St Botulph's	43	North Hykeham	18
St Peter's Eastgate	42	Haddington	13
St Mary's	33	Stapleford	43
St Martin's	70	Swinderby	30
St Mark's	24	Thorpe-on-the-Hill	25
St Michael's	50		——
	——		474
	459		
		Deanery of Longoboby	
Deanery of Graffoe		Billinghay	60
Aubourn	26	Waterside	17
Haddington	7	Dogdike	23
Bassingham	61	Walcot	40
Boultham	21	Blankney	40
Carlton-le-Moorland	38	Boothby Graffoe	23
Doddington	14	Bracebridge	18
Whisby	13	Branston	72

Place	House-holds	Place	House-holds
Canwick	20	Kirkby-La-Thorpe St Denis	21
Sheepwash	1	Kirkby-La-Thorpe St Peter	18
Coleby	45	Kyme	63
Dunston	38	N. Kyme	35
Harmston	48	Leasingham	22
Kirkby Green	22	Roxholme	11
Metheringham	48	Old Sleaford	10
Navenby	54	Quarrington	17
Nocton	39	Rauceby	22
Potter Hanworth	45	Chapel of St James S. Rauceby	21
Scopwick	32	Rowston	33
Skinnand	5	Ruskington	55
Timberland	38	Silk Willoughby	42
Waddington	70	Swarby	21
Washingborough	no figure	Crofton	3
Welbourn	no figure		
	‾‾‾		‾‾‾
	798		1030

Deanery of Lafford

		Deanery of Loveden	
Anwick	32	Ancaster	9
Asgarby	17	Sudbrook	8
Ashby-de-la-Launde	18	Willoughby	7
Aswarby	22	Beckingham	36
Aunsby	16	Fenton chapel and hamlet	31
Bloxholm	no figure	Stragglethorpe ditto	10
Brauncewell	12	Sutton hamlet	10
Dunsby hamlet	5	(Long) Bennington	97
Bloxholm hamlet	1	Foston chapel	42
Burton Pedwardine	25	Brant Broughton	40
Cranwell	no figure	Carlton Scroop	26
Digby	53	Caythorpe	41
Dorrington	44	Frieston hamlet	15
Evedon	13	Claypole	77
Ewerby	50	Fulbeck	46
Great Hale	67	Hough-on-the-Hill	38
Little Hale	36	Brandon chapel and hamlet	9
Heckington	107	Gelston hamlet	8
Helpringham	56	Hougham	39
Howell	14	Marston chapel and hamlet	61
Ingoldsby	48	Leadenham	62
		Normanton	19

Place	House-holds	Place	House-holds
Stubton	22	Burton Coggles	35
Westborough	38	Careby	24
Dry Doddington chapel		Castle Bytham	28
and hamlet	25	Holywell and Aunby chapel	
	———	& hamlet	15
	816	Counthorpe hamlet	11
		Colsterworth	27
Deanery of Grantham		Woolsthorpe hamlet	9
Allington	19	Corby	32
Barkston	39	Creeton	14
Barrowby	43	Edenham	62
Belton	27	Scottlethorpe hamlet	18
Boothby Pagnell	21	Grimsthorpe hamlet	8
Denton	no figure	Elsthorpe hamlet	10
Grantham	252	Suthorpe hamlet	1
Braceby chapel & hamlet	12	Gunby	14
Gonerby chapel & hamlet	52	Irnham	17
Londonthorpe chapel & hamlet	19	Bulby hamlet	14
Manthorpe chapel & hamlet	17	Hawthorpe hamlet	6
Great Ponton	37	Lavington (Lenton)	22
Harlaxton	58	Keisby hamlet	13
Honington	26	Osgodby hamlet	12
Little Ponton	13	Little Bytham	23
Ropsley	30	Bytham Grange hamlet	2
Little Humby hamlet	7	North Witham	15
Sapperton	no figure	Lobthorpe chapel	no figure
Sedgebrook	36	'Shester', hamlet	3
Allington hamlet	21	South Witham	33
Somerby	32	Stainby	21
Humby chapel & hamlet	8	Stoke N. and S.	22
St Anne chapel & hamlet	1	Easton chapel & hamlet	21
Stroxton	12	N. Stoke chapel & hamlet	16
Syston	24	Swayfield	25
Welby	34	Swinstead	40
Wilsford	34	Westby	24
Woolsthorpe	37	Witham on the Hill	38
	———	Manthorpe chapel & hamlet	18
	911	Toft chapel & hamlet	13
		Lound chapel & hamlet	12
Deanery of Beltisloe			———
Bitchfield	24		762

Place	House-holds
Deanery of Aveland	
Aslackby	44
Milnthorpe hamlet	10
Graby hamlet	5
Billingborough	65
Bourne	174
Cawthorpe hamlet	22
Dyke hamlet	27
Dembleby	11
Dowsby	24
Graby hamlet	3
Dunsby	32
Folkingham	50
Loughton hamlet	17
Hacconby	26
Stainfield hamlet	12
Haceby	40
Horbling	56
Bridgend hamlet	8
Kirkby Underwood	26
Morton	48
Hanthorpe hamlet	24
Newton	18
Osbournby	43
Pickworth	26
Rippingale	51
Ringstone chapel & hamlet	2
Sempringham	13
Pointon chapel & hamlet	48
Scott Willoughby	4
Stow	3
Swaton	59
Spanby chapel & hamlet	6
Threckingham	31
Walcot	no figure
	——
	1028

Place	House-holds
Deanery of Stamford	
St Mary's	41
St Michael's	52

Place	House-holds
St John's	31
St George's	30
All Saints	59
	——
	213
Deanery of Ness	
Barholm	14
Baston	57
Thetford hamlet	1
Braceborough	21
Shillingthorpe hamlet	1
Banthorpe hamlet	1
Carlby	17
Deeping St James	157
Frognall hamlet	6
Walderham Hall hamlet	3
Market Deeping	90
West Deeping	27
Greatford	27
Langtoft	60
Stowe	6
Tallington	20
Thurlby	51
Northorpe hamlet	22
Obthorpe hamlet & chapel	7
Uffington	52
Casewick hamlet	1
	——
	641
Deanery of Holland	
Algarkirk	72
Fosdyke hamlet	84
Benington	69
Bicker	80
Boston	471
Butterwick	45
Crowland	77
Donington	127
Northorpe hamlet	21
Eaudike hamlet	13

Place	House-holds	Place	House-holds
Fleet	50	*Deanery of Gartree*	
Fen End hamlet	9	Asterby	28
Frampton	112	Belchford	53
Toft hamlet	3	Bucknall	52
Freiston	147	Cawkwell	3
Gedney	94	Coningsby	221
Gedney Fen End chapel & hamlet	32	Dalderby	no figure
Gosberton	107	Donington-on-Bain	31
Holbeach	147	Edlington	36
Holbeach Hurn hamlet	8	Gautby	19
Holbeach Drove hamlet	7	Goulceby	27
Kirton	228	Haltham-on-Bain	25
Brothertoft hamlet	10	Hemingby	53
Leake	127	Horsington	37
Leverton	48	Kirkby-on-Bain	53
Moulton	90	'Cristede' hamlet	16
Moulton Chapel hamlet	41	Langton	24
Pinchbeck	200	Minting	36
Quadring	88	Ranby	15
Westhorpe hamlet	10	Roughton	30
Skirbeck	no figure	Stainton	17
Spalding	154	Stenigot	14
Cowbit hamlet	54	Stixwold	60
Surfleet	64	(Gt.) Sturton	26
Sutterton	67	Tattershall	236
(Long) Sutton	111	Tattershall Thorpe hamlet	68
Lutton hamlet	48	Thimbleby	40
Sutton St Edmund hamlet	62	Waddingworth	19
Sutton St James hamlet	55	Woodhall	no figure
Swineshead	209		———
Toft	no figure		1239
Tydd	40	*Deanery of Horncastle*	
Weston	50	Baumer	59
Whaplode	115	Sturton grange hamlet	1
Whaplode Drove hamlet	29	Little Sturton hamlet	1
Wigtoft	84	Horncastle	164
Wrangle	76	Toynton chapel & hamlet	18
Wyberton	54	(W.) Ashby chapel & hamlet	44
Brothertoft hamlet	8	Mareham-on-the-Hill chapel & hamlet	22
	———	Wood Enderby chapel & Hamlet	24
	3897		

Place	House-holds	Place	House-holds
Low Toynton	12	Hareby	12
Mareham-le-Fen	87	Hundleby	33
Martin (?)	12	Lusby	16
Moorby	19	Mavis Enderby	43
Scrivelsby	19	Miningsby	15
Thornton	no figure	Raithby	18
Wilksby	6	Revesby	no figure
Wispington	18	Sibsey	96
	——	Frith Bank hamlet	24
	506	Spilsby	48
		Steeping Parva	39
		Stickford	52
Deanery of Hill		Stickney	90
Ashby Puerorum	21	Thorpe (St Peter)	42
Aswardby	18	Toynton All Saints	40
Bag Enderby	17	Toynton St Peter	48
Brinkhill	no figure	West Keal	46
Claxby Pluckare	12	Laythorpe hamlet	6
Fulletby	18	W. Keal Cotes hamlet	18
Greetham	16		——
Hagworthingham	46		832
Hameringham	19		
Harrington	12		
Langton-by-Spilsby	25		
Lettisbie Ketsby?	10	*Deanery of Candleshoe*	
Oxcombe	10	Addlethorpe	44
Salmonby	15	Ashby by Partney	34
Sausthorpe	21	Bratoft	25
Scrafield	8	Scrimthorpe hamlet	9
Somersby	14	Burgh-le-Marsh	92
South Ormsby	30	Candlesby	24
Tetford	40	Croft	59
Winceby	10	Sutton End hamlet	8
	——	Driby	10
	362	Firsby	26
		Friskney	69
		Gunby	15
Deanery of Bolingbroke		Ingoldmells	39
Bolingbroke	40	Irby (in-the-Marsh)	12
East Keal	48	Orby	42
Cotes hamlet	7	Partney	51
Hagnaby	8	Scremby	18
Halton (Holgate)	43		

Place	House-holds	Place	House-holds
Skegness	14	Mumby	50
Skendleby	27	Mumby Chapel hamlet	36
Steeping Magna	30	Saleby	22
Sutterby	8	Staney (? Stain)	2
Wainfleet All Saints	56	Sutton in the Marsh	46
Wainfleet St Mary	38	South Reston	13
Wainfleet chapel	no figure	Swaby	17
Welton-le-Marsh	34	Theddlethorpe All Saints	44
Winthorpe	55	Theddlethorpe St Helen	45
	———	Thoresby (South)	6
	839	Tothill	14
		Trusthorpe	39
		Ulceby	7
Deanery of Calcewaith		Fordington hamlet	3
Aby	14	Well	1
Alford	101	Willoughby	16
Rigsby chapel and Well and		Bonthorpe hamlet	6
Tothby hamlets inc. in Alford		Mawthorpe hamlet	5
Rigsby hamlet	16	Hasthorpe hamlet	4
Anderby	32	Habertoft hamlet	5
Authorpe	24	Sloothby chapel & hamlet	31
Beesby (in-the-Marsh)	31	Withern	no figure
Belleau	10		
Claythorpe hamlet	21		———
Bilsby	40		1170
Thurlby hamlet	14		
Asserby hamlet	6	*Deanery of Louthesk*	
Calceby	18	Alvingham	30
Claxby	12	Burwell	22
Claythorpe	20	Walmsgate chapel & hamlet	8
Cumberworth	27	Carlton (Great)	36
Farlesthorpe	20	Carlton (Little)	12
Gayton-le-Marsh	50	Castle Carlton	21
Haugh	no figure	Calcethorpe	4
Hogsthorpe	70	Cadeby hamlet	2
Huttoft	80	Grimoldby hamlet	1
Legbourne	44	Cockerington (North)	70
Mablethorpe St Mary & St Peter	32	Cowcroft hamlet	3
Maltby-le-Marsh	31	Cockerington St Leonard	32
Markby	20	Conisholme	20
Hannah chapel & hamlet	15	Covenham St Bartholomew	33
Hagnaby chapel & hamlet	10	Covenham St Mary	39

Place	House-holds	Place	House-holds
Farforth	9	S. Elkington	18
Maidenwell hamlet	4	Dunsthorpe hamlet	4
Fotherby	30	Acthorpe hamlet	1
Fulstow	69	Fanthorpe hamlet	1
Northorpe hamlet	8	Cotes Grange hamlet	1
Easton hamlet	8	S. Somercoates	44
Easthorpe hamlet	3	Scupholme hamlet	10
West Thorpe hamlet	20	Stewton	12
Marsh Chapel, chapel and hamlet	55	Tathwell	31
Gayton-le-Marsh	9	Cadwell hamlet	2
Grainthorpe	24	Dovendale hamlet	1
Wragholme hamlet	24	Utterby	30
Ludney hamlet	12	Welton-le-Wold	24
Grimoldby	45	Withcall	13
Hallington	24	Wyham	1
Haugham	17	Cadeby hamlet	1
Keddington	44	Yarborough	32
Louth Park hamlet	7		
Kelstern	22		1403
Little Grimsby	4		
Ludborough	38	*Deanery of Grimsby*	
Manby	40	Aylesby	45
Muckton	35	Ashby	13
N. Elkington	8	Fenby hamlet	10
? Acthorpe hamlet	1	Barnoldby-le-Beck	24
N. Ormsby	21	Beelsby	13
Ormsby Abbey hamlet	1	Bradley	32
N. Reston	12	Brigsley	25
Beckhouse hamlet	3	Cabourne	12
N. Somercoates	60	Clee	22
Northorpe hamlet	26	Utterby hamlet	18
Raithby (cum-Maltby)	21	Houll hamlet (Oule)	14
Ruckland	4	Thrunscoe hamlet	16
Worlaby Grange hamlet	1	Weelsby hamlet	6
Saltfleetby All Saints	31	Cuxwold	10
Three Bridges hamlet	3	East Ravendale	11
Saltfleetby St Clement	13	Grainsby	21
Saltfleetby St Peter	31	Great Coates	34
Skidbrooke	18	(Great) Grimsby St James & St	
Saltfleethaven hamlet	29	Mary	145
Northend hamlet	10	Hatcliffe	6
		Gunnerby hamlet	5

Place	House-holds	Place	House-holds
Hawerby	7	Ferriby (South)	56
Beesby hamlet	5	Goxhill	90
Healing	13	Grasby	28
Holton-le-Clay	24	Habrough	51
Humberston	52	Halton (E.)	96
Irby upon Humber	20	Horkstow	33
Laceby	53	Immingham	66
Little Coates	10	Keelby	47
Newton (Wold)	22	Cotham hamlet	1
N. Coates	37	Killingholme	75
Rothwell	24	Kirmington	31
Scartho	22	Limber magna	60
Swallow	20	Nettleton	67
Swinhope	6	Riby	44
Tetney	90	Saxby All Saints	34
(N.) Thoresby	50	Somerby	5
Autby hamlet	1	Stallingborough	150
Waithe	16	Thornton (Curtis)	89
Waltham	41	Ulceby	71
W. Ravendale	1	Wootton	29
		Worlaby	48
	——	Wrawby	50
	996	Glanford Bridge hamlet	60
			——
Deanery of Yarborough			1907
Barnetby-le-Wold	31		
Barrow on Humber	106		
Barton on Humber with chapel of		*Deanery of Walschcroft*	
Barton St Mary	207	Binbrook St Mary	25
Bigby	22	Claxby	40
Kettleby hamlet	1	Croxby-le-Vale	11
Thorpe hamlet	5	E. Rasen	64
Glanford Bridge hamlet	9	E. Wickham	1
Bonby	35	Irford	1
Brocklesby	21	Kelsey St Mary	57
Limber parva hamlet	15	Winghale hamlet	1
Newsham hamlet	1	Kelsey St Nicholas	31
Cadney	52	Kingerby	16
Howsham hamlet	38	Kirkby	8
Newstead hamlet	1	Owersby End hamlet	22
Croxton	18	Osgodby hamlet	38
Elsham	64	Linwood	43

Place	House-holds	Place	House-holds
Middle Rasen Drax	38	New Pasture hamlet	2
Middle Rasen Tupholme	56	Bleasby hamlet	7
Newton-by-Toft	16	'Howdon' hamlet	4
Normanby-le-Wold	24	Lissington	36
N. Willingham	53	Collow hamlet	1
Owersby	53	Ludford magna	17
Stainton-le-Vale	16	Towes hamlet	1
Tealby	97	Thorpe hamlet	1
Thoresway	26	Ludford parva	11
Thorganby	15	Panton	20
Thornton-le-Moor	11	Hardwick hamlet	2
Cant hamlet	6	Rand	7
Beasthorpe hamlet	1	Fulnetby hamlet	15
Toft-next-Newton	18	Hallthorpe hamlet	1
Usselby	18	Sixhills	24
Walesby	20	Grange hamlet	2
Risby hamlet	8	Snelland	15
Otby hamlet	3	two (unnamed) hamlets	7
W. Rasen	50	Sotby	24
	——	Stainfield	21
	887	Stainton	16
		Reasby hamlet	6
		Langworth hamlet	12
Deanery of Wraggoe		Newball hamlet	10
Apley	9	W. Barkwith	13
Bardney	100	W. Torrington	23
Southrey hamlet	52	Wickenby	17
Benniworth	42	Westlaby hamlet	3
Biscathorpe	17	Willingham (South)	39
Bullington	2	Wragby	35
Goltho hamlet	8		——
Burgh on Bain	9		815
Girsby hamlet	1		
E. Barkwith	22		
E. Torrington	18	*Peculiars*	
Hatton	27	Sleaford (R.D. Lafford)	145
Holton Beckering	37	Holdingham hamlet	20
Beckering hamlet	13	Asgarby (R. D. Bolingbroke)	14
Kirmond-le-Mire	14	Melton Ross (R. D. Yarborough)	21
Langton-by-Wragby	34	Scamblesby	25
Legsby	16	N. Kelsey	100
Collow hamlet	2	Melton Manor within par. of	

Place	House-holds	Place	House-holds
Binbrook St Gabriel's (R. D. Walschcroft)	25	Formby hamlet no figure	
		Andleby hamlet no figure	
S. Carlton cum Thurlby S. Carlton (Archdeaconry of Stow)	16		520
Thurlby	25	Total of the rural deaneries	21,985
Caistor town	63	Total of the county excluding the archdeaconry of Stow	
Howton-le-Moor chapel	33		
Clixby chapel	33		
Hundon hamlet no figure			22,505

INDEX

Names of families follow the names of places. Counties are given for places outside Lincolnshire

Ingham, 45
Ingoldmells, 56, 163, 167
Irby, family, 72
　Anthony, 23, 109
　another, 109
　Leonard, 107, 109–12, 114–15, 173
　-on-Humber, 47
Ireland, levies for, 117
　soldier from, 98
Irford priory, 41, 47, 55–6
Irnham, 78, 104
　hall at, 150

Jackson, John, 72
Johnson, William, 36, 147
Joye, John, 103

Katherine (Howard), queen of England,
　124, 152
　(of Aragon), queen of England, 31, 153
Kelsey, South, 150, 158
Kemp, Francis, 103
Kendall, Dr, vicar of Louth, 26, 36–7
Kesteven, 3, 5, 7, 48, 67–8, 78, 93, 167
Ketsby, 104, 150
Kettleby, 6–7, 55, 78
　Henry VIII at, 152
Kiddall (Kydall), of Ferriby, South,
　Thomas, 55
　Thomas, of London, 8
Kirkby, la Thorpe, 57
　Underwood, survey of, 68–70, 77
Kirkstead, abbey of, 51
　abbot of, 36, 40, 46, 50
Kirtleton, Matthew, 113
Kirton, wapentake, 5, 78
　in Lindsey, grammar school at, 146
Knaith, hall at, 151
Knights Hospitallers, order of, 16, 25
Kyme, 71
　priory, 25, 39–41, 52, 55, 59, 61
　Eau, Appletreeness on, 15
　family, 64
　Guy, 30, 32

Laceby, 44
Lacy, Henry, 107
　Thomas, 107
　Thomas, of Granchester, 107
Lancaster, duchy of, bondmen of the, 166
　council of the, 74
　duchy court, 53

lands of the, 5, 32, 49, 53, 91, 135
　officials of the, 162
Herald, at Lincoln, 29
Langtoft, 47–8
Langton-by-Wragby, 170
Latimer, Hugh, bishop of Worcester,
　154, 184
Laughton, 166
　school at, 146
Lawrence, Robert, 60
Lawres, rural deanery, 187
Layton, Dr John, 41
　Dr Richard, 23, 41
Leadenham, Stragglethorpe, near, 8
Leake, 48
Leech, William, 30–1, 33, 36–7
Legbourne, 48, 60
　priory, 25, 27, 53
Legh, Dr Thomas, 23, 41
Legsby, 51
Leicestershire, 3, 66–7
Leke, Francis, 58
Leland, John, *antiquary*, 3, 134, 151
Leverton, poor relief at, 97–9
Lincoln, 1, 9, 27–8, 34, 38, 65, 79–81, 89,
　113
　apprenticeship in, 128–30
　archdeaconry of, 9, 11, 16, 66, 176, 187
　Bail, 127
　bakers of, 127–8
　Beaumont's Fee or Rent, 127
　bishop of, *see* Atwater, Bullingham,
　　Chaderton, Cooper, Holbeach,
　　Longland, Taylor, Watson, White,
　　Wickham
　Burghmanmote, 120–1
　buscage, 124
　Cantilupe college, 9
　cathedral, 19–21, 174–7,
　　Burghersh chantry in, 20, 140, 175
　　chantry priests in, 20
　　Close, 127
　　dean and chapter, 20, 175–6
　　dean of, *see* Heneage
　　ecclesiastical courts, 175–6
　　grammar school in Close, 140–1
　　poor clerks of, 20
　　prebendaries, 19
　　provost, 20
　　residence of canons, 19–21
　　St Hugh's shrine in, 20
　　Song School of, 140–1

Willoughby, family, (*cont.*)
  Peregrine, 12th baron Willoughby d'Eresby, 75–6, 118, 154–7, 181, 186
  Robert, 13th baron, 145
  Susan, 154–7
  William, 10th baron, 151
  William, son of Sir Christopher, 33
  of Parham, Charles, 1st baron, 92–3, 118, 151, 153, 173, 181, 186
Wilsford, 15
Wilson, Dr Thomas, secretary of state, 103, 113, 115, 131, 138
wine, imports, 87–8, 156
Wingfield, Charles, 173
  Sir John, 108
  Robert, 47, 106, 112
Winteringham, 65
Winthorpe, 56
Wiseman, John, 24, 40–1, 56
Witham, river, 4, 78, 81, 83, 85, 88
  on-the-Hill, 78, 156
  South, 2
wolds, the, 2–3, 5, 66, 77
Wolsey, George, killed at Horncastle, 27, 31
  Thomas, cardinal, 34

wool, production, 3
  exports, 87
Woolsthorpe, 55
Wraggoe wapentake, 27
Wrangle, 146, 163
Wray, Sir Christopher, 67, 173, 181
  Sir William, 67, 104, 118, 186
Wymark, John, 13
  Robert, 122
Wymbish, Thomas, 53
Wyse, Grace, 45

Yarborough, rural deanery, 25, 181
Yarmouth, co. Norfolk, 82
Yates, William, 101
Yaxley, Francis, 107
  Richard, of Boston, 183
  Rose, 183
  William, 183
Yoell, Thomas, 36
York, 1, 23, 81, 89, 98, 125, 152
  Cecily, Duchess of, 136
  -shire, 81
    brewers of, 4
    clothiers of, 3, 83
    East Riding of, 2
    rebels in, 28–9